GW01237009

JULIE
BIUSO
—— •• ——
COOKS

VEGETABLES

JULIE BIUSO COOKS

VEGETABLES

Hodder & Stoughton
AUCKLAND LONDON SYDNEY TORONTO

This book is specially for two very wonderful people,
my dear father and my dear late mother.

Copyright © 1991 Julie Biuso
First published 1991
ISBN 0 340 549025

All rights reserved. No part of this publication may be reproduced or
transmitted in any form or by any means, electronic or mechanical,
including photocopy, recording, or any information storage and retrieval
system, without permission in writing from the publisher.

Illustrations by Donna Hoyle.
Typeset by Typeset Graphics Ltd, Auckland.
Printed and bound by GP Print Ltd, Wellington,
for Hodder and Stoughton Ltd, 44-46 View Rd,
Glenfield, Auckland, New Zealand.

CONTENTS

ACKNOWLEDGEMENTS

For kindly providing the table and plate used in the cover photograph, my thanks respectively to Country Antiques, 489 Manukau Road, Auckland, and Milly's Kitchenware Shop, 289 Ponsonby Road, Auckland.

For his enthusiasm and skill in producing the wonderful cover photograph, my special thanks to Ian Batchelor, 14-16 Beresford Street, Auckland.

I would also like to thank Julie Dalzell, editor of *Cuisine* magazine (Level 2, Windsor Court, 136 Parnell Road, Auckland) for her enthusiastic support and personal encouragement over the past five years.

Thank you to Shelley Clements, editor of *More* magazine (17B Hargreaves Street, Auckland) for her interest and valuable promotional support.

I can't leave out Alice Worsley from Radio i (107 Great North Road, Auckland), can I? (She would never talk to me again!) Thanks for your tremendous support over the years.

I also want to thank my literary agent Ray Richards for believing in me and making this book possible. To Tom Beran, my publisher from Hodder and Stoughton, a special thanks for his hours of attentive and thorough work.

These acknowledgements wouldn't be complete without an expression of tremendous thanks for the continued loyal support, understanding, advice, criticisms, practical help and sheer hard work from my partner Remo, and the enthusiasm (when it comes to food) from our son Luca. I know the meals didn't always make it on time — but we certainly shared a few great ones, didn't we!

Kind thanks to you all and to all those, too numerous to mention, who have helped me over the years and, more specifically, on this book. Cheers!

INTRODUCTION

One of my earliest and fondest memories has me sitting with my brothers and sisters on the front porch of our old farmhouse, shelling homegrown peas for Christmas lunch. We basked in the sun, laughing and teasing each other, and quickly popping into our mouths any tiny peas that missed the colander. Those peas, grown in our huge vegetable garden tended mostly by my father but at times by the whole family, seem to me the best I've ever had.

The sweet corn, snapped off the plant, shucked, de-silked and in the cooking pot before you knew it, was milky and deliciously sweet. Even the dreaded green vegetables — Popeye's spinach and silver beet — didn't taste half so bad freshly picked, quickly cooked and tossed in plenty of butter, salt, pepper and nutmeg. We loved the misshapen carrots and parsnips and roared with laughter whenever we found a three-legged one, especially if the 'middle leg' was shorter than the other two!

I learned a lot about freshness, quality and taste from my parents and our vegetable garden. For instance, overblown cauliflowers would be watery and tasteless; old ones would be smelly to cook and strong to taste, and they'd be left on the dinner plates. In the vegetable garden I discovered how important it is to learn from your mistakes and cope with the disappointment. I learned patience: you can't hurry nature and vegetables can't be 'willed' to grow.

With my mother I experienced the delightful anticipation of watching something grow, knowing it will soon be in the cooking pot, then on the table for all to enjoy. I felt her joy and thankfulness when the garden provided enough health-giving, full-of-taste vegetables to feed the whole family. From my mother I learned that sooner is better than later — use vegetables when they are at their peak, rather than leaving them to rot. And, of course, from my dear mother I learned to cook.

When it came to vegetables, the importance of freshness and quality rang through loud and clear in our family. It is something so deeply ingrained in me that I've never had to 'learn' it. If I walk into a shop and detect even a whiff of rotting produce, I automatically walk out. If I see leeks trimmed of their roots and showing brown ends, cabbages and lettuces pared right back, or spring onions chopped back to a third of their natural length, I feel the anger welling inside me. These vegetables aren't fresh — they're days, if not weeks, old. How dare the shopkeeper try and pull the wool over our eyes?

Although it's the perfect solution, we don't all have the space, the time or the inclination to grow our own vegetables. But there is another way: learning to recognise and demand truly fresh produce. Expect the freshest and best, and don't accept anything less. Next time you're offered fruit or vegetables that are obviously wilted or showing signs of decay, and therefore deprived of their health-giving properties, say loudly 'No, that's not fresh enough, haven't you got anything fresher?' Enquire when the fresh produce arrives and say you'll be back then. And go back then. I can guarantee you'll be looked after — they wouldn't dare offer you anything substandard, because they know you have the courage to announce to a shop full of customers that the goods aren't fresh.

Unfortunately, this approach doesn't work in the supermarket. Everything is scrubbed, wrapped in plastic or sprayed with water to make it look fresh, fresh, fresh. Any signs of decay are lopped off with a knife. Potatoes are washed, we are told, for our convenience. It's certainly not convenient when those poor potatoes, robbed of their protective dusty coating, turn green in a matter of days. Nor, when forced into plastic bags, they develop a sour taste and rot within a week because the air can't circulate.

What's happening? Have good health and good taste been replaced by 'convenience'? Are we going to sit back quietly and let it continue or even escalate? Are we going to let our food be irradiated just so that it can sit longer on shop shelves?

Whoever coined the phrase 'Fresh is best' got it exactly right. When it comes to vegetables, not just for the visual pleasure and good taste, but for the sake of our health, it is vitally important.

Julie Biuso
Auckland, 1991

BEGINNINGS

In this section you will find, quite literally, 'the beginnings' to a meal: things to dip or dunk, finger-licking morsels to nibble on, stylish starters and seasonal specialties, and of course soups, some light and refreshing, others a meal in themselves.

❖

DIP, DUNK, SCOOP OR NIBBLE
SPRING AND SUMMER STARTERS
THREE WAYS WITH AVOCADOS
SOMETHING DIFFERENT FOR
AUTUMN AND WINTER
LIGHT AND REFRESHING SOUPS
WINTER SOUPS
BIG SOUPS
CHILLED SOUPS

❖

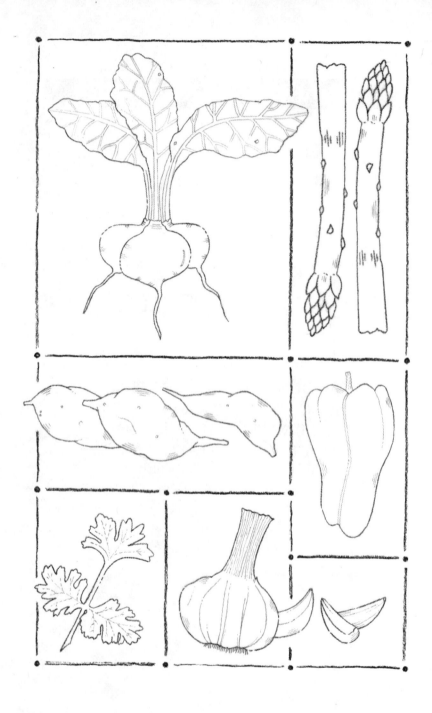

Dip, Dunk, Scoop or Nibble

Here's a selection of finger-licking morsels if ever there was one. Dips have been around a long time and it's understandable why. Served with crisp vegetables, like celery and carrot, they make an inexpensive, healthy snack. Gado Gado, an Indonesian specialty, enlarges on this concept — so much so, that it's easily turned into a meal.

If you've only tried tinned dolmades, packed in salt or brine, these juicy, nutty-tasting little bundles of grape leaves will come as a revelation: 'So that's what they're meant to taste like.'

The other bits and bobs in this section are good for dunking, scooping, spreading or nibbling.

... And if you've not yet considered eating raw broad beans, you might be pleasantly surprised if you do.

❖

GADO GADO AND SAUCES

MUSHROOMS IN
LEMON MARINADE

CHARRED PEPPERS

MARINATED EGGPLANTS

WHITE BEAN AND
ROSEMARY PURÉE

DOLMADES

MARINATED GARLIC CARROTS

BROAD BEANS ALLA GENOVA

❖

GADO GADO

Gado Gado, a selection of vegetables and titbits, served with a pungent, spicy, peanutty dipping sauce, is an excellent dish to have in your repertoire. Its versatility lends to feeding either a small group as a starter, or a large group as a 'nibble'; guests can select, dunk and nibble as the whim takes them. By adding extra protein in the form of eggs or tofu, the dish can be made substantial enough to constitute a meal that is perfect in hot weather.

Vegetable platter
Choose a selection of the following:
3 new potatoes, steamed, peeled and sliced
200 g green beans, topped and tailed (leave raw or blanch briefly)
2 carrots, peeled and cut into sticks
½ cucumber, peeled and cut into chunks
½ cup cauliflower florets (leave raw or blanch briefly)
½ fresh pineapple, skinned and sliced
1 cup fresh bean sprouts
½ cup shredded cabbage, softened (see below)

Extras
4 eggs, hard-boiled, shelled and quartered
150 g tofu (bean curd), cut into oblong shapes (fresh or shallow-fried)
krupuk (shrimp wafers), fried in hot oil until puffy, drained, then stored airtight until required

Put the cabbage in a large bowl and pour boiling water over. Leave for 1 minute, drain, rinse and shake dry. Dry off on kitchen paper; this leaves the cabbage crunch-tender but more digestible.

Arrange the chosen vegetables, and any extra items, on a large platter. Serve with one of the following dipping sauces.

Java Dipping Sauce

Although not strictly Indonesian, this dark and aromatic, spicy and nutty sauce is my favourite.

8 tablespoons soy sauce
6 small stalks lemon grass, or 6 strips lemon peel
2 star anise
25 g raw sugar
½ cup (approx.) hot water
1 cup crunchy peanut butter
2 tablespoons lemon juice
1 teaspoon sambal olek (chilli paste)
2 cloves garlic, crushed

Combine the soy sauce, lemon grass, star anise, raw sugar and hot water in a small saucepan. Stir the mixture over a gentle heat until the sugar dissolves. Simmer for 10 minutes and strain, discarding the lemon grass and star anise.

Combine the liquid with the peanut butter, lemon juice, chilli paste and garlic. Blend in a food processor or by hand. If the sauce is very thick, add a little more hot water to bring it to a dipping consistency. Transfer to a container, cover and refrigerate until required (keeps for several days).

Keeping Fresh Ginger

Fresh ginger softens and rots quite quickly when stored in the refrigerator, particularly when it is stored in plastic.

The trick is to store it in absorbent paper, such as kitchen paper, loosely wrapped, and in the least-cool part of the fridge, like the vegetable crisper or shelves on the door. The paper absorbs any moisture (a plastic bag would lock it in, causing rotting), keeping the ginger cool and dry. It can last many weeks this way.

Fresh ginger can also be frozen, just as it is, in a container or plastic bag. Grate it while still frozen and use in stir-frys, etc.

Another idea is to store a 'clump' of peeled ginger in a bottle of sherry. Use it to give a boost to Chinese-style dishes.

Ginger and Soy Dipping Sauce

The fresh taste of ginger gives this sauce a lift. It is particularly good with pineapple or other fruits like banana, mangosteen, nashi, watermelon and crisp apples.

¼ cup peanut oil
1 onion, finely chopped
2 large cloves garlic, crushed
4 small, dried red chillies, crushed
small knob of fresh ginger, roughly chopped
175 g roasted, shelled peanuts
3 tablespoons soy sauce
1 tablespoon brown sugar
¾ cup (approx.) hot water

Heat the peanut oil in a frypan over a gentle heat. Add the onion and fry until soft and a pale gold colour.

Add the garlic, chilli and ginger. Cook for a few minutes, then tip into a food processor or liquidiser and add the peanuts, soy sauce, brown sugar and ¼ cup hot water. Process until smooth, adding more hot water if necessary to bring it to a dipping consistency.

Store, covered and refrigerated, until required (keeps for 2–3 days).

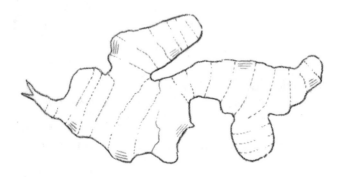

Coconutty Tamarind Sauce

The addition of coconut cream gives this sauce a richness the others lack.

2 tablespoons peanut oil
1 onion, finely chopped
8 small, dried red chillies, crumbled
1 teaspoon blachan (shrimp paste) (optional)
1½ cups tinned coconut cream
½ cup crunchy peanut butter
¼ cup tamarind liquid
¼ teaspoon salt

Heat the peanut oil in a frypan over a gentle heat. Add the onion and fry until soft and a pale gold colour. Add the chillies and blachan, if using. Fry for 5 minutes, stirring often.

Blend in the coconut cream by degrees, then blend in the peanut butter, tamarind liquid and salt. Bring to a gentle boil, then cook gently, stirring often, until it is thickish. Cool and store, covered and refrigerated, until required (keeps for 2 days).

Tamarind

Tamarind, the fruit of a tropical tree, is used to provide an acid, sweet-sour flavour. It's sold in a sticky mass of pulp and seeds. Reconstitute tamarind by soaking a large knob of it in a cup of very hot water. Leave for 15 minutes, then squeeze with the fingers to separate the seeds from the pulp. Rub through a sieve and use it to flavour curries, chutneys, pickles, sauces and drinks.

MUSHROOMS IN LEMON MARINADE

Serves 6

These delectable little mushrooms are great hot or at room temperature. If they are not for immediate consumption, cool, then store refrigerated (they keep for 2–3 days).

100 ml olive oil
¼ cup water
½ teaspoon salt
freshly ground black pepper to taste
50 ml lemon juice
1 tablespoon finely chopped oregano or marjoram
  (or ½ tablespoon dried oregano or marjoram)
1 bay leaf
500 g small, white button mushrooms

Put the olive oil, water, salt, black pepper, lemon juice and herbs into a large frypan. Bring to the boil, uncovered, then tip in the mushrooms. Cook at a lively boil for 7–10 minutes, or until cooked through, flipping the mushrooms over in the reducing liquids.

Using a slotted spoon transfer the mushrooms to a dish. Continue reducing the liquids over a high heat, swirling the pan from time to time, until the oil and liquids have reduced and formed an emulsion. Pour over the mushrooms and serve hot, or leave them to cool to room temperature.

Storing Mushrooms

If given the option of buying mushrooms in a plastic bag or in a brown paper bag, always choose the latter. Mushrooms stored in plastic (at room temperature or in the fridge) quickly sweat and become soggy, then rotten.

Store them either in an unsealed brown paper bag or unsealed in a large plastic bag or container lined with absorbent kitchen paper.

CHARRED PEPPERS

Serves 6–10 as an antipasto dish

Roasting peppers enhances their wonderfully sweet flavour. This easy recipe is redolent of rosemary and garlic and makes a tasty, colourful addition to an antipasto selection.

4–6 red and yellow peppers, halved, cored and deseeded
6 cloves garlic, split in half
1 large sprig rosemary, broken into four pieces
bay leaves
¼ teaspoon salt
50 ml extra virgin olive oil

Put the peppers, cut side upwards, in a large, heavy-based casserole. Distribute the garlic and rosemary amongst the peppers and put ½ bay leaf inside each half. Sprinkle over the salt and pour on the olive oil.

Set the casserole over a high heat and allow the olive oil and peppers to get very hot. Cover with a lid and transfer to an oven preheated to 180°C. Cook for about 30–40 minutes, or until the peppers are very tender and lightly charred.

Serve at room temperature, with bread for scooping or mopping up the juices. The peppers store well, covered and refrigerated, for 1–2 days.

Roasting Peppers

Roasting peppers over a gas flame, a hot barbecue or in a hot oven causes the skin to char and blister, making it easy to peel off. The charring brings out a nutty, sweet, slightly smoky flavour.

To roast peppers, sit them on an oven rack in an oven preheated to 200°C, and cook for about 20 minutes, turning occasionally with tongs, or until they are blistered and charred. Transfer to a board and when cool peel off the skins and slip out the cores and seeds.

They can be used immediately, or kept for several days, covered and refrigerated. They are delicious with a vinaigrette, plain, or flecked with herbs, or dotted with capers, olives, anchovy pieces, etc. Serve as a nibble, or atop pizza or croûtes.

MARINATED EGGPLANTS

Serves 4

Garlic, herbs, olive oil and lemon juice give excellent flavour to this Greek eggplant dish. It can be served as a vegetable accompaniment to a simple lamb dish, as part of a Mediterranean meal, or the eggplant halves can be cut into quarters and served with olives, feta cheese, chick-peas, etc. as part of a 'mezze' (nibbles) platter. They keep well for 1–2 days, providing they are refrigerated, but bring them to room temperature before serving.

2 large eggplants, trimmed
salt
¼ cup olive oil
2 large cloves garlic, finely chopped
2 tablespoons finely chopped fresh marjoram or oregano
    (or use 1 tablespoon of either dried herb)
freshly ground black pepper to taste
½ lemon

Cut the eggplants in half lengthwise, then score the cut surfaces in a diamond pattern. Sprinkle the cut sides with salt, then lay upside down in a colander and drain for 30 minutes. Squeeze, shake off excess moisture and pat dry.

Lightly oil a roasting tin. Put in the eggplants, cut side upwards, then drizzle with the olive oil. Sprinkle over the garlic and herbs, sprinkle lightly with salt and grind over black pepper. Turn the eggplant slices over, then bake them in an oven preheated to 180°C for 45–60 minutes, or until they are crisp on the base and tender.

Carefully turn them over with a fish slice, then continue cooking for 15 minutes, or until very tender and a good deep golden-brown colour. Squeeze over a little lemon juice, and serve them hot, or at room temperature.

Dégorger

This means to rid foods of bitter or strong flavours. The most common vegetable to be subjected to the dégorging process is eggplant. It is first halved, sliced or cubed, salted well, then left to drain in a colander for 30–40 minutes. It's a good idea to put a plate underneath the colander to collect the liquid. The eggplant pieces are then dried with kitchen paper before the recipe is continued.

Bitter cucumbers are also greatly improved either by soaking in water, or by salting and draining. It may sound like an old wives' tale, but I've been told that if you cut the cucumber from the blossom end only (the blossom end is the opposite end to the stalk end), the cucumber will not be bitter.

Antipasto

This Italian word means a dish, or dishes (the plural is antipasti) served before the 'pasti' or main meal. There are zillions of things, simple and elaborate, raw and cooked, hot and cold, which fall into this category, but the most simple ones are olives, salami, and cured hams or pork products.

Mezze

Mezze are the Greek and Middle Eastern versions of antipasti and tapas, consumed as a 'nibble' before the main meal. They are often, I might add, much to the regret of many a tourist, accompanied by a shot or two of ouzo or aniseed liqueur (an ouzo-induced hangover is one of the worst kinds!).

Mezze include toasted, salted chick-peas, olives, cubes of feta cheese, little pastry do-dahs, cured meats, fishy things, cucumber chunks, etc.

To Soak or Not to Soak

Years ago, when the dried beans in this country were always as hard as bullets, it was imperative to soak all varieties in water before attempting to cook them.

These days we must eat lots more pulses (a faster turnover of stock), or drying methods must be improved, because most beans hardly require a soaking at all. The only pulse I continue to soak for a lengthy period is chick-peas.

The old salting rule still applies, though; don't salt the beans or peas until they are tender, otherwise they will never become tender.

Growing Rosemary

I could grow parsley, basil, coriander, thyme, mint and oregano from seed, but not rosemary. That is, until I eventually got tired of nicking it from roadside gardens, and took the time to read about its requirements.

I can tell you it doesn't like a rich, humusy soil. Various rosemary bushes, all bright-eyed and bushy-tailed, fresh from the nursery, have curled up their toes and died in my composty mixtures. Now I grow it in sandy, even stony soil, and for a treat I dig in a few crushed eggshells and water it occasionally. It grows like a weed.

To Chop or Crush

Some recipes call for chopped garlic. This is stronger than crushed garlic, probably because you use more of it, and because the pieces are bigger when they hit your palate. If you want a milder taste, use less garlic and crush it.

WHITE BEAN AND ROSEMARY PURÉE

Serves 12 as an antipasto dish

The smooth texture of this garlicky purée is offset perfectly by the interesting tang of lemon and surprise bursts of chilli.

225 g small dried white beans (use cannellini, haricot or navy beans), rinsed, then soaked for 3 hours in cold water
1 tablespoon tomato concentrate
2 small dried chillies (use the tiny 'Bird's Eye' chillies)
3 tablespoons extra virgin olive oil
1 large clove garlic, finely chopped
1 tablespoon finely chopped rosemary
½ teaspoon salt
1 tablespoon lemon juice

Transfer the beans to a large saucepan and pour on a litre of water. Stir in the tomato concentrate and add one chilli, crumbled. Bring to the boil, then turn the heat down and cook gently for about 30 minutes, or until tender (may take up to an hour).

Drain, reserving some of the cooking liquid. Mash the beans or purée them in a food processor, using a little of the cooking liquid to turn the mixture into a purée.

Finely chop the second chilli. Heat the olive oil in a medium-sized saucepan over a medium heat and add the garlic, rosemary and chilli. Sauté for 2–3 minutes. Pour into the bean purée, add the salt, blend together, then tip all the mixture back into the saucepan.

Cook for 2–3 minutes, stirring, then blend in the lemon juice. Cover with a lid, remove from the heat and allow to cool. Refrigerate until required (keeps for 2 days).

Serve as a nibble or antipasto dish accompanied by crusty French bread, fresh pita pockets or hot (or cold) dry toast.

DOLMADES

Makes about 40

These stuffed vine leaves not only make an interesting nibble to serve with drinks, but they are also good for picnics. Alternatively, include them in Greek-Middle Eastern menus. They keep for 2–3 days, providing they are covered and refrigerated.

400–500 g preserved vine leaves
3 tablespoons olive oil
1 large onion, very finely chopped
½ cup short-grain rice, washed and drained
2 tablespoons pinenuts
2 tablespoons currants
2 tablespoons finely chopped parsley
2 tablespoons finely chopped mint
¼ teaspoon salt
freshly ground black pepper to taste
1 cup water mixed with juice of a lemon and 3 tablespoons olive oil
unsweetened yoghurt (optional)

Carefully separate the vine leaves under running water. Rinse well, then place them in a bowl of cold water. Plunge several leaves at a time into a large saucepan of boiling water, leave for 1–2 minutes, then remove with tongs and transfer to a bowl of cold water. When all are done, drain and shake them dry, then snip off any stems.

Next make the filling. Heat the olive oil in a large frypan and add the onion. Cook very gently until the onion is soft and a light golden colour. Stir in the rice, cook for 1–2 minutes, stirring, then add the pinenuts, currants, parsley, mint, salt and black pepper to taste. Blend in ¾ cup water, then cover with a lid and cook very gently for about 12 minutes, or until most of the liquid has been absorbed and the rice is nearly tender.

Place the vine leaves smooth side downwards on a clean bench. Put a small blob (about ¾ teaspoon) of the filling in the middle of each leaf. Carefully fold the stem end and sides of the leaf over the stuffing, then roll up tightly, moulding the dolmades into shape.

Use any torn leaves to line a large, heavy-based frypan; then put the dolmades in the pan, in one layer, seams tucked underneath. Pack them in as closely as possible to prevent them unrolling during cooking. Cover the top with more leaves. Pour over the mixed water, lemon juice and olive oil. Position a plate on top to hold them in place and cover with a lid. Bring to a gentle boil, then turn the heat to low and simmer very gently for about an hour, or until the dolmades are very tender. Remove from the heat and leave to cool (don't remove the lid). When cool, transfer to a container, cover and chill until serving time. If liked, accompany them with a bowl of thick yoghurt (see page 111).

MARINATED GARLIC CARROTS

Serves 6 as an antipasto dish

These sprightly carrots make a great contrast to a selection of rich antipasto dishes.

200 g young carrots, peeled
1 tablespoon red wine vinegar
¼ teaspoon salt
freshly ground black pepper to taste
1 clove garlic, crushed
1 tablespoon finely chopped marjoram (optional)
1 tablespoon extra virgin olive oil

Cut the carrots into very fine julienne (the same length as a match but half the thickness). Soak them in ice-cold water for 30 minutes. Drain, shake well, then pat dry on kitchen paper.

Mix the red wine vinegar, salt, black pepper, garlic and marjoram together in a small bowl. Whisk in the olive oil. Drop in the carrots, toss well and marinate (covered and chilled) for an hour before serving.

BROAD BEANS ALLA GENOVA

There can be no simpler start to a spring meal than this rustic Genoese offering. The first time it was suggested to me, I was a little sceptical, but nonetheless intrigued. However, I quickly became a fan.

It was many years ago, in an old trattoria in the 'seedy' part of town near the port of Genoa, that some friends and I were persuaded to try something other than the house specialty of freshly caught fish. We were presented with a carafe of 'gut-rot' red wine, a slab of salty, pungent, white sheep's cheese, a calico-wrapped log of coarse-textured salami studded with black peppercorns and reeking of garlic, and a basket of freshly picked, young broad beans.

Our host sliced some salami thickly, crumbled the cheese and snapped open a few beans and told us to try the three ingredients together. The combination, I can tell you, is quite remarkable.

The young beans are delicately nutty to taste, and milky, though slightly astringent. The sweet-hot fat and spice of the salami chases the astringency away, then the tang and salt of the cheese bite into the mouth, alarming the tastebuds but finishing with a lingering saltiness which makes the mouth salivate, begging for the milkiness of the beans to soothe it. And so it goes on. Before you know it you will have devoured great quantities of all three, not to mention copious draughts of any rough red you may happen to serve with it.

Choose a well-seasoned, coarse-textured salami, preferably one with chunkier pieces of sweet fat, but avoid hot-spiced ones flavoured with chilli. The cheese should be fresh, tangy-sharp and crumbly in texture. Reasonable substitutes are a good Welsh Caerphilly, a dry (not crumbling), low-salt feta, or perhaps a white Cheshire cheese. The beans must be young and fresh. A youngish, lively Chianti goes well with this, as does a new Beaujolais. But a gutsier wine, providing it is red, will not be out of place.

Spring and Summer Starters

I think it was the American pop group the Byrds who sang the song ... 'to each and everything there is a season'. How true!

Spring sees artichokes arriving at the market, first the smallish buds, tender enough to be shaved wafer-thin and eaten raw with nothing else but a dousing of vinaigrette. And later, towards the end of the season, the heavy, well-formed artichokes which respond well to steaming and braising. That's the time the classic Roman treatment – Artichokes Roman Style – comes into its own.

Summer sees tomatoes, deep red and bursting with juice, and peppers and sweet corn sweeter than ever.

It's when vegetables are at their peak that the start of a meal can be centred on them.

❖

ARTICHOKES ROMAN STYLE

TOMATOES STUFFED WITH TUNA

SUNBURST SALAD

FRESH SWEET CORN ON
GARLIC CROÛTES

❖

ARTICHOKES ROMAN STYLE

Serves 4

It's not just the rich, full flavour that makes these artichokes a knockout, but their visual impact contributes as well. The artichokes are trimmed, but the stems are left on, and they are presented 'bottoms up' with the stems pointing in the air. The ideal temperature at which to serve them is when they are no longer hot, but not quite completely cooled either.

4 large artichokes, with stems attached
juice of 1 lemon mixed with 2 litres of water
2 large cloves garlic, peeled and finely chopped
1 rounded tablespoon finely chopped mint
½ teaspoon salt
freshly ground black pepper to taste
3 tablespoons finely chopped parsley
¼ cup extra virgin olive oil

Cut off the top third of each artichoke and discard. Spread the leaves apart, opening and loosening the artichokes. Remove the mauve-coloured leaves in the centre, then press the soft, yellowish leaves away from the centre until a cavity is formed and the choke is revealed. The choke is the collection of fibrous hairs, which should be totally scraped out as it is inedible, even after cooking. Use a pointed teaspoon to remove it, but take care to remove only the hairy fibre, because directly below this is the meaty base of the artichoke (referred to as the fond or heart). As the artichokes are prepared, plunge them into the acidulated water.

In a bowl mix the garlic, mint, salt, black pepper and parsley. Set aside one third of this mixture and press the rest into the cavities of the artichokes.

Choose a heavy-based casserole just large enough to contain the artichokes. Place them in the casserole with stems pointing up. Rub the rest of the herb mixture over the outside of the artichokes. Drizzle over the olive oil and add enough water to come about one third of the way up the leaves. Put on a lid and cook over a medium heat for about 45–60 minutes, or until tender and easily pierced by a skewer.

Transfer to a serving dish, arranging them with the stems up. If the juices in the pan are on the thin side, simply reduce over a high heat until an emulsion forms, then pour it over the artichokes.

Remember that the stems are edible, too; they have a slightly earthier taste than the leaves.

Artichoke Tips

Always use a stainless steel knife (not a carbon one) to cut artichokes; carbon taints them, causing blackening to the artichoke and knife. (If you accidentally use a carbon steel knife, clean it after with ½ lemon; it will remove the black and the nasty metallic smell.)

Use the cooked artichoke leaves for dunking into a dip. Try a vinaigrette flavoured with orange rind and orange juice; a sour cream dip flavoured with capers, garlic and black pepper; or a herby, garlicky vinaigrette.

TOMATOES STUFFED WITH TUNA

Serves 4–6 as a main course, or 6–8 as a starter

These tomatoes make a good starter for a summer's meal, or, accompanied by a bowl of crisp salad leaves and a loaf of 'country bread', an admirable light lunch. They can be prepared well in advance, even the day before if necessary; store in a covered container in the refrigerator and serve chilled.

6 large (or 12 medium) tomatoes, skinned
2 x 185 g tins tuna, drained
1 teaspoon Dijon-style mustard
2 tablespoons capers, drained
1 tablespoon lemon juice
1 tablespoon finely chopped parsley (or dill)
½ teaspoon salt
plenty of freshly ground black pepper
½ cup (approx.) mayonnaise

Dressing
4 tablespoons juice from tomatoes
6 tablespoons extra virgin olive oil
½ teaspoon salt
pinch of castor sugar
freshly ground black pepper to taste

Cut a cap off the tomatoes and set aside. Carefully scoop out the seeds and as much pulp as possible. Drain the seeds and pulp in a sieve set over a bowl and reserve the juice for the dressing. Turn the empty tomatoes over and leave them to drain.

Put the tuna in a bowl and break up the flakes with a fork. Blend in the mustard, capers, lemon juice, parsley, salt and black pepper and as much mayonnaise as necessary to bind the ingredients together.

Shake any liquid from the tomatoes, then fill with the tuna mixture. Put on the caps, then transfer to a container, cover and chill for 2–3 hours.

Blend the tomato juice, olive oil, salt, castor sugar and black pepper together in a small bowl. When ready to serve, arrange the tomatoes on individual plates, whisk the dressing and spoon over. Serve immediately.

SUNBURST SALAD

Serves 4

This roasted pepper salad, dressed with walnut oil and orange rind, and garnished with hard-boiled eggs, capers and olives, really captures the spirit of summer.

6 peppers of assorted hues
2 eggs, at room temperature
juice of ½ lemon
grated rind of ½ orange
1 tablespoon snipped chives
¼ teaspoon salt
plenty of freshly ground black pepper
1 teaspoon capers, drained
4 tablespoons walnut oil
several black olives
paprika

Sit the peppers on an oven rack in an oven preheated to 200°C, and cook for about 20 minutes, turning occasionally with tongs, or until they are blistered and charred. Transfer to a board and allow to cool. Peel off the skins and slip out the cores and seeds. Slice the peppers into strips and arrange on a large plate.

Hard-boil the eggs, shell them and cut into quarters. Arrange in the centre of the peppers.

In a small bowl whisk the lemon juice, orange rind, chives (reserve a few for garnishing), salt, black pepper and capers, then whisk in the walnut oil. Spoon over the peppers and eggs. Decorate with the olives and reserved snipped chives, then sieve a little paprika over. Serve immediately with good crusty bread.

FRESH SWEET CORN ON
GARLIC CROÛTES

Serves 4

Who said sweet corn need always be served on the cob? When it's plentiful and cheap, it's time to be experimental. The following idea is simply superb. A good bottle of Sémillon makes a delicious partner.

3 fresh corn on the cob
½ cup cream
few pinches of salt
freshly ground black pepper to taste
¼ teaspoon sugar
knob of butter
2 tablespoons snipped chives or chopped parsley

Peel off the husks from the sweet corn and remove all the silks. If the sweet corn is young and just-picked there is no need to cook it first. Otherwise, cook for 10–15 minutes in unsalted, gently boiling water. Drain, then use a sharp knife to cut the corn off the cobs. This can be prepared in advance.

Put the cream, salt, black pepper, sugar and butter in a small saucepan and set over a medium-high heat. Cook until reduced by half (until you have approx. ¼ cup). Add the prepared sweet corn and chives or parsley, and cook for 1–2 minutes until heated through and creamy in consistency.

Arrange the hot garlic croûtes on plates and spoon over the creamy sweet corn mixture. Serve immediately.

Garlic croûtes
bread for toasting
garlic butter

Toast the bread to a deep golden colour. Spread with garlic butter and stamp into rounds with a cutter, or cut into triangle shapes. Use hot.

'Put the Water on to Boil First'

It's true! Just like Mum said! Bring the water to the boil first before going down to the corn patch to pick corn. As soon as the sweet corn is cut from the plant, the sugar starts turning to starch, so the sooner you get it in the pot the sweeter it's going to be. (The same applies to green peas.)

The other old wives' tale is true, too; don't salt the water until the corn is cooked, or the kernels will toughen.

Spicy Corn

Here's a quick, savoury trick using sweet corn.

Cook 4 cobs of sweet corn and scrape off the kernels while still warm. Melt a knob of butter in a smallish frypan and add ½ teaspoon each of cinnamon and garam masala, a few pinches of salt and ¼ teaspoon chilli powder. Stir-fry for 1–2 minutes, then add the prepared corn. Cook, stirring often, till it is heated through.

This is good on toasted muffins with bacon and avocado, or alongside cooked tomatoes, or with ham steaks, with a kumara salad, or with a tasty, tossed green salad.

Whole Barbecued Corn

This is a delicious treatment for sweet corn.

Carefully peel back the husks, then pull off the silks. Wash under running water. Fold the husks back over the corn, then tie them tightly with kitchen string (not nylon-coated string!). Soak the prepared corn in a bowl of cold water for 10 minutes, then shake dry. Cook for 15–20 minutes over a hot barbecue, turning occasionally. Serve with fresh butter.

31

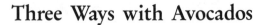

Three Ways with Avocados

An avocado's an avocado's an avocado ...
I fell in love with them years ago ... what more can I say?

❖

AVOCADO WITH BLACK
OLIVE PURÉE
....
TOMATOES STUFFED WITH
AVOCADO ON GARLIC CROÛTES
....
AVOCADO WITH ORANGE
TOMATO DRESSING

❖

AVOCADO WITH BLACK OLIVE PURÉE

Serves 4–8

This garlicky olive purée not only looks stunning in the cavities of the avocados but also makes a pleasant contrast to their smooth texture.

1 generous cup soft, black olives, halved and stoned
1 medium tomato, skinned
1 large clove garlic, roughly chopped
1 teaspoon lemon juice, plus a little extra
1 tablespoon coarsely chopped fresh basil (or parsley)
freshly ground black pepper to taste
2 tablespoons olive oil
4 ripe but firm avocados

The olive purée is easily made in a food processor (otherwise chop the ingredients very finely by hand).

Put the olives, tomato, garlic, lemon juice, basil (or parsley), black pepper and olive oil in a food processor and whizz until chopped and smooth. Cover and set aside until required. (The purée will keep, refrigerated, for several days.)

When ready to serve, cut open the avocados and extract the stones. Position them on plates, and smear the cut surfaces with a little lemon juice. Fill the cavities with the olive mixture, mounding it in the shape of an olive stone. (Serve any extra mixture separately in a side bowl.)

Serve immediately with hot fingers of toast or soft, warm pita bread.

Wobbling Avocados

Having trouble with wobbling avocados? If they wobble around on the plate, cut off a small sliver from the rounded part. They will then sit flat.

TOMATOES STUFFED WITH AVOCADO ON GARLIC CROÛTES

Serves 4

This makes a light and delicious start to a summer's meal.

8 medium tomatoes, skinned
1 large ripe avocado
salt
freshly ground black pepper to taste

Dressing
grated rind of ½ lemon
1 tablespoon lemon juice
¼ teaspoon salt
¼ cup olive oil
freshly ground black pepper to taste
pinch of castor sugar
1 teaspoon finely chopped basil (or chives or parsley)
1 teaspoon finely chopped mint

Garlic croûtes
4 slices toast bread
1–2 cloves garlic, peeled and crushed
30 g butter, softened

Cut a cap off each tomato and set aside. Carefully scoop out the seeds and as much pulp as possible. Drain the seeds and pulp in a sieve set over a bowl and reserve the juice. Turn the empty tomatoes over and leave to drain.

Cut the avocado in half. Discard the stone, then scoop out the flesh with a teaspoon and place in a bowl. Add 1 teaspoon of the strained tomato juice, season lightly with salt and black pepper, and mash with a fork. The dish may be prepared 1–2 hours ahead to this point, providing the stuffing and tomatoes are covered in plastic and refrigerated.

When ready to serve, spoon the avocado mixture into the tomatoes and top with the tomato caps. Position the garlic croûtes on individual plates, top with the tomatoes and spoon over the dressing. Serve immediately.

Dressing

Mix all the ingredients together, adding 1–2 teaspoons of the strained tomato juice. This may be mixed ahead of time, but add the herbs at the last minute to ensure they keep a good colour.

Garlic croûtes

Blend the butter and garlic together. Toast the bread and spread with the butter. Cut off the crusts and cut the bread into rounds using a cutter, or into small squares. Use immediately.

Avocado Advice

The avocado is called a fruit because it grows on trees, but in composition it is more like a vegetable. It contains more fat than any other fruit — about 20 per cent (but no cholesterol), traces of minerals, traces of many vitamins (A, B_6, C), very little starch and practically no sugar.

Buy avocados under-ripe. That way you can ripen them at home and consume them at their peak (they often become badly bruised in shops and vegetable markets because of overhandling and squeezing and testing for ripeness). Ripen them at room temperature or, to speed up the process, place them in a brown bag and leave them in a warm spot. They are ready to eat when they yield to gentle hand pressure.

It's best not to refrigerate them until they are ripe, as the ripening enzymes can be destroyed by excess cold. Once ripe, store them refrigerated; they will last for several days. Remember, once cut, to brush them with lemon juice to prevent discolouring.

AVOCADO WITH ORANGE
TOMATO DRESSING

Serves 6

This is one of my favourite ways with avocados. The buttery richness of the avocado is kept in check by the freshness of the orange, and the warm, clove-like basil and clear tomato taste combine to make a stunning summer first course.

4 tablespoons olive oil
3 spring onions, finely chopped
1 large clove garlic, crushed
1 teaspoon raw sugar
1 teaspoon tomato purée
½ teaspoon salt
freshly ground black pepper to taste
6 small ripe tomatoes, skinned and finely chopped
1 tablespoon finely chopped basil, plus a few whole leaves to garnish
grated rind of 1 orange
juice of 1–2 oranges (use the second orange to thin the dressing to a pouring consistency)
3 ripe but firm avocados

Put the olive oil, spring onions, garlic, raw sugar, tomato purée, salt and black pepper, along with four of the prepared tomatoes, in a saucepan. Stir together, then set over a medium heat and cook gently, uncovered, until pulpy, for about 12 minutes.

Add the chopped basil, orange rind and juice to the mixture, then fold through the remaining two tomatoes. Cool and set aside until required. (The sauce may be prepared several hours ahead. Even keeping it overnight is fine, providing it is kept refrigerated.)

When ready to serve, cut open the avocados, extract the stones and position on plates. Spoon over the dressing, filling the cavities and letting the excess dressing form a pool on the plate. Decorate with basil leaves and serve immediately. Good with thinly sliced, buttered, grainy bread.

Something Different for Autumn and Winter

When the predictable cold weather fare starts to bore you, delve into this eclectic collection; you're bound to find something that's either affordable or easy to make, or different.

❖

CELERIAC SALAD WITH
HERB MAYONNAISE
....
JACKET-BAKED BEETROOT WITH
SOURED LEMON CREAM
....
LEEKS VINAIGRETTE
....
OVEN-BAKED MUSHROOMS
....
WILTED SPINACH AND
MUSHROOM SALAD

❖

CELERIAC SALAD WITH HERB MAYONNAISE

Serves 6–8

For a light lunch this dish makes a pleasant accompaniment to slices of ham off the bone.

500 g celeriac
¾ cup homemade mayonnaise
2 tablespoons finely chopped fresh herbs (choose from parsley,
    chives, lemon thyme, thyme, chervil, marjoram, tarragon)
¼ teaspoon salt
freshly ground black pepper to taste
few squirts lemon juice

Using a sharp knife chop off the thick brown skin on the celeriac, being sure to remove all traces of roots. Grate the celeriac coarsely, either by hand or in a food processor. Work quickly with the celeriac once cut, as it soon discolours (a few squirts of lemon juice can delay this).

Mix the mayonnaise, herbs, salt, black pepper and lemon juice in a bowl, and mix in the celeriac. Cover the bowl and chill for at least 2 hours before serving (overnight is fine). Before serving toss again, then transfer to a clean serving bowl.

Celeriac

Celeriac is closely related to celery and is often known as 'turnip-rooted celery'. But unlike celery, the stems and leaves of the plant are not eaten. Celeriac forms a white-fleshed, globular root, which can grow up to 15 cm in diameter, and this is the part which is eaten.

The flavour is more delicate than that of celery, but it is just as useful. It can be grated raw and used in salads, or steamed, boiled, mashed, puréed, or added to soups and stews.

When choosing celeriac, check for freshness; it should feel firm to the touch and should not sound hollow when tapped.

JACKET-BAKED BEETROOT WITH
SOURED LEMON CREAM

Serves 6

Here's a stunning idea for small beetroot. The contrast between the deep-coloured beets and the soured cream is eye-catching, particularly when the beetroot just begins to bleed into the cream.

Serve this as an unusual starter in winter, or as a vegetable accompaniment to Sauerbraten (spicy-sweet, marinated beef dish) or similar-style dishes.

6 medium (even-sized) beetroot
250 g sour cream
grated rind of 1 lemon
grated rind of 1 lime (or use 2 lemons)
1 teaspoon lemon juice
few pinches of salt
freshly ground black pepper to taste
2 tablespoons snipped chives

Trim excess stalks from the beetroot tops, but be sure not to nick the skin, as the beetroot will bleed during cooking and lose its deep colouring. Do not trim the tapering root.

Wash carefully, then wrap each one tightly in tinfoil and sit them on an oven rack in an oven preheated to 180°C. Cook, turning once with tongs, for 1½ hours, or until tender.

Meanwhile, mix the sour cream, lemon and lime rinds, lemon juice, salt, black pepper and half of the chives. Remove the beetroot from the foil, then wrinkle the skin and peel off. Trim the ends. Put the beetroot on serving plates and cut each through the top, three-quarters of the way through, into four quarters, so that each beetroot opens up like a flower. Spoon a little sauce into the centre of each, sprinkle with chives and serve within 15 minutes.

LEEKS VINAIGRETTE

Serves 6

This unusual way with leeks makes an attractive light starter to a winter's meal, or, if teamed with other dishes, it is superb as the basis of a light meal (for example, try it with a hard-boiled egg and olive salad, dressed with a creamy mayonnaise and a spinach and mushroom salad).

6 slim young leeks, with roots intact
salt
1 large tomato, skinned
1 teaspoon green peppercorns, drained
plenty of freshly ground black pepper
1 teaspoon white wine vinegar
½ teaspoon Dijon-style mustard
3 tablespoons olive oil

Use a large knife to trim the leaf tips of the leeks, then remove any coarse outer leaves. Trim the roots, taking care not to cut them off entirely, as they will hold the leeks together during blanching. Cut each leek in two lengthwise, then rinse thoroughly under running cold water. Shake dry, then trim the leeks to a uniform length to fit the serving plates. If the leeks have had their roots chopped off, tie each leek half with a plastic and metal tie-tag before cooking, then slip this off after draining.

Bring a large saucepan of water to the boil, add a few pinches of salt, then plunge in the leeks. Don't cover the pan but allow the water to return to the boil, then cook for 7–10 minutes, or until fork-tender. Drain and refresh with plenty of cold water, drain again, then shake out as much water as possible. Leave to drain in a colander, then transfer to a tray lined with a double thickness of kitchen paper. Cover with plastic wrap and refrigerate until required. (The leeks can be prepared a day in advance.)

Cut the tomato in half, scoop out the seeds and put them into a small sieve set over a bowl. Extract as much juice from the seeds as possible, then discard them. Cut the tomato flesh into fine slivers, then cover and set aside.

When ready to serve, add the green peppercorns, ¼ teaspoon salt, black pepper, white wine vinegar, mustard and olive oil to the tomato juice in the bowl. Whisk well.

Arrange two leek halves on each plate. Add the slivered tomato to the dressing, blend well and spoon over the leeks. Serve immediately.

Skinning Tomatoes

When tomatoes are eaten fresh, as in a salad, there is usually no need to remove the skins (remove them if they are tough), but if they are used in soups, sauces or vegetable stews, it is advisable to do so. The skin tends to separate from the flesh during cooking and float to the surface when it is cooked, looking unappetising and tasting tough. Also, cooked tomato skins are not easily digested.

The idea is to heat the tomato in water so it swells. This makes the skin taut and causes it to burst. The ripeness of each tomato varies, so it is best to plunge them, one at a time, into a saucepan of boiling water (easiest done with tongs or a slotted spoon); allow 6–15 seconds. Lift out and plunge into a bowl of cold water and peel. (If the tomato is difficult to peel, repeat the process.) If the peeled tomato looks fluffy or furry, it was in the water too long and has started to cook; cut the seconds down for any other tomatoes.

Never remove the skins from tomatoes which are to be baked in the oven: it holds them together and they will collapse without it.

OVEN-BAKED MUSHROOMS

Serves 4

A food processor or blender makes quick work of this light and tasty mushroom filling. Accompanied by a tangy salad and a loaf of crunchy bread, these mushrooms make fine autumnal fare.

8 large (approx. 400 g) open-cup mushrooms (mature button ones)
salt
freshly ground black pepper to taste
1 large clove garlic, crushed
⅓ cup cream
1 tablespoon coarsely chopped parsley
1 tablespoon snipped chives
1 teaspoon chopped marjoram (optional)
1 large egg yolk
2 slices (approx. 100 g) ham, de-rinded and chopped (optional)
1 cup fresh breadcrumbs (if not using ham increase breadcrumbs to 1¼ cups)
½ cup freshly grated Parmesan cheese
knob of butter

Gently rinse or wipe the top of the mushroom caps, then cut off the stalks. Rinse the stalks and shake dry, then chop roughly. Put in a food processor or blender with 1 teaspoon salt, some black pepper, the garlic, cream, parsley, chives, and marjoram if used. Process until well chopped, then add the egg yolk and ham if used. Process until smooth, transfer to a bowl and blend in the fresh breadcrumbs by hand. (If the crumbs are mixed in by machine the mixture becomes tacky.)

Sprinkle the insides of the mushrooms with a little salt and grind over a little black pepper. Divide the mixture between the mushrooms, spreading it on with a knife. Sit them in an oiled roasting tin, sprinkle over the Parmesan cheese and dot with butter. Bake for about 25 minutes, or until tender and lightly golden on top, in an oven preheated to 200°C. Serve hot.

Parmesan Cheese (Parmigiano-Reggiano)

True Parmesan cheese (Parmigiano-Reggiano) has an inviting aroma and a slightly salty, spicy flavour and a granular texture. As you eat it the small granular pieces dissolve and burst into flavour on your tongue.

It leaves all Parmesan look-alikes for dead. For instance, how many of the Parmesan-style cheeses would you consider serving as a fresh cheese? No doubt few would make the grade; most are highly seasoned, or soapy, waxy, dry, hard, coarse-textured or inferior in some other way. Use them as a grating cheese if you must, but not in Italian recipes calling for the incomparable Parmigiano-Reggiano.

Buy Parmesan cheese in the piece and treble-wrap it tightly in tinfoil. Pop it into a plastic bag and store it in the least-cool part of the fridge (usually the door). If storing for a long period, remove the foil every so often, wipe the rind clean and cover with fresh foil. For long-term storage, wrap as described above and freeze; it will emerge nearly as good as fresh-cut cheese!

Parmesan cheese has many uses in the kitchen. It is used to flavour cooked and uncooked foods, and in stuffings and sauces for vegetable, pasta and meat dishes. It is mixed with crumbs and sprinkled over gratins to provide a crisp, evenly brown topping (Parmesan browns well but does not run or turn stringy when cooked). The same crumb coating is applied to meats and vegetables before frying, and of course it is served atop pasta, gnocchi, rice and soups.

To serve as a fresh cheese it should be in peak condition, not drying or hard. Serve it with fresh, juicy pears, figs, crisp apples, or cured meats, like prosciutto and salami.

Remember, Parmesan cheese is extremely good for you, so don't feel guilty about using heaps of it (don't send me the bill, though!). It is quickly digested, easily assimilated and low in calories; it's even safe for babies.

WILTED SPINACH AND
MUSHROOM SALAD

Serves 6

This interesting salad of wilted spinach makes an ideal starter to a rich winter's meal.

3 slices wholemeal bread, crusts removed
¼ cup frying oil
salt
300 g spinach, well washed and torn into bite-size pieces (discard the stalks)
¼ cup black olives, halved and stoned
¼ cup olive oil
250 g small button mushrooms, washed and sliced (leave whole if very small)
freshly ground black pepper to taste
1 teaspoon green peppercorns, drained
2 tablespoons red wine vinegar

Cut the wholemeal bread into small dice for croûtons. Heat the frying oil in a large frypan, and when hot add the croûtons and fry, turning occasionally, until they are lightly browned. Using a slotted spoon, remove the croûtons and drain briefly on crumpled kitchen paper. Sprinkle with salt, then set aside until required.

Put torn spinach leaves and black olives in a bowl, then set aside, covered with plastic wrap, until required (refrigerate if preparing more than an hour in advance).

When ready to cook, heat a frypan with the olive oil. When it is quite hot, add the mushrooms and cook quickly over a very high heat until they 'squeak' and turn brown. Grind over black pepper, sprinkle with ¼ teaspoon salt and the green peppercorns, then pour on the red wine vinegar. It will hiss and roar. Swirl the pan, then pour it over the salad; quickly toss together. Sprinkle over the croûtons, dish onto separate plates and serve immediately.

Light and Refreshing Soups

A bowl of light, refreshing soup makes an invigorating start to a meal.

The following multi-season soups provide just the right titillation; whetting the appetite without overloading the stomach.

WATERCRESS SOUP WITH
LEMON CROÛTONS

SPICY SPINACH SOUP

SIMPLE VEGETABLE SOUP

TOMATO AND ORANGE SOUP

SPICED APPLE AND
YOGHURT SOUP

SORREL AND SPINACH SOUP

WATERCRESS SOUP WITH LEMON CROÛTONS

··

Serves 4

This soup, with its pretty pale green colour, lightness and refreshing taste, makes a lovely start to a spring meal.

To prevent the soup from curdling (the acid from the onion and the milk often react), soften the onion very well in the butter and heat the milk to boiling point, then cook the soup gently.

2 large bunches watercress
30 g butter
1 medium onion, finely chopped
2 tablespoons plain flour
250 ml water
1 litre milk
½ teaspoon salt
¾ teaspoon arrowroot
50 ml cream

Lemon croûtons
4 slices stale white bread, crusts removed
oil for frying
¼ teaspoon salt
¼ teaspoon freshly ground black pepper
finely grated rind of 1 lemon

Trim off the watercress stalks just below the point where the leaves start. Fill the sink with cold water and immerse the watercress. Wash quickly, discarding any yellowing leaves and thick stalks, then chop finely.

Melt the butter in a large saucepan and add the onion. Cover with a lid and cook very gently until the onion is very soft and transparent (about 12 minutes). Add the watercress, cover the pan with a lid and cook for approximately 15 minutes or until the watercress has softened; stir occasionally.

Draw the pan off the heat, add the flour, blend in, then pour on the water. Cook gently for 5 minutes.

Meanwhile, heat the milk in a separate saucepan until it is just under boiling point, then tip it into the watercress. Add the salt, then simmer very gently, uncovered, for 12–15 minutes.

Purée the soup in batches in a food processor or blender; then, if a very smooth finish is required, pass it through a coarse sieve.

The soup may be prepared ahead to this point, but should not be kept at room temperature for more than an hour. If necessary, refrigerate the soup when cool and reheat gently when required.

Return the soup to the cleaned pan, set over a gentle heat, then add the arrowroot blended with the cream and 2 tablespoons of the soup. Bring just to the boil, stirring, then ladle it into hot soup bowls. Garnish with lemon croûtons and serve immediately.

Lemon croûtons

Cut the bread into small cubes. Heat a 1-cm depth of oil in a large frypan and add the cubes of bread. Cook quickly, tossing with a slotted spoon, until they are a light golden brown.

Lift the croûtons out of the oil using the slotted spoon and drain them briefly on kitchen paper. Tip onto a clean piece of paper and sprinkle over the previously mixed salt, black pepper and lemon rind. Shake the paper to coat the croûtons evenly.

The croûtons can be prepared 2–3 hours before required; store uncovered at room temperature.

Keep the Croûtons Crunchy

Creamed soups are nicely complemented by croûtons, as their crispness offsets the smooth, creamy texture (they add a few calories though!).

If you are serving a soup in a tureen, don't sprinkle on the croûtons until the tureen is on the table, and your guests or family are ready to eat, as the croûtons quickly turn soggy.

SPICY SPINACH SOUP

Serves 4

This is certainly not what you expect spinach soup to be, but it is most intriguing — spicy, nutty and refreshing. And it's quick to make, too.

1½ tablespoons peanut oil
1 rounded tablespoon coarsely grated fresh ginger
2 teaspoons peanut butter
300 g spinach, trimmed, well washed and finely chopped
salt
½ teaspoon garam masala
½ teaspoon ground turmeric
½ teaspoon moscovado or dark brown sugar
1 teaspoon cornflour
1 tablespoon light soy sauce

Heat the peanut oil in a large saucepan over a medium heat. Drop in the ginger and stir-fry gently for 2 minutes. Add the peanut butter, stir to dissolve, then fry for another minute. Pour on 1 litre hot water, bring to the boil, then drop in the spinach. Sprinkle in a generous ¼ teaspoon salt, return to the boil, then simmer, covered, for 5 minutes.

In a small bowl mix the garam masala, turmeric, sugar, cornflour, soy sauce and a few tablespoons of liquid from the soup. Pour into the soup, mix well, then leave to simmer, partially covered, for 10 minutes. Serve hot.

Cooking Spinach

Leafy vegetables, like spinach, can be cooked with just the water left clinging to them after washing. Put them into a saucepan, set over a medium heat and stir the spinach often until it has wilted, or is cooked to your liking.

Salt added to the spinach as it cooks will minimise the chalky taste it sometimes possesses.

SIMPLE VEGETABLE SOUP

Serves 6

There are times in life when I crave for something simple, uncomplicated and unadulterated. This soup, which is full of goodness, fits the bill perfectly. Needless to say, the vegetables should be fresh (don't make it a home for withered leftovers rattling around in the vegetable crisper — deposit these on the compost!).

1 onion, finely chopped
knob of butter
1 clove garlic, crushed
¼ teaspoon curry powder
2 stalks celery, finely sliced
2 carrots, peeled and sliced into thin rings
1 large potato, peeled and cubed
piece of butternut pumpkin (about same size as the potato)
1½ teaspoons salt
1 teaspoon tomato purée
1 cup cauliflower florets, chopped
6 leaves silver beet, finely chopped
2 spring onions, with greenery, finely sliced (optional)
1 tablespoon finely chopped parsley or basil

Put the onion and butter in a large saucepan with a tablespoon of water. Cover and cook gently until the onion is soft and transparent. Add the garlic and cook for another minute, then stir in the curry powder. Cook for 1 minute, stirring, then add the celery, carrot and ¼ cup water. Cover, bring to the boil, then cook gently for 5 minutes.

Add the potato and pumpkin, then pour on 3 litres cold water. Stir in the salt and tomato purée, then bring to the boil. Simmer, partially covered, for 20 minutes, then add the cauliflower and silver beet and simmer for another 20 minutes.

Finally add the spring onions and parsley or basil, and cook for 10–20 minutes, or until all the vegetables are tender.

If you like, serve it as a light meal, with Parmesan cheese and hot garlic, or herb, bread to accompany.

TOMATO AND ORANGE SOUP

Serves 4

It's surprising how easily simple ingredients can be turned into such a spectacular soup. This is tomato soup like you've never had before.

2 x 400 g tins Italian tomatoes, mashed (or 1 kg outdoor tomatoes, coarsely chopped)
1 small onion, finely chopped
1 small carrot, finely diced
3 sprigs fresh thyme (or ¼ teaspoon dried thyme)
finely grated rind of ½ lemon and ½ orange
pinch of sugar
¼ teaspoon salt
1 litre chicken stock, preferably homemade (or substitute vegetable stock or water)
45 g butter
45 g plain flour
juice of 1 orange
150 ml cream (optional)
snipped chives (optional)

Put the tomatoes in a large saucepan with the onion, carrot, thyme, lemon and orange rinds, sugar, salt and stock. Cover and bring to the boil, then simmer gently, partially covered, for 30 minutes; stir occasionally. Pass the soup through a mouli-légumes into a bowl (or strain, then process the solid matter).

Put the butter in the cleaned saucepan, set over a low heat and allow to melt. Draw off the heat and tip in the flour. Stir well, then pour in about one third of the soup. Blend together, then mix in the remaining soup. Bring to the boil, stirring, lower the heat and cook for 5 minutes. Add the orange juice and check the seasoning.

If required, the soup can be prepared 24 hours in advance to this point. Cool quickly, cover and chill; reheat gently.

If you are using cream (the cream enriches the soup, making it more velvety, but it lightens the colour and adds calories!) pour it in, then gently reheat the soup. Serve hot, garnished with chives. If liked, crunchy, hot bread makes a good accompaniment.

SPICED APPLE AND YOGHURT SOUP

Serves 4

This is a simple, warming soup, made from virtually nothing —
just the sorts of 'bits and pieces' you might have on hand at any
given time.

1 medium onion, finely chopped
1 stalk celery, finely sliced
1 large apple (choose something tart, like a Granny Smith), peeled
  and finely chopped
2 knobs of butter
2 tablespoons finely chopped mint, plus a few leaves for garnishing
1 level tablespoon fresh curry powder
2 tablespoons plain flour
5 cups light chicken stock, vegetable stock or vegetable water
1 teaspoon salt (add a little more salt if the stock or vegetable water
  is unsalted)
1 cup plain, unsweetened yoghurt
crisp pita bread

Place the onion, celery and apple in a large saucepan with the
butter. Cover and cook gently for about 15 minutes, or until soft.
Add the finely chopped mint, then increase the heat to medium
and stir in the curry powder. Cook for 1–2 minutes, stirring, then
remove the pan from the heat and blend in the flour. Pour on
the stock and add salt. Set over a high heat and stir until it is
boiling. Turn the heat to low, partially cover and simmer for 15
minutes.

  Purée the soup in batches, in a food processor or blender, then
return it to the cleaned pan. Reheat, stirring, then remove it from
the heat and blend in the yoghurt. Serve garnished with mint
leaves and accompanied by crisp pita bread.

  If you want to prepare the soup in advance, cook and purée
it, but don't add the yoghurt. Reheat when required, remove from
the heat, then swirl in the yoghurt (the yoghurt will curdle if
it is cooked with the soup).

SORREL AND SPINACH SOUP

Serves 4

Sorrel leaves have a pleasant, lemony tang and add interest to soups and salads. If it is not available in your area, try to get hold of some sorrel seeds from a nursery, as it's very easy to grow.

300 g sorrel
300 g spinach
1 medium onion, finely sliced
30 g butter
2 level tablespoons plain flour
900 ml light chicken stock or vegetable water
½ teaspoon salt (or a little more if the stock or vegetable water
*   is unsalted)*
3 tablespoons liquid cream (optional)

Prepare the sorrel and spinach first. Remove stalks and wash well, then chop finely.

Put the onion in a saucepan with the butter, cover with a lid and set over a low heat. Cook until soft but not coloured. Stir in the sorrel and spinach, cover the pan and cook for about 12 minutes or until the vegetables are wilted. (Don't be alarmed by the change in colour; sorrel loses its brightness when cooked.) Remove the pan from the heat and sprinkle over the flour. Stir in the stock by degrees, blending well, add the salt and stir until boiling. Then turn down the heat and simmer, uncovered, for 5 minutes.

Purée the soup in batches, in a food processor or blender, then pass it through a large sieve (this gives a smoother texture). Reheat, stir in the cream and serve hot.

Garlic croûtons make a good addition.

❖ Winter Soups

There's nothing like a bowl of hot soup to revive you in chilly weather. Winter soups make the perfect use for all those prolific winter vegetables like parsnips, carrots, cauliflower, leeks, spinach and silver beet when they are at their peak and least expensive.

❖

BROCCOLI AND
CAULIFLOWER SOUP

CURRIED PARSNIP SOUP

JERUSALEM ARTICHOKE SOUP

CREAM OF SILVER BEET SOUP

ORANGE, CARROT AND
MINT SOUP

LEEK AND POTATO SOUP

CREAM OF SPINACH SOUP

❖

BROCCOLI AND CAULIFLOWER SOUP

Serves 6

This is a good, homely winter soup; it's cheap, easy to make and feeds plenty. The curry powder is optional; it helps warm the cockles of the heart on a cold night, although the soup is more delicate without it.

2 knobs of butter
1 medium onion, finely chopped
1 clove garlic, crushed
1 stick celery, finely chopped
1½–2 teaspoons curry powder (optional)
4 tablespoons plain flour
350 ml chicken stock
2 teaspoons salt
2 bay leaves
700 g broccoli, trimmed and cut into small florets
1 small cauliflower, trimmed and cut into small florets
2–3 strips lemon rind
½ cup cream

Put the butter in a large saucepan with the onion, garlic and celery. Cover with a lid and cook gently until it is soft (add a spoonful of water if it looks as if the mixture might catch on the base of the pan). Stir in the curry powder (if using), cook for 1 minute, then mix in the flour. Blend in the stock, add the salt and bay leaves and pour in 2 litres water.

Bring to the boil, stirring often, then add the broccoli and cauliflower. Cover, reboil, then simmer, partially covered, for 20 minutes, or until it is very tender.

Strain into a bowl, discard the bay leaves, then purée the solids in a food processor or blender and return them to the cleaned pan with the strips of lemon rind. Blend in the liquids and return to the boil. Add the cream, simmer for 1–2 minutes, then serve.

This soup is excellent with cheesy-flavoured bread.

CURRIED PARSNIP SOUP

Serves 4

Curry and parsnips might sound an odd combination but, believe it or not, this soup is absolutely delicious! The colour is also pleasing — it's a pretty, creamy, pale pea-green. Remember it in winter when parsnips are plentiful and cheap, and serve it with a loaf of crusty bread or garlic bread.

900 g parsnips, trimmed and peeled
40 g butter
1 large onion, finely chopped
1 large clove garlic, crushed
1 rounded tablespoonful curry powder
1 medium potato, peeled and diced
1.25 litres chicken stock or vegetable water
1 teaspoon salt, or to taste
150 ml cream
1 teaspoon chopped fresh coriander (or substitute either mint or
*   parsley)*

Cut the parsnips into wedges, then into thin slices, discarding any woody cores. Gently melt the butter in a large saucepan, then add the parsnips, onion and garlic. Add 1–2 tablespoons water, cover with a lid and cook gently for 12–15 minutes, or until wilted and softish.

Stir in the curry powder and cook for 1–2 minutes, stirring occasionally, then add the potato cubes. Stir to coat these in the curry mixture, then pour in 1 litre of the stock or vegetable water and add the salt.

Bring to the boil, removing any 'scum' as it rises. Simmer, partially covered with a lid, for about 25 minutes, or until the vegetables are tender. Cool for a few minutes, then blend in batches, in a food processor or blender, until smooth.

Return the soup to the cleaned pan and check the consistency. If the soup is very thick (this alters, depending on the starch content of the vegetables), blend in the extra stock.

If you want to freeze the soup, prepare it ahead to this point; cool, then freeze. When required, thaw it slowly, reheat and finish off. Blend in the cream and coriander and reheat gently, stirring often.

JERUSALEM ARTICHOKE SOUP

Serves 4

A delicate-tasting soup that makes a pleasant start to a winter's meal.

1 large onion, finely sliced
60 g butter
350 g large Jerusalem artichokes (the bigger and more evenly
*   shaped they are, the easier they are to peel)*
900 ml milk
¾ teaspoon salt
300 ml hot water
freshly ground black pepper to taste
2 tablespoons cream
finely chopped parsley to garnish

Put the onions in a saucepan with the butter, cover with a lid and cook over a gentle heat, until the onion is soft, but not coloured.

Peel the artichokes and slice thinly, then add them to the onions. Toss to coat them in the buttery mixture.

Heat the milk and tip into the artichokes, then add the salt and hot water. Set on a very low heat, partially covered. (Don't cover completely, as it will boil over.) Simmer very gently for 25 minutes, or until tender, then purée in batches, in a food processor or blender, or pass through a mouli-légumes. Return to the cleaned pan.

Reheat the soup, taste, and add a little black pepper, or more salt if required. Stir the cream through, dish into hot bowls and garnish with parsley. If liked, serve with a bowl of crisp, lightly salted croûtons.

Jerusalem Artichokes

Jerusalem artichokes, a tuber native to North America, look like a gnarled piece of fresh ginger and have an interesting, nutty-earthy flavour. They are not related to globe artichokes, although some say there is a similarity of taste.

Jerusalem artichokes are easily turned into a delicate soup, but they are also good soused in a vinaigrette, sautéed (see recipe on page 199), turned into fritters, 'souffléed', baked, sauced, or used raw in salads.

They tend to darken once peeled or cut, but putting them into lightly acidulated water during preparation, or cooking them in either acidulated water or milk, lessens the discolouration.

Silver Beet Idea

Looking for something different to do with silver beet? Borrow an idea from the Italians and sauté it in olive oil.

Separate the stems from the leaves, wash well and chop coarsely. Sauté the stems in a frypan with a little olive oil for about 10 minutes. Then add the chopped leaves. Cook for a few minutes, tossing from time to time, or until tender. Grind over plenty of black pepper, sprinkle with salt and squirt on a little lemon juice. Serve hot.

For a soup recipe using silver beet, see page 58.

CREAM OF SILVER BEET SOUP

Serves 4

This soup makes good use of home-grown silver beet. The recipe. doubles well and freezes successfully.

500 g silver beet, well washed and roughly chopped
salt
1 medium onion, finely chopped
2 knobs of butter
2 level tablespoons plain flour
750 ml light stock or vegetable water
200 ml milk
75 ml cream

Plunge the silver beet into a saucepan of well-salted boiling water and cook uncovered for 7 minutes. Drain, reserving the cooking water for the soup.

Meanwhile, put the onion and butter in a saucepan, cover with a lid and cook gently, until the onion is soft but not coloured. Remove the pan from the heat and stir in the flour. Blend in the stock or cooking water, return to the heat and bring to the boil. Add the silver beet and ½ teaspoon salt.

Simmer the soup on a low heat, partially covered, for about 20 minutes, or until the silver beet is very tender.

Purée in batches, in a food processor or blender, then return it to the cleaned pan. Heat the milk separately and blend slowly into the soup, then add the cream. Heat gently, recheck the seasoning, then serve immediately with crusty bread.

ORANGE, CARROT AND MINT SOUP

Serves 4

This is a good winter soup which is tasty and inexpensive. It's the sort of thing you can whip up without having to trek to the shops, as the main ingredients are standard winter fare: oranges, carrots and onions.

knob of butter
400 g carrots (about 4 big ones), peeled and sliced thinly
1 large onion, peeled and sliced
1 litre light chicken stock or vegetable water
approx. 1 teaspoon salt
2 large oranges, squeezed (scant ½ cup juice)
1 tablespoon finely chopped mint
¼ cup cream (optional)
mint leaves to garnish

Melt the butter gently in a large saucepan and add the carrots and onion. Cover with a lid and leave on a low heat, stirring occasionally, until the vegetables are softened but not coloured or browned (about 15 minutes).

Add the stock and ¾ teaspoon salt, then bring to the boil and simmer, partially covered, for 20–30 minutes, or until the vegetables are really soft. Take off the heat and cool for a few minutes.

Strain the vegetables through a sieve set over a bowl, then transfer to a food processor or blender. Process until smooth. Set the sieve over the clean pan and push the vegetables through. Then pour in the liquid and stir to blend.

Add the orange juice and mint and check to see if more salt is needed. Reheat gently, then pour into heated bowls. If cream is liked, dribble a little over each bowl of soup and stir at once, clockwise, to form a swirl. Decorate with sprigs of mint.

If the soup appears thin (this depends on the type of carrots), mix 1–2 tablespoons arrowroot with a little water, add to the soup and bring to the boil. Cook for 1–2 minutes, then serve.

LEEK AND POTATO SOUP

Serves 8

A good winter stand-by — filling, nourishing, tasty and inexpensive. See Crème Vichyssoise, page 71, for the deluxe, chilled version.

4 medium leeks
50 g butter
4 medium potatoes, peeled and thinly sliced
1¾ teaspoons salt
1 litre water
500 ml milk, heated
liaison (optional), gives the soup a smooth finish
a little finely chopped parsley or snipped chives
2 egg yolks
3 tablespoons cream

Use a large knife to cut off the tops of the leeks, then shave off any tough parts and remove any coarse outer leaves. Trim off the roots, and cut each leek in two lengthwise, then rinse thoroughly under running water. Slice thinly.

Melt the butter in a large saucepan, then add the leeks. Toss them in the butter over the heat for 3–5 minutes, then lay the potatoes on top. Don't stir the potatoes through the leeks, because if they sit on the base of the pan they can catch. Cover the pan with a lid and cook on a very gentle heat for 20 minutes.

Stir through the salt, then add the water and hot milk. Bring it just to boiling point, stirring often, then immediately turn the heat to low. Partially cover with a lid and cook very gently for 20 minutes.

Purée in batches, in a food processor or blender, and return to the cleaned pan.

If using the liaison, blend egg yolks and cream in a small bowl and add a ladleful of the hot soup. Pour this into the soup, stirring, and set the pan over a medium heat. Keep stirring until the soup thickens slightly (do not allow it to boil or it will curdle).

If you are not using the liaison, reheat the soup only. Ladle into hot bowls and garnish with a little chopped parsley or a few snipped chives.

Egg and Cream Liaisons Get the 'Heave-ho'

Cream soups are often 'finished' with a mixture of egg yolk and cream, referred to as an egg and cream liaison. This binds the soup rather than thickening it, and introduces a smooth, velvety texture.

However, these days most of us want to unload our cholesterol, not beef it up with hidden 'fats'. So, in my regular family meals, egg and cream liaisons are dispensed with; then, when used for a special occasion soup, their incomparable velvety richness can be lingered over, 'oohed' and 'ahhed' over and thoroughly enjoyed.

Curdling the Liaison

When adding an egg and cream liaison to a soup, it is wise to have both egg yolk and cream at room temperature. Mix them in a small bowl and add 2–3 tablespoons of the hot soup. Pour into the soup and stir well. If the soup contains just vegetables, or meat and stock and no flour, the soup must not be allowed to boil after the liaison is added. If it does, the egg yolk will cook (curdle).

But if the soup is roux-based or contains another starch like arrowroot, it is safe to bring the soup to the boil, as the starch stabilises the mixture (prolonged boiling will eventually cause it to break down).

If you do curdle the soup, either sieve, blend or process it, or change its name and fob it off as 'Chinese Raindrop Soup' or some other fantastic name.

CREAM OF SPINACH SOUP

Serves 4

This is a simple, good-flavoured spinach soup.

450 g fresh spinach, well washed and roughly chopped
salt
30 g butter
1 medium onion, finely chopped
1 small clove garlic, crushed
3 level tablespoons plain flour
600 ml light stock or vegetable water
freshly ground black pepper to taste
freshly grated nutmeg to taste
300 ml milk
75 ml cream

Plunge the spinach into a saucepan of well-salted, boiling water and cook, uncovered, for 5 minutes (use a wooden spoon to push the spinach under the bubbling water as it rises). Drain, reserving the water for the soup.

Wipe out the pan, drop in the butter and add the onion. Cover with a lid and cook over a gentle heat until the onion is soft, but not coloured. Add the crushed garlic and cook for another 1–2 minutes.

Remove the pan from the heat and stir in the flour, then blend in the stock or vegetable water and bring to the boil. Season with 1 teaspoon salt, a little black pepper and a few grates of nutmeg. Add the spinach, then simmer on a low heat for 15 minutes. Purée in batches, in a food processor or blender, and return to the cleaned pan.

Heat the milk in a saucepan and carefully blend into the soup. Check the seasoning. Swirl in the cream, grate a little nutmeg over the top and serve immediately.

Alternatively, ladle into bowls, dribble a little cream over each bowl of soup, stir at once, clockwise, to form a swirl, and grate over a little nutmeg.

❖

Big Soups

Sometimes a soup is so BIG (nourishing and filling) that it is a meal in itself. The next three soups, starting with the 'Big Daddy' of all soups, Minestrone, are just that.

❖

MY FAVOURITE MINESTRONE

CRISPY-TOPPED PUMPKIN SOUP

CHICKEN AND
SWEET CORN SOUP

❖

MY FAVOURITE MINESTRONE

This recipe makes enough to serve about 10 people — but you can serve it to smaller groups over a period of days (it keeps about 3 days providing you only heat up the amount you intend to serve; reserve the rest chilled in the refrigerator).

3 tablespoons olive oil
2 medium onions, finely chopped
2 large cloves garlic, crushed
150 g bacon (rind removed), finely chopped (optional)
2 sun-dried tomatoes in oil, finely chopped (optional)
1 tablespoon finely chopped marjoram (or use 1 teaspoon dried marjoram)
1 tablespoon finely chopped thyme (or use a scant teaspoon dried thyme)
1 cup full-bodied red wine
175 g small, dried white beans, soaked several hours in 1.5 litres cold water
400 g tin Italian tomatoes, mashed
500 ml tinned tomato juice
salt
1 large carrot, peeled and finely sliced
1 stick celery, finely sliced
1 medium potato, peeled and diced
1 small piece pumpkin, peeled, seeds removed, and cubed (should yield 1 cup cubed pumpkin)
1 cup cauliflower florets, chopped
8 silver beet leaves (or a bunch of spinach), chopped
1 cup freshly grated Parmesan cheese

Extras
1–2 tablespoons pesto or pistou (recipes on page 288—289)
   or 2 tablespoons finely chopped basil

Heat the olive oil in a roomy saucepan and drop in the onions, garlic, and bacon, if using. Cook gently for about 10 minutes, or until the bacon fat starts to run. Add the sun-dried tomatoes, if using, and the marjoram and thyme. Cook for another minute, then pour in the red wine and the beans and soaking liquid.
   Bring to the boil and add the Italian tomatoes (with their juice), tinned tomato juice, plus 2 litres of cold water and 1 teaspoon

salt. Reboil, partially cover with a lid and simmer for 2 hours. Add the carrot and celery, return to simmering point and cook for 20 minutes, then add the potato, pumpkin and cauliflower. Bring back to the boil and cook for about 30 minutes, or until the vegetables are tender.

Lastly, add the silver beet or spinach and simmer for about 20 minutes, or until cooked. Check the seasoning, adding more salt if necessary. If it is not for immediate consumption, cool the pot of soup quickly in a sink filled with cold water, then cover and chill until required.

Reheat over a gentle heat and when hot, swirl in 3 tablespoons Parmesan cheese. If adding pesto, pistou or basil, spoon it on top of the soup. Ladle into soup bowls and serve with the remaining Parmesan cheese.

Fresh is Best

Minestrone is one of those things best made without a recipe; what it calls for is fresh seasonal vegetables (not withered remains of a miscalculated week's shopping) and time. This *is* important; an insufficiently cooked minestrone will taste raw. The trick is to cook it long and slow, drawing out all the flavours, so the vegetables and liquid meld together.

Adding Pasta to Minestrone

To make minestrone soup more substantial, ½ cup small pasta can be added along with the silver beet, but (and this is a *big* but) the pasta will not improve in the soup; it will turn flabby and, eventually, slimy. Therefore, only add pasta to the whole soup if you intend all the soup to be served, or, if it is for a smaller group, to the amount of soup you are reheating and serving.

CRISPY-TOPPED PUMPKIN SOUP

Serves 4

This requires a little more effort than regular pumpkin soup, but it makes absolutely scrumptious winter fare. The presentation of the soup, which is cooked in the shell, always rouses favourable comment. Serve it as a main course, preceded by 'nibbles', and follow with an interesting salad.

4 small, green buttercup pumpkins, weighing approx. 500 g each
salt
300 g (2 medium) potatoes, peeled and diced
1 litre water
4 tablespoons cream
¾ cup finely grated Gruyère cheese
freshly ground black pepper to taste

Garlic croûtons
1 tablespoon oil
2 large knobs of butter
4 slices grainy bread, crusts removed and cut into large squares
1 tablespoon crushed garlic
salt
freshly ground black pepper

Using a sharp knife, slice a cap off each pumpkin. Use a sharp-pointed teaspoon to scoop out any flesh. Set the pumpkin tops aside and put any flesh in a large saucepan. Use the teaspoon to dig out pips and pith, then gouge out as much flesh as possible by scraping the sides and bases of the pumpkins. (Take care not to pierce the pumpkin shells.) Sit the pumpkins in a shallow, ovenproof dish and sprinkle the insides lightly with salt.

Put all the flesh in the saucepan and add the potatoes, water and 1½ teaspoons salt. Bring to the boil, turn the heat down, then partially cover with a lid and simmer gently for 40 minutes.

Either purée in a food processor or blender, or mash the mixture with a potato masher. (A food processor gives the smoothest texture, but a few unexpected lumpy bits add interest.) If required the soup can be prepared up to this point 24 hours in advance; cool, cover and refrigerate the soup, and wrap and chill the pumpkins (bring them to room temperature before finishing off).

When ready to finish off, bring the soup to boiling point, then ladle it into the pumpkins. Spoon 1 tablespoon cream over the surface of each, and scatter over the garlic croûtons, then the Gruyère cheese. Grind over some black pepper. Put the pumpkins in an oven preheated to 200°C and bake for about 25 minutes, or until the cheese is bubbling and brown on top. (If the topping hasn't browned after 25 minutes, grill it briefly.)

Transfer the pumpkins to individual dishes and serve. (A note of caution — the soup is very hot underneath the cheese crust.) If you like, the pumpkin caps can be baked with the pumpkins and served alongside them.

Garlic croûtons
Heat the oil in a large frypan over a medium heat and drop in a large knob of butter. Add the cubes of bread and cook, stirring often, until lightly browned. Drop in the second knob of butter and the crushed garlic. Sprinkle over a little salt and grind on a little pepper. Continue cooking, stirring often, until the croûtons are browned and the garlic is lightly browned, crisp and nutty-smelling. (Take care not to burn the garlic.) Transfer to a plate. The croûtons can be made 2–3 hours before required and if stored at room temperature, uncovered, they will remain crisp.

Cheesy Globs

Save the rinds from Parmesan cheese, wipe them clean and store in a plastic bag in the fridge or freezer. Cut into chunks and add to a thick vegetable soup, like minestrone, during the last hour of cooking; the rinds soften into melting 'globs' of cheese — an absolute treat!

CHICKEN AND SWEET CORN SOUP

Serves 4–6

The following is a super-tasty, nourishing soup. Using a whole chicken makes good, flavoursome stock, but not all of this is utilised in this recipe. Either use the stock in another dish or freeze it for later use. There will also be a little chicken meat left over to use in crêpes, stuffed vegetables or other dishes.

Stock
1 small chicken
3 litres water
small piece fresh ginger, peeled
1 large onion, coarsely chopped
2 stalks celery, coarsely sliced
1 teaspoon black peppercorns
2 teaspoons salt

Soup
2 cups (2 x 310 g tins) tinned cream-style sweet corn
½ teaspoon salt
¼ teaspoon freshly ground black pepper
4 spring onions, finely sliced
2 teaspoons finely grated fresh ginger
1 teaspoon sesame oil
1 chicken stock cube
3 tablespoons cornflour mixed with 3 tablespoons water
1–2 spring onions, finely sliced, for garnishing (optional)

Cut the chicken into quarters and pull off as much fat and skin as possible. Rinse under running water, then place in a large saucepan. Add the remaining stock ingredients and bring to the boil. Skim off any 'scum', then turn the heat to low and simmer gently, partially covered, for 1½ hours, turning the chicken pieces over from time to time.

Lift the chicken pieces out of the stock and place them on a board. When they are cool enough to handle, remove the meat from the bones, discarding any skin, fat and sinews. Dice the meat across the grain. (Use about a cup of meat; cool, cover and refrigerate the remainder.)

Strain the remaining stock and place 6 cups of it in a clean saucepan. (Cool, cover and refrigerate or freeze the remaining stock.) Add the sweet corn, salt, pepper, spring onions, fresh ginger, sesame oil and crumbled stock cube. Bring to the boil and simmer for 1–2 minutes, then add the cornflour and water and stir until boiling. Lower the heat, add the chicken, allow it to heat through, then serve garnished with a little chopped spring onion.

Salting the Soup

Some people say seasoning a soup to perfection is the most difficult part of soup-making. I'm inclined to agree. When clear, flavourless liquids, like water and milk, or bland, starchy ingredients, like potatoes or rice, or vegetables with a high water content, like zucchini and leafy greens, are used, more salt is required.

Add the salt by degrees, stirring it in well, then wait a few minutes, stir again and taste. No soup should taste bland or tasteless; continue seasoning and tasting until the flavour is more pronounced or drawn out.

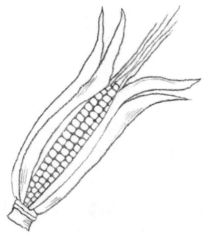

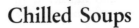

Chilled Soups

Cold soups used to be scoffed at by many, but, probably due to the universal acceptance of soups like Vichyssoise and Gazpacho, they are now scoffed up!

And why not? In hot or humid weather there can be no better way to revive jaded palates than with an icy-cold bowl of soup.

CRÈME VICHYSSOISE
CREAMY AVOCADO SOUP
ICED MUSHROOM SOUP

CRÈME VICHYSSOISE

Serves 8

Vichyssoise is a refinement of the French peasant soup of leek and potato. This chilled version, enriched with cream, has a velvety texture (it is processed, then sieved) and a delicate flavour. Served icy, not just cold, on a balmy evening, it is soothing and satisfying. Match it with a crisp white wine with good acid (nothing too fruity) to leave the palate clean.

6 young leeks
30 g butter
4 medium potatoes, very finely sliced
1 stick celery, finely sliced (optional)
1 tablespoon finely chopped parsley
2 teaspoons salt (if the stock is salted, use less salt)
2 litres homemade chicken stock
250 ml cream
finely snipped chives

Use a large knife to cut off the tops of the leeks, then shave off any tough parts, or remove any coarse outer leaves. Trim off the roots, then cut each leek in two lengthwise and rinse thoroughly under running water. Slice finely.

Melt the butter in a large saucepan, then add the leeks. Toss the leeks in the butter, then cover with a lid and cook for 10–15 minutes over a low heat, stirring often, until the leeks are soft (be careful not to let them brown).

Add the potatoes, celery if used, parsley, salt and stock. Bring to the boil, stirring, then simmer, partially covered, for 30 minutes or until the vegetables are tender. Allow to cool.

Purée in batches, in a food processor or blender, until very smooth, then pass through a sieve and discard any fibrous matter. Whisk in most of the cream, check the seasoning, then chill in the refrigerator until required. Alternatively, place the soup in the freezer until it is icy. Before serving, swirl in a little more cream and scatter over a few snipped chives.

CREAMY AVOCADO SOUP

Serves 4

With its cool, creamy green hues this chilled soup makes an ideal summer starter. If it should curdle when the cream is added, warm the first cup of chicken stock before pouring it in; this will 'loosen' the cream particles and the soup will blend together smoothly.

1 medium onion, finely chopped
2 tablespoons lemon juice
3 large avocados
1 teaspoon salt, or to taste
1 tablespoon finely chopped tarragon
1 tablespoon snipped chives
1 tablespoon finely chopped parsley
1 cup liquid cream
4 cups grease-free homemade chicken stock

This soup is quickly made in a food processor. Process the onion with the lemon juice until creamy, then add the avocado flesh, salt, and all the herbs, except for a few chives (reserve these for garnishing). Process until smooth, then pour in the cream and 1 cup chicken stock through the feed tube.

Transfer to a bowl and blend in the remaining chicken stock. Chill well, covered, for 2 hours. Before serving, stir well to blend, then ladle into chilled bowls. Garnish with a few snipped chives.

Going Green

If herbs like parsley are chopped in a food processor or blender with other ingredients they will turn the mixture green. Sometimes this can enhance the food, as in the case of avocado dips or mixtures, green pea or green vegetable soups, green sauces, etc. But sometimes it can look very unappetising, as is the case when meatballs are tinged with a greenish hue (it looks as if the meat is off). In the latter case, it is better to add the chopped herbs to the mixture after processing; the herbs will then colour the mixture attractively with little flecks of green.

ICED MUSHROOM SOUP

Serves 4

This is a delightful soup which captures the delicate flavour of mushrooms. It's a versatile recipe too; it freezes well, and is equally delicious well chilled on a hot summer's day and piping hot in winter.

6 spring onions, trimmed and roughly chopped
30 g butter
1 large clove garlic, crushed
3 tablespoons plain flour
4 cups chicken stock or vegetable stock
1 teaspoon salt, or to taste
300 g fresh button or field mushrooms, wiped clean and roughly
  chopped
½ cup cream
1 tablespoon snipped chives

Put the spring onions in a large saucepan with the butter and garlic and cook gently over a low heat, covered with a lid, until the vegetables are very soft. Stir in the flour and cook for 1–2 minutes, stirring with a metal spoon. Blend in the stock and salt and stir until the soup comes to the boil. Simmer gently for 10 minutes.

Purée the mushrooms in batches (leave them a little bit chunky for a more interesting texture), in a food processor or blender, using the spring onion broth to help liquefy the mixture. When all the soup is puréed, return it to the saucepan and add the cream. Heat gently, stirring, and simmer for 2–3 minutes. Serve hot, or, alternatively, well chilled, sprinkled with chives.

LUNCHEON, SUPPER AND MAIN COURSE DISHES

Using vegetables as the basis of a meal, rather than as an adjunct to a meat course, is a concept well worth embracing. But it's one many people have difficulty with.

For most vegetarians it's usually a smooth progression from eating less meat, to eating meat rarely, to not eating it at all (very few meat-eaters abandon it overnight), and meals to replace those made with meat seem to evolve as a matter of course. It's harder for those trying to 'give up' or 'cut down' on meat, because meat, for most of us, has long been the central part of the meal, with vegetables pegged on as an afterthought. When you're entrenched in the 'meat and three veg' syndrome, it's pretty hard to break out of it, especially when not all family members share your ideas. But the freedom, once you do, can change your whole approach to food. Suddenly balance of colour, contrasts of texture and taste present more of a challenge, and more of an inspiration. At first it might seem daunting, but with a little practice, 'composing' a meal within this loose structure becomes second nature.

Let's start with a clean plate and think about how you might like to fill it: With something substantial, grand enough to constitute a whole meal? (look under the Mediterranean Salads, Something More Substantial and Potatomania sections). With something 'big' enough to replace meat, contrasted with a few vegetable dishes in minor roles? (check out the Crêpes, Tarts, Pies and Pastry Things, and Eggcellent dishes). Or with a lighter meal, or something which can be put together in a flash? (check out Simple But Scrumptious).

75

Turning crêpes, pastry, pulses, grains, starch vegetables, eggs and cheese into light meals, luncheons, suppers and dinners is one of the most creative, delightful facets of vegetable cookery.

❖

EGGCELLENT EGGS
TARTS, PIES AND PASTRY THINGS
THREE WAYS WITH CRÊPES
MEDITERRANEAN SALADS
POTATOMANIA
SIMPLE BUT SCRUMPTIOUS
SOMETHING MORE SUBSTANTIAL

❖

Eggcellent Eggs

Making a meal from vegetables and an egg or two results in some of the quickest, most nutritious and most delicious dishes I know (don't try and say that too fast!).

Frittatas and tortillas and dishes based on soft-boiled or hard-boiled eggs, or made with fried or scrambled eggs, really extend the repertoire of recipes suitable for family or casual meals.

❖

HARD-BOILED EGGS WITH
SCRUMMY SAUCE
ONION TORTILLA
ARTICHOKE FRITTATA
ASPARAGUS FRITTATA
HUEVOS TAPATIOS
PIPERADE

❖

HARD-BOILED EGGS WITH SCRUMMY SAUCE

Serves 4

This dish is so called because it really is scrumptious to eat. An added bonus is how quick it is to prepare. Try it on a night when you need speedy nourishment, but refuse to open a can. Alternatively, serve it as part of an Asian or vegetable meal.

4–5 eggs, at room temperature
3 tablespoons oil
2 medium onions, finely sliced
1 teaspoon chilli powder (or 1 teaspoon hot pepper sauce)
400 g ripe tomatoes, peeled and chopped
1 teaspoon raw sugar
¼ teaspoon salt
juice of 1 lemon

Hard-boil the eggs, then shell them and set aside.

Heat the oil in a saucepan over a medium heat and add the onions. Cook gently until lightly browned. Add the chilli powder and fry for 1 minute, stirring, then add the tomatoes and raw sugar. Cook gently, uncovered, until the tomatoes have turned to a pulp. Season with the salt and lemon juice, and cook for another 2–3 minutes.

Slice the eggs in half lengthwise and add to the sauce. Reheat gently, spooning the sauce over the eggs, then serve immediately.

Gently Does It

Hard-boiled eggs are a misnomer. If you literally boil eggs until hard, the whites will have turned tough and rubbery; they should be cooked in gently boiling water only, and never overcooked (overcooked eggs are difficult to digest).

When you first lower them into the water, carefully roll the eggs around the pot for a few seconds. This sets the yolk in the centre.

ONION TORTILLA

Serves 4–6

Spanish tortillas don't have a lot in common with Mexican tortillas. The former are round, flat omelettes, often potato-based, and are found all over Spain. The following tortilla, made with onions, is particularly sweet and light.

4 tablespoons olive oil
3 medium onions, finely sliced
freshly ground black pepper to taste
3 large eggs
1 teaspoon milk
¼ teaspoon salt

Put 3 tablespoons of the olive oil in a large saucepan and add the onions. Cook over a low-medium heat, stirring often, until wilted and lightly golden (about 15 minutes). Grind over a little black pepper. Cover the pan and turn the heat to low. Cook for about 10 minutes or until the onions are very tender. Transfer to a bowl and beat in the eggs, milk and salt.

Wipe out the pan, pour in the last tablespoon of olive oil and heat gently. Pour in the onion mixture. Cook over a gentle heat, until it is well browned on the base. Slide under a heated grill to brown the top. Loosen from the pan and turn onto a plate. Serve at room temperature.

Stop Cracking Up

To prevent the shells from cracking during cooking, use the point of a dressmaking pin to prick the rounded end of each egg, where there is a small air-sac. The pin hole acts like an escape valve; as the contents of the egg swell during cooking, they force the air out of the air-sac, preventing the shells from cracking.

Having the eggs at room temperature and bringing them slowly to the boil also helps.

ARTICHOKE FRITTATA

Serves 6

This is wonderfully nutty and is as good cold as it is hot. Success lies in using well-trimmed, young, slim artichokes; mature artichokes are too fibrous for this dish. Serve this frittata for a spring luncheon, or cut into tiny morsels and serve with drinks.

4 young artichokes
juice of 1 lemon, mixed with 2 litres of water
2 tablespoons olive oil
5 eggs
¾ cup freshly grated Parmesan cheese
freshly ground black pepper to taste
1 tablespoon finely chopped marjoram (or ½ teaspoon dried marjoram)

Trim the artichoke stems, then cut off the top third of each and discard. Pull off the tough outside leaves, leaving only the very tender leaves near the centre. Slice the artichokes in half and scrape out any choke (fibrous hairs). Drop into acidulated water as they are done, then shake off any excess water, and cut into wafer-thin slices.

Set a large frypan over a medium-high heat and add the olive oil. When it is hot, drop in the artichokes. Sauté for about 15 minutes, stirring often, or until they are a light golden brown colour. Pour in ½ cup water, stir with a spoon, then put on the lid and lower the heat. Cook gently for about 30 minutes, or until very tender.

Meanwhile, lightly beat the eggs in a bowl and add the Parmesan cheese, black pepper and marjoram. Pour this over the artichokes in the frypan and cook over a low-medium heat until partially set and golden on the base. Loosen the frittata from the pan, then cover the pan with a large plate, flip over, lift off the pan, and slide the frittata back into the pan to cook the second side. Cook until golden, then slide out onto a serving plate.

ASPARAGUS FRITTATA

Serves 4

Light and flavoursome, this thin frittata makes a great spring-time nibble or lunch dish. Use pencil-thin asparagus; save the fat ones for dunking into melted butter and Parmesan cheese.

350 g very slim asparagus spears
salt
5 eggs, at room temperature
freshly ground black pepper to taste
6 tablespoons freshly grated Parmesan cheese
4–5 tablespoons olive oil

Trim the asparagus and wash well. Plunge into a saucepan of lightly salted, boiling water. Cook uncovered until tender (don't undercook them; if they are crunchy the frittata will break apart).

Break the eggs into a bowl and beat them lightly with a fork. Add ¼ teaspoon salt, some black pepper and the Parmesan cheese. Carefully blend in the whole asparagus.

Heat 4 tablespoons of the olive oil in a large, shallow frypan over a low-medium heat. Pour in the asparagus mixture. Cook gently, until the base is golden brown, loosening the frittata from the sides and base of the pan as it cooks.

When it is nearly set on top, slip it out onto a plate. If the frypan seems dry, add a little more olive oil and swirl it around. Cover the frittata with another plate, lift the top plate off, then slide it back into the frypan. Cook until the underside is set and golden. Slide onto a clean plate and serve hot or warmish.

Frittata

Knowing how to make a frittata, a flattish Italian egg dish, can get you out of many a meal-time crisis. In no time at all, and with few ingredients, you can have a nutritious, tasty dish. Flavour it with Parmesan cheese, herbs, mushroom, potatoes, onions, spinach, tomatoes, artichokes, peppers, zucchini, asparagus, ham, bacon or spicy sausage.

The trick lies in using a well-oiled pan, cooking the vegetables first and not making the frittata too thick.

HUEVOS TAPATIOS

Serves 4

This is an unusual, tasty and filling dish made by stacking a spicy beef mixture with avocados and chilli sauce on hot tortillas. The tortilla stacks are then topped with fried eggs! Accompany this with a 'juicy' salad, perhaps one made with oranges.

3 tablespoons oil
1 small onion, finely chopped
2 large cloves garlic, crushed
1¾ teaspoons ground cumin seeds
1½ teaspoons chilli powder
salt
700 g prime minced beef
¾ cup tinned tomatoes, mashed
2 ripe but firm avocados
1 tablespoon lemon juice
1–2 fresh green chillies, deseeded and very finely chopped
2 small tomatoes, skinned and diced
2 tablespoons chopped fresh coriander
4 tortillas
¼ cup oil
4 eggs

Heat the oil in a frypan over a medium heat. Add the onion and fry for 5 minutes, stirring occasionally, then add the garlic. Cook gently until soft and lightly golden in colour.

Add the prepared cumin, chilli powder and 1 teaspoon salt and fry for 1–2 minutes. Increase the heat to high and add the beef. Break up the meat with a fork and continue to cook until it is no longer pink. Blend in the tinned tomatoes. Turn the heat to low, cover and cook very gently for 15 minutes. If the mixture appears watery, reduce it, uncovered, over a medium heat.

The meat may be prepared a day ahead to this point; cool, cover and chill. Reheat when required.

Meanwhile, cut the avocados in half, extract the stones and scoop out the flesh. Mash in a bowl with the lemon juice, ¼ teaspoon salt and chopped chillies. Blend in the fresh diced tomatoes and coriander.

Heat the tortillas in a hot, ungreased, heavy-based frypan (I find a small black crêpe pan ideal) for about 30 seconds each side. Lay the tortillas on individual plates. Heat ¼ cup oil in a large frypan. Break the eggs into a cup, then lower them into the oil. Fry until the egg whites are set, splashing a little hot oil over them as they cook. Lightly sprinkle with salt.

Spread the meat sauce over the warm tortillas, cover with the avocado mixture, then top each tortilla with an egg. Serve immediately.

Hot and Dry

Long, thin-fleshed chillies can be strung up and dried at room temperature; they'll last for ages. Thread them up through the stalk, using a needle and strong cotton, and leave them in a darkish, airy spot until completely dry. Then transfer to a container or hang them up in the kitchen.

If the chillies are dried in the sun or in the light, they will lose their strong colour, but will still be good to use.

Remember to give your hands a thorough wash after dealing with chillies.

Freezing Hot Stuff

If chillies aren't always available in your area, it's a good idea to keep some in the freezer. Wash them, dry them with kitchen paper and pop them into a plastic bag; seal well.

Unfortunately, frozen chillies are only good to use in recipes where they are cooked, as they tend to become limp once thawed. It's easier to split, deseed and chop them while they are still frozen.

Porous Shells

Be careful where you store eggs.

Eggshells are porous and can absorb strong odours. If possible, store eggs in an egg carton, in the closed drawer of the refrigerator, away from bacon, onions, blue cheese or other strong-smelling foods (butter, cream and milk are also easily tainted).

How Fresh is That Egg?

Old eggs are bad eggs. If in doubt carry out the following quick test:

Immerse the egg in a bowl of cold water.

If it sinks or lies on its side, it is fresh ... eat it!

If it stands on the pointed end, it is beginning to go off ... better use it fast!

If it floats, don't even offer it to the dog ... it's dead!

Make Them Last Longer

To make eggs last longer, store them with the pointed end facing down (as they come in the carton, usually). This prevents the air cell from breaking, which helps maintain the quality of the egg.

PIPERADE

Serves 6

This Basque dish of cooked tomatoes and peppers, bound together into a soft, creamy emulsion with fresh eggs, is perfect for a late summer's brunch. I say 'late summer' because the secret of the dish lies in having full-flavoured, sun-ripened tomatoes and wonderfully sweet peppers (hothouse vegetables will make this dish insipid).

2 tablespoons olive oil
1 large onion, finely sliced
4 cloves garlic, crushed
6 large peppers (red and green), cored, deseeded and finely diced
1 kg ripe tomatoes, skinned, cored and diced
scant ½ teaspoon salt
plenty of freshly ground black pepper
1 tablespoon finely chopped basil (optional)
4 eggs, at room temperature

Heat the olive oil in a large frypan over a low-medium heat. Add the onion and fry gently until golden, stirring often. Add the garlic and cook for a few more minutes, then add the prepared peppers. Cook for 15 minutes, stirring occasionally, then add the tomatoes. Cook for about 45 minutes, stirring often (especially towards the end of cooking), or until it is thick and pulpy. Stir through the salt, black pepper and basil, if using.

If you are making the dish ahead of serving time (up to a day in advance is fine), add the salt and pepper at this point, but add the basil when reheating as the flavour will be fresher. Cool, cover and refrigerate, then reheat in a clean frypan when required.

Break the eggs into a bowl, beat with a fork, then pour into the pepper mixture. Cook gently, stirring, until the eggs are well combined and just cooked; the mixture should remain creamy and must not be overcooked. Serve immediately, accompanied by hot bread, brioche or croissants. Bacon and ham also make admirable partners.

Tarts, Pies and Pastry Things

Making your own rich shortcrust pastry may sound like a difficult task to some and a drag to others, but I hope, at least once in your life, you do get to eat it (even if it's not you who makes it!) because it is quite splendid.

On the other hand, there is such good quality filo pastry, made commercially, that only those with patience-a-plenty and time-to-kill need attempt it.

As for the recipes? The Asparagus and Camembert Tarts are obviously a spring treat, the Sweet Corn Filo Pies and Pissaladière call out for summer and the Leek and Apple Pie belongs in winter. The other two are multi-seasonal.

❖

LEEK AND APPLE FILO PIE

ASPARAGUS AND
CAMEMBERT TARTS

SWEET CORN FILO PIES

PISSALADIÈRE

SPINACH IN FILO

SWEET ONION TART

❖

LEEK AND APPLE FILO PIE

Serves 6–8

This is an unusual combination — leeks, apples and Gruyère cheese — but teamed up with a crisp, fruity, juicy salad, like Witloof and Orange Salad (page 256), it makes very good eating.

3 medium leeks
4 potatoes (about 600–700 g), peeled and cut into chunks
salt
approx. 60 g butter
1 large green apple, peeled, cored and sliced
9 large sheets filo pastry
freshly ground black pepper to taste
175 g Gruyère cheese, thinly sliced
12 small sage leaves (or a few pinches of dried sage)

First prepare the leeks. Use a large knife to cut off the tips of the leaves, then remove any coarse outer leaves. Trim the root end, then cut each leek in two lengthwise. Rinse thoroughly under cold running water, then shake dry and slice.

Put the potatoes in a pan, cover with cold water, add a little salt and bring to the boil. Cook until tender, drain and cut into small cubes.

Melt a knob of butter in a large frypan and add the sliced leeks. Cook for about 15 minutes over a medium heat, shaking the pan occasionally. Add the apple slices and a few pinches of salt. Cook for another 1–2 minutes.

Melt the remaining butter in a small pan. Brush 4 sheets of filo pastry with melted butter, stacking them as you go. Nestle them into an ovenproof dish (approx. 33 cm long by 21 cm wide by 5 cm deep), then put in the potatoes. Sprinkle well with salt and grind on some black pepper. Lay the Gruyère cheese on top, then cover with the leek and apple mixture and the sage leaves.

Brush the remaining 5 sheets of filo pastry with melted butter, stacking them as you go, then place them on top of the pie, nestling them in to fit the dish. Trim off the excess pastry, brush the top with melted butter, then score the surface into 'diamonds' with a small knife. Bake in an oven preheated to 180°C for 30–40 minutes, or until a very good golden brown. Cut into wedges and serve hot.

ASPARAGUS AND CAMEMBERT TARTS

Makes approx. 10 tarts

Whenever I serve these tarts they are, not surprisingly, a roaring success; golden, flaky pastry housing a melt-in-the-mouth creamy Camembert and asparagus mixture just can't fail! Team them up with an interesting, fruity-type salad to balance the richness.

400 g fat asparagus, washed, trimmed and soaked
salt
4 spring onions, finely sliced
1 clove garlic, crushed
knob of butter
2 egg yolks
¼ cup cream
½ cup fresh white breadcrumbs
125 g Camembert cheese, cubed (leave rind on)
good grating fresh nutmeg
freshly ground black pepper
5 sheets (750 g) frozen, pre-rolled puff or rough puff pastry
1 egg, beaten with a pinch of salt

Plunge the asparagus into a saucepan of lightly salted, boiling water. Cook uncovered for 1 minute. Drain, refresh with cold water, then leave to drain again. Pat dry with kitchen paper, then cut into short lengths.

Place the spring onions and garlic in a saucepan with the butter. Cover and cook over low heat until soft. Mix the yolks and cream together in a bowl and add the asparagus, cooled spring onion mixture, breadcrumbs, Camembert cheese, a generous ¼ teaspoon salt, and grated nutmeg and ground black pepper to taste.

Meanwhile, thaw the pastry sheets and cut 10 rounds approx. 10.5 cm in diameter and another 10 rounds approx. 11.5 cm in diameter. Prick the bases of the smaller rounds with a fork and dab the edges with a little cold water. Spoon the filling on to the pastry rounds, mounding it up and keeping it in from the edges. Place the larger rounds of pastry on top and gently press the edges of the pastry rounds together to seal. Use a small knife to 'knock the edges up'.

Make a decorative border by marking vertical indentations on the edges of the 'knocked up' dough. Cut a small hole in the centre of each tart to allow steam to escape; this stops the pastry becoming soggy. Use the knife to mark a lattice pattern on top of each tart. If the pastry is soft, refrigerate for 30 minutes.

Brush with the beaten egg and bake in the top third of a hot oven preheated to 225 °C for 15 minutes, or until well browned and crisp. Serve hot.

'Knocking Up' Pastry Edges

This means to make light indentations on the edge, or edges, of pastry with a small sharp knife.

If the edges of the pastry are pressed too hard or squashed during shaping, or gummed up with egg wash, the pastry cannot rise properly. By loosening the extreme edges, without breaking the seal, the pastry can live up to its name of 'puff' pastry.

Flan Ring is Best

A flan ring placed on a baking tray produces a crisper base to the pastry, as any moisture can freely run out from underneath the flan ring and evaporate. In a flan dish, the moisture is trapped in the dish, underneath the pastry, and it can cause the pastry to become soggy.

SWEET CORN FILO PIES

Makes about 50 triangles

Creamy sweet corn given a rev-up with a little curry powder makes an easy, inexpensive and tasty filling in these filo pastries.

knob of butter
1 small onion, finely chopped
1 tablespoon curry powder, or to taste
1 small tin cream-style sweet corn
¼ teaspoon salt
4 tablespoons fresh breadcrumbs (or a little more)
1 small egg, lightly beaten with a pinch of salt
approx. 50 g butter
200 g filo pastry sheets

Place the knob of butter in a small saucepan, add the chopped onion and 1 teaspoon water. Cover the pan and cook on a low heat for about 7 minutes, until the onion is softened but not browned. Add the curry powder and cook for another minute, stirring. Remove from the heat and mix in the sweet corn, salt and breadcrumbs, then beat in the egg.

As filo pastry dries out quickly, work with half the sheets at a time. Cut the sheets into 4 long strips with scissors and stack them neatly. Lay 8–10 strips of filo on a clean, dry work surface (keep the remaining filo strips covered with a clean cloth). Brush each strip gently with melted butter, then place a knob of the filling about 3 cm in from the edge on the left-hand side. Fold the pastry over from the right side, enclosing the filling, so the bottom edge meets the left edge, forming a triangle. Continue folding over at right angles to make a multi-layered triangle. Tuck in any overhanging pastry underneath.

Lay the pastries on a baking tray lined with non-stick baking paper, and brush with a little melted butter. Bake for about 15 minutes in an oven preheated to 180°C, or until a good golden brown. Serve hot.

If you want to make these pastries ahead of time, you can store them in an airtight container in the fridge for up to 2 days. Or you could store them in the freezer for up to 6 months. The pastries can also be cooked a few hours in advance, then reheated briefly when required.

PISSALADIÈRE

Serves 8

Here's an interesting tart to try in the summer months when basil is plentiful. It is best served with something light and refreshing, like a mixed leaf salad with a lemony dressing.

2 large cloves garlic, roughly chopped
1 large bunch basil (should weigh about 40 g after stalks are removed)
6 tinned anchovy fillets, drained (optional)
1 tablespoon white wine vinegar
2 egg yolks, at room temperature
1 cup fresh breadcrumbs
salt
freshly ground black pepper to taste
100 ml olive oil
a 20 cm flan ring or dish lined with rich shortcrust pastry (see recipe, page 302)
350–400 g (about 10) small tomatoes, skinned, cored and halved
60 g finely grated Gruyère or Cheddar cheese

In a food processor or blender, combine the garlic, basil leaves, and anchovies if you are using them. Add the white wine vinegar and blend until smooth. Drop in the egg yolks and breadcrumbs and season with a few pinches of salt (omit salt if anchovies are used) and a good grinding of black pepper. Dribble in the olive oil through the feed tube with the machine running.

Spread the mixture on top of the pastry, then arrange the tomatoes on top, rounded side facing up. Scatter over the cheese.

Bake the tart for about 45 minutes in an oven preheated to 190 °C, or until it is well browned. Remove from the oven, cool for 5 minutes, then slide onto a cooling rack. Flip off the flan ring (or cool in the flan dish). Serve hottish.

SPINACH IN FILO

Makes about 50 triangles

Spinach and feta is a much-loved combination, but I've given these pastries a new twist by flavouring them with dill and fennel and a topping of nutty sesame seeds.

1 kg spinach, washed well and coarsely chopped
1 large onion, very finely chopped
70 ml olive oil
175 g (approx. 1 cup) feta cheese, drained and well crumbled
½ teaspoon fennel seeds
1 tablespoon finely chopped dill
1 tablespoon finely chopped parsley
freshly grated nutmeg to taste
¼ teaspoon salt
freshly ground black pepper to taste
200 g filo pastry
approx. 75 g butter, melted
1 large egg yolk, lightly beaten with 1 teaspoon water
sesame seeds for sprinkling on top

Put the prepared spinach into a saucepan with just the clinging water. Cover with a lid and set over a medium heat until the spinach wilts. Drain, then when it is cool use your hands to wring out as much moisture as possible.

Put the onion in a frypan with the olive oil. Cover with a lid and cook gently until it is soft and transparent. Blend in the spinach, feta, fennel seeds, dill, parsley, nutmeg, salt and black pepper.

As filo pastry dries out quickly, work with half the sheets at a time. Cut the sheets into 4 long strips with scissors and stack them neatly. Lay 8–10 strips of filo on a clean, dry work surface (keep the remaining filo strips covered with a clean cloth). Brush each sheet gently with melted butter, then place a knob of the filling about 3 cm in from the edge on the left-hand side. Fold the pastry over from the right side, enclosing the filling, so the bottom edge meets the left edge, forming a triangle. Continue folding over at right angles to make a multi-layered triangle. Tuck in any overhanging pastry underneath.

Lay the pastries on a baking tray lined with non-stick baking paper. Brush with the beaten egg, then sprinkle generously with sesame seeds.

Bake in an oven preheated to 180 °C for about 15 minutes, or until a good golden brown. Serve hot.

If you want to make these pastries ahead of time, either store the uncooked pastries, well wrapped in plastic wrap, in the fridge for up to 3 days, or alternatively store them in the freezer for up to 6 months. The pastries can also be cooked a few hours in advance, then reheated briefly when required.

How to Deal with Frozen Spinach

It's handy to have a packet of frozen puréed spinach in the freezer for times when fresh spinach is not available.

If you don't require the whole packet, saw off what you need with a sharp, serrated knife and refreeze the remainder. Thaw the spinach in a microwave, very gently in a saucepan, or at room temperature.

Once it is thawed, wring out as much moisture as possible, working with small lumps at a time, squeezing it in the palms of your hands. If the spinach still seems sloppy, place it in a dry frypan and toss it over a medium heat, to drive off excess moisture.

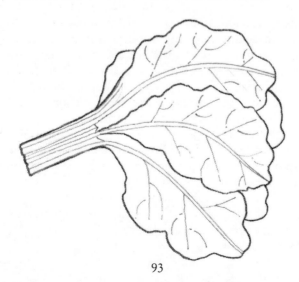

SWEET ONION TART

Serves 6

This tart has been a favourite of mine for nearly two decades; crisp, short pastry encasing sweet, creamy onions. Ambrosia! Serve it as a lunchtime dish with a crispy, fruity salad (for example, the Witloof and Orange Salad, page 256, or the Watercress, Spinach and Grapefruit Salad, page 254).

50 g butter
1 tablespoon oil
600 g onions, peeled and finely sliced
¼ teaspoon salt
freshly ground black pepper to taste
good grating fresh nutmeg
3 egg yolks
150 ml cream
a 20 cm flan ring or dish lined with rich shortcrust pastry (see
*   recipe, page 302)*

Melt the butter in a large saucepan and add the oil, then the onions. Cook over a low-medium heat, uncovered, stirring from time to time, until the onions are a pale golden colour. This will take at least 25 minutes and should not be hurried, as the slow colouring develops the onions' naturally sweet flavour. Towards the end of cooking take care not to let the onions catch and burn.

Mix in the salt, black pepper and nutmeg, then blend in the egg yolks and cream. Pour into the chilled pastry case. Bake in an oven preheated to 200°C for about 35 minutes, or until the pastry is golden brown and the custard set and golden.

Remove the tart from the oven and leave it to firm for 10 minutes. Either serve it in the dish, or remove the flan ring and slide the tart on to a serving plate. Serve hot or warmish.

Although the tart is best eaten when freshly cooked, the pastry can be made and lined into the flan ring or dish a day ahead and kept chilled (or frozen). The filling can be made a day in advance also; keep it refrigerated, but bring it to room temperature before cooking.

Three Ways with Crêpes

This one is self-explanatory; here are three uses for crêpes, incorporating 'bits and pieces'.

The recipe for crêpe batter and the 'How to' is on page 300.

❖

MUSHROOM CRÊPES

SAVOURY STUFFED CRÊPES

CRÊPE STACK 'ITALIANO'

❖

MUSHROOM CRÊPES

Serves 4 (makes about 24 crêpes)

These crêpes are given good, robust flavours from rosemary, red wine and garlic. Serve with spinach salad and a full-flavoured red wine.

1 quantity crêpe batter (page 300)
butter
1 large onion, finely chopped
1 tablespoon finely chopped rosemary sprigs
¼ cup dry red wine
450 g button mushrooms, sliced very thinly
2 tablespoons plain flour
½ cup light stock or vegetable water
¼ teaspoon salt
freshly ground black pepper
1 tablespoon finely chopped parsley
¼ cup freshly grated Parmesan cheese

Make up the crêpes as described.

Melt a large knob of butter in a large frypan over a medium heat. Add the onion and rosemary, and cook until golden brown. Pour in the red wine and let it evaporate. Turn the heat to high and add the mushrooms. Cook, tossing often, until the mushrooms ooze juice.

Continue to cook until all but a scant 2 tablespoons of the juice has evaporated. Sprinkle over the flour, stir in, then blend in the stock or vegetable water. Add salt and black pepper and bring to the boil, stirring. Cook for 2–3 minutes, until thick and creamy, then add the parsley.

Lay the crêpes out on a clean surface (easiest done in two batches) and spread about 2 tablespoons of the mushroom mixture on each one. Fold in half, then in half again, forming triangles.

Generously butter a large, shallow, ovenproof dish and put in the crêpes in rows, slightly overlapping. Brush lightly with a little melted butter and sprinkle over the Parmesan cheese.

The crêpes may be prepared ahead to this point; wrap and refrigerate but bring them to room temperature before cooking.

Bake in an oven preheated to 180°C for 12–15 minutes, or until heated through and crisp. Serve immediately.

SAVOURY STUFFED CRÊPES

··

Serves 4 (makes about 24 crêpes)

This is a good family dish which uses up small quantities of 'left-overs' (dare I use the word!).

1 quantity crêpe batter (page 300)
25 g butter
100 g button mushrooms, thinly sliced
1 tablespoon plain flour
175 ml light chicken or vegetable stock
good pinch of salt
plenty of freshly ground black pepper
2 tablespoons cream
3 hard-boiled eggs, finely chopped
225 g ham off the bone, finely shredded (or 1 cup cooked, well-drained, chopped spinach or silver beet)
1 tablespoon finely chopped parsley
few grates nutmeg
extra butter for greasing and glazing
2 tablespoons freshly grated Parmesan cheese

Make up the crêpes as described.

Melt the butter in a saucepan over a medium heat, then add the mushrooms. Cover with a lid and cook slowly for 5 minutes until the mushrooms give out liquid. Remove the pan from the heat and add the flour, then blend in the stock, salt and black pepper. Bring to the boil, stirring, and cook for 1–2 minutes. Add the cream, and cook until the mixture is like a thick cream. Add the eggs, ham, parsley and nutmeg.

Lay the crêpes on a dry work surface and spread the mixture over them. Roll up into cigar shapes (probably easiest done in two batches). Place, tightly packed, in layers in a large, shallow, buttered ovenproof dish. Brush the top of the crêpes with butter and sprinkle over Parmesan cheese.

The dish may be prepared up to 24 hours ahead to this point; cover with plastic wrap and refrigerate, but bring it to room temperature before cooking.

When you are ready to cook, preheat an oven to 180°C and cook the crêpes for about 15 minutes or until they are heated through and crisp on top. Serve immediately.

CRÊPE STACK 'ITALIANO'

Serves 3–4

This is like a speedy version of lasagne, but made with crêpes instead of pasta. The crêpes are layered up with tasty ingredients, smothered with Parmesan cheese and baked briefly. Instead of the ham in the recipe, try one of any of the following (you'll need about a cupful): chopped salami; cooked, puréed spinach; chopped chicken; chopped, blanched asparagus; chopped, sautéed mushrooms; chopped, hard-boiled egg.

3 tablespoons olive oil
2 cloves garlic, crushed
1 tablespoon finely chopped parsley
¾ cup tinned Italian tomatoes, well mashed
¼ teaspoon salt
freshly ground black pepper
1 tablespoon tomato concentrate
small knob of butter, plus a little extra for greasing the dish
16 crêpes (see page 300)
150 g ham off the bone, finely shredded
50 g freshly grated Parmesan cheese
100 g firm mozzarella cheese, grated (buy vacuum-packed cheese)

Put the olive oil and garlic in a saucepan, and cook gently until the garlic turns a pale biscuit colour. Immediately add the parsley, stir, then add the tinned tomatoes, salt, black pepper and tomato concentrate. Cook gently for about 15 minutes, stirring occasionally, or until the oil separates from the tomatoes and the mixture is pulpy.

Lightly butter a roasting tin or dish and place 2 crêpes on the base. Form 2 crêpe stacks by spreading each with a little tomato sauce, then a sprinkling of ham, Parmesan and mozzarella cheese. Layer up, spreading the top crêpes with tomato sauce and a good sprinkling of Parmesan cheese. Dot the top with a little butter.

The crêpes may be prepared up to 24 hours in advance to this point. Cover with plastic wrap and refrigerate, but bring them to room temperature before cooking.

When you are ready to cook, preheat an oven to 180 °C and bake the crêpes for 15–20 minutes, or until heated through and crisp on top.

Treating a New Crêpe Pan

A crêpe pan has slightly sloping sides, whereas an omelette pan has rounded sides (it makes it easier to turn the omelette out), but one pan can do both jobs providing a little care is taken.

Choose a heavy pan (cast-iron is ideal). Treat the new pan by filling it with cooking oil and leaving it overnight. Next day, heat the pan until it is just hot, then pour off the oil. Wipe it out with kitchen paper and use.

If sticking occurs, clean the pan with kitchen paper dipped in a little oil and salt. If you must wash the pan in water, dry it thoroughly afterwards and rub with oil.

Tomatoes: Sun-ripened and Tinned

Whenever a dish calls for tomatoes which are to be cooked, imported tinned tomatoes, preferably the Italian 'San Marzano' variety, are preferable to indifferent fresh ones (they are redder, riper and more full-flavoured than most tomatoes we grow in this land).

But if tomatoes are called for in a salad, use fresh ones (preferably outdoor tomatoes as they should have the best flavour) as tinned ones, even if they taste better than flavourless, hot-house tomatoes, are too sloppy.

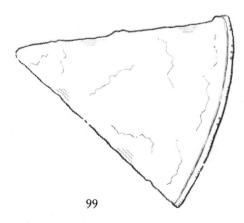

Mediterranean Salads

These are some of my favourite recipes in this book (I am a confessed olive oil and garlic addict after all!).

The aromas and flavours are assertive and gutsy; there's nothing meek or mild about this lot. And because all the flavoursome juices encourage dipping, dunking and mopping up with bread, an easy conviviality develops amongst those sharing any one of these dishes.

MY FAVOURITE RATATOUILLE

Serves 6–8

In late summer, when peppers and tomatoes are at their peak, and eggplants are moderately priced, there is no finer dish than the colourful, flavoursome vegetable stew, ratatouille. Serve it with plenty of fresh bread to mop up the juices.

2 medium eggplants
salt
2 medium onions, finely sliced
2 cloves garlic, finely chopped
several basil leaves
200 ml olive oil
3 large peppers (if available use one red, one green and one yellow),
*   cored, deseeded and cut into strips*
500 g ripe tomatoes, skinned and diced
500 g small zucchini, sliced into thick chunks
freshly ground black pepper to taste

Cut the eggplants into rounds, then into large cubes. Sit them in a colander and sprinkle with salt. Leave to drain for 40 minutes.

Put the onions, garlic and basil into a large saucepan with 100 ml olive oil. Cook over a very low heat, stirring often, for about 20 minutes, or until tender. Add the peppers, cover the pan with a lid and cook gently for 15 minutes. Add the tomatoes and cook, with the lid on, for a further 30 minutes.

Pat the eggplant cubes dry with kitchen paper. Heat 100 ml olive oil in a frypan over a medium heat and when it is hot add the eggplant cubes. Cook, tossing often until lightly browned and tender. Add to the tomato mixture along with the zucchini, ¾ teaspoon salt and a good grinding of black pepper.

Mix everything together, bring to a gentle boil, then turn heat to low. Partially cover with a lid and cook gently for about 30 minutes, or until very tender. If the ratatouille is very liquid, cook without a lid. Serve hot or at room temperature.

Although delicious when freshly made, the ratatouille keeps well for at least 2 days; cover when cool and store refrigerated, but bring it to room temperature before serving.

MY SECOND-FAVOURITE RATATOUILLE

Serves 6–8

There are as many ways to make ratatouille as there are to roast a leg of lamb. The preceding recipe is more textured, keeping the vegetables in shape, but this version is softer and pulpier, with a very sweet flavour and fragrance.

2 medium eggplants
salt
2 onions, finely chopped
100 ml olive oil
2 cloves garlic, crushed
2 large red peppers, cored, deseeded and cut into chunks
freshly ground black pepper to taste
400 g ripe tomatoes, skinned, cored and finely diced
1 teaspoon fresh coriander seeds
12 whole basil leaves

Cut the eggplants into rounds, then into large cubes. Sit them in a colander and sprinkle with salt. Leave to drain for 40 minutes.

Put the onion in a large saucepan with the olive oil, and cook very gently for about 15 minutes, or until it is soft. Add the garlic, eggplant cubes and red peppers, ½ teaspoon salt and some black pepper. Cover and cook very gently for 30 minutes, stirring occasionally.

Remove the lid and add the tomatoes and coriander seeds. Cook uncovered for a further 15 minutes, or until the vegetables are tender. Transfer to a serving bowl and stir the basil leaves through the mixture while it is still hot. Serve at room temperature. Store as in the preceding recipe for ratatouille.

FENNEL NIÇOISE

Serves 6

Fennel is a versatile vegetable, becoming quite celery-like in flavour once cooked. Stewed with tomatoes, olives, herbs and olive oil, it is succulent and tasty.

4 fennel bulbs (should weigh about 1.2 kg)
5 tablespoons olive oil
1 large onion, finely sliced
2 cloves garlic, finely chopped
400 g tin Italian-style tomatoes, mashed
¼ teaspoon salt (increase salt to ½ teaspoon if olives are omitted)
1 tablespoon finely chopped marjoram (or ½ teaspoon dried marjoram)
1 bay leaf
freshly ground black pepper to taste
½ cup black olives (optional)
2 tablespoons finely chopped parsley

Prepare the fennel by trimming away the root end, removing stems and any bruised or coarse parts. Wash well, then slice into thick wedges.

Place 2 tablespoons olive oil in a medium-sized saucepan and set on a low heat. Add the onion and garlic, cover with a lid and cook gently until softened (about 10 minutes). Remove to a plate and add the rest of the oil to the saucepan. Increase the heat to medium-high and add the fennel. Cook uncovered, stirring often, for about 10 minutes, or until lightly browned.

Return the onions and garlic to the pan and add the tomatoes, salt, marjoram, bay leaf and black pepper. Stir well to combine the ingredients, bring to the boil, then simmer, uncovered, for 15–30 minutes, or until tender (depends on the maturity of the fennel). Mix in the black olives, if you are using them, and the parsley. Serve hot or at room temperature.

PROVENÇAL SALAD

Serves 6–8

In this dish, new potatoes and black olives are added to stewed onion, tomatoes and peppers, then topped with nutty-tasting strips of fried, garlicky eggplant. Teamed with a crusty loaf of bread and a refreshing salad it easily constitutes a casual summer's meal.

1 large eggplant, sliced into rounds
salt
500 g small new salad potatoes, scrubbed
1 large onion, finely sliced
approx. 150 ml olive oil
¼ cup black olives, halved and stoned
500 g ripe tomatoes, skinned, cored and diced
6 peppers (preferably 2 each green, red and yellow), cored, deseeded
*   and cut into thick chunks*
3 large cloves garlic, finely chopped

Sit the eggplant slices in a colander and sprinkle them with salt. Leave to drain for 40 minutes.

Position the potatoes in a metal colander or steaming basket and set over a saucepan of boiling water (the colander or steaming basket should nearly fit the pot). Sprinkle lightly with salt, cover tightly with a lid or double thickness of tinfoil, and steam over vigorously boiling water until tender. Allow 12–15 minutes for tiny, freshly dug potatoes, but up to 30 minutes for large ones.

When they are just tender, remove the colander or steaming basket from the pot and when the potatoes are cool enough to handle, peel and cut them into cubes.

Put the onion in a large saucepan with 100 ml olive oil and cook gently for about 15 minutes, or until tender, stirring occasionally. Add the black olives, tomatoes and peppers to the pan, then bring everything to the boil. Cover with a lid and cook gently for 30 minutes, stirring occasionally.

Add the potatoes to the pan along with ¼ teaspoon salt. Cook uncovered for another 5 minutes, then set aside while preparing the eggplant.

Pat the eggplant slices dry with kitchen paper, then heat 50 ml olive oil in a large frypan over a medium heat. When the oil is hot, add the eggplant slices to the pan, turning to coat them in the oil. Cook to a good golden brown. Turn heat to low and cook until tender. If the pan is dry, dribble in a little more olive oil, then sprinkle over the chopped garlic. Turn the eggplant slices in the garlic oil and cook for 1–2 minutes until the garlic is a pale nut-brown colour (take care not to let it burn).

Remove the eggplant slices to a board, then pour any remaining oil and garlic over the salad. Cut the eggplant slices into strips and arrange them on top of the salad. Serve at room temperature.

Extra Eggplant Ideas

Serve the cooked slices spread with tapenade (a black olive and garlic purée); or douse with a basil and garlic vinaigrette; or make a special vinaigrette with balsamic vinegar, basil and garlic and use this to anoint the eggplant slices. All these are delicious with pita pockets or French bread.

Confine Those Splatters

If you're frying something that is wet or moist, like sliced eggplant or zucchini for example, the fat is going to splatter.

A splatter screen (a round, flat piece of fine metal mesh with a long handle) is a good investment. Placed over the frypan or saucepan it will stop most of the splatters leaping out of the pan, but because it is made of mesh, steam can still pass through. (When you put a lid on top of the pan to confine splatters, you trap in steam, which creates moisture and frying ceases.)

Failing a splatter screen, a piece of absorbent kitchen paper also works well (because is is not round, steam can escape from the sides). However if you cook with gas this can be very dangerous, as the flame may ignite the kitchen paper.

CAPONATA

Serves 12 as an antipasto dish or 6 as a salad

Remo, my husband, and I have more fights about this dish than any other. He says my celery is too long, the eggplant cubes too small and it's either undercooked or overcooked, or something else is wrong. However, none of this deters me from making it, because, without fail, he demolishes the lot!

2 large eggplants (should weigh about 1 kg)
salt
approx. ½ cup olive oil
6–10 sticks celery, cut into 2–3 cm lengths
1 large onion, finely sliced
⅓ cup tomato concentrate
1 tablespoon sugar
freshly ground black pepper to taste
1¼ cups good quality red wine vinegar
2 tablespoons capers, drained
½ cup pimento-stuffed green olives, drained

Cut the eggplants into large cubes. Place in a colander, sprinkle generously with salt and leave to drain for 40 minutes. Turn out on to kitchen paper and pat dry.

In a large, deep saucepan heat most of the olive oil over a high heat until a faint haze is given off. Drop in half the eggplant cubes. Stir to coat them in the oil, lower the heat to medium and fry until a light golden brown. Tilt the pan, lift out the eggplant cubes with a slotted spoon and transfer them to a side bowl. Add a little more oil to the pan and repeat the process with the remaining cubes.

Next fry the celery chunks until they are lightly browned, using a little more oil if the pan is dry. Transfer to the bowl with the slotted spoon. Lower the heat, add the onion, cover with a lid and cook gently until it is softish and lightly coloured.

Dilute the tomato concentrate with 4 tablespoons water. Mix in the sugar, ½ teaspoon salt, some black pepper and the red wine vinegar. Pour into the pan and mix in the capers, olives, fried eggplant cubes and celery.

Bring to a gentle boil, lower heat and cook gently for 15–30 minutes, stirring occasionally, or until tender. Leave to cool and serve at room temperature.

Because of the high vinegar content, this dish keeps well (covered and refrigerated) for 3–4 days. (If you've got a 'Remo' in the house of course it won't last that long!)

Scrumptious Eggplant

Here's a super-scrummy way to treat eggplant.

Prepare them in the normal way, slicing and salting them. Then either fry the slices in oil, or brush with oil and barbecue them. While they are still warm, anoint them with a little homemade pesto. Scoff up with plenty of bread as an indulgent treat, or cut into smallish pieces and serve as a finger-licking nibble (provide napkins or paper serviettes as they are a little messy to eat).

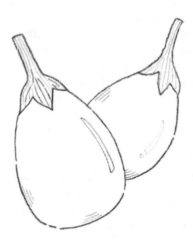

PASTA SALAD NIÇOISE

Serves 6–8

This is an interesting, substantial, late summer, main course salad. Although best served just after it has been made, while still warmish, it's perfectly good made a day ahead and served chilled.

1 large eggplant
salt
oil for frying
4 peppers of assorted hues
¼ cup finely chopped fresh basil leaves, plus several whole leaves
extra virgin olive oil
1 tablespoon balsamic vinegar (or red wine vinegar)
freshly ground black pepper to taste
1 clove garlic, crushed
400 g tomatoes, roughly chopped
¼ cup black olives, halved, stoned and chopped
2 tablespoons chopped flat-leaf parsley
400 g fusilli (twisty pasta coils)

Slice the eggplant into rounds, salt lightly and layer up in a colander. Leave to drain for 40 minutes, then pat dry with kitchen paper.

Heat a frypan over a medium-high heat with a little frying oil and when hot lower in as many eggplant slices as will fit in one layer. Cook both sides until they are a rich golden brown, turning with tongs (add more oil when the pan dries out). Cook the remaining eggplant this way. When cool, cut the slices into strips.

Sit the peppers on an oven rack in an oven preheated to 200 °C and cook for about 20 minutes, turning occasionally with tongs, or until they are blistered and charred. Transfer to a board and allow to cool. Peel off the skin and slip out the cores and seeds. Slice the peppers into strips, then put them in a bowl with the fresh basil.

Mix 2 tablespoons extra virgin olive oil with the chosen vinegar, ¼ teaspoon salt, plenty of freshly ground black pepper and the garlic. Pour this over the peppers and toss lightly. Spoon the pepper mixture over the eggplant strips. Cover and leave at room temperature while preparing the tomatoes and pasta. (If serving chilled, cool, cover and chill.)

Pass the tomatoes through a mouli-légumes (or a metal sieve) into a bowl. Mix in 2 tablespoons extra virgin olive oil, plenty of black pepper, a few pinches of salt and the chopped olives and parsley.

Cook the pasta in plenty of well-salted boiling water until just 'al dente'. Drain well, tip into a large bowl and pour on the tomato sauce. Toss well. (If not serving immediately, cool, cover and chill.)

Gently transfer the pasta to a large serving bowl, shaping it in a ring. Gently toss the eggplants and peppers together and spoon them into the centre of the dish. Decorate with a few basil leaves and serve. This salad is good with a bottle of gutsy red wine.

Balsamic Vinegar

This superior vinegar, a speciality of Modena, Italy, is made using a centuries-old technique. The juice of trebbiano grapes is boiled down to a sweet syrup, then poured into wooden barrels. It is left for at least 5 years, and in some cases, for many years more. The resulting vinegar is aromatic, spicy and sweet-sour to taste. Add it to dressings, sauces, vegetable dishes and meat dishes.

EGGPLANT WITH YOGHURT AND GARLIC DRESSING

Serves 6

Here's a dish which makes an admirable late summer, vegetable main course. Accompany it with a chick-pea or dried bean salad, an interesting salad like Cucumber and Feta Salad (page 246) and warmed pita bread.

2 medium eggplants (about 750 g each), sliced into rounds
salt
approx. ¼ cup olive oil
1 large onion, sliced
1 green pepper, cored, deseeded and sliced
1 clove garlic, crushed
3 large tomatoes, skinned, cored and diced
½ teaspoon salt
freshly ground black pepper to taste

Sauce
1 cup natural, unsweetened yoghurt
1 tablespoon finely chopped mint
2 cloves garlic, crushed

Layer the eggplant slices in a colander, sprinkling them well with salt. Leave to drain for 40 minutes. Pat dry with kitchen paper.

Heat 2 tablespoons olive oil in a large, heavy-based casserole over a medium heat. Add several slices of eggplant and cook on both sides until browned. Transfer them to a plate and repeat with the rest of the slices, adding more oil as necessary.

Put the onion, green pepper and garlic in the casserole with 1 tablespoon olive oil. Cover with a lid and cook gently until tender. Stir in the tomatoes, salt and black pepper, then carefully blend through the eggplant slices; don't worry if they break apart — it's all part of the charm of the dish.

Cover and cook on low heat for about 20 minutes, stirring occasionally, or until the eggplant is tender. Allow to stand, covered, for 5 minutes. Remove the lid and spoon the sauce down the centre. Serve hot, or at room temperature.

Sauce

Line a small sieve with a piece of kitchen paper and sit it over a bowl. Pour in the yoghurt and leave it to drain for an hour. Carefully turn the yoghurt into a clean bowl and stir through the mint and garlic.

To Thicken Yoghurt

To make plain yoghurt thick and velvety, like Greek yoghurt, it is necessary to drain off the whey.

Line a small sieve with a piece of kitchen paper or, if straining longer than 4 hours, with clean muslin, and sit it over a bowl. Pour in the yoghurt, cover with a plate and leave to drain for at least an hour, but up to 36 hours.

Carefully turn the yoghurt into a clean bowl and use as desired. After an hour the yoghurt is thicker and sauce-like. After 36 hours it is very dense and creamy and can be shaped into small 'blobs', dusted with chopped herbs, paprika or ground pepper, and served as a fresh 'cheese', drizzled with extra virgin olive oil or walnut oil. Serve with pita pockets or pumpernickel bread. The thickened yoghurt can also be mixed with capers, spices, lemon rind, garlic, green peppercorns, gherkin, olives, etc., and used as a dip or a sauce.

The whey, which contains worthwhile nutrients, can be used in baking bread, muffins, etc.

BEAN AND TUNA SALAD

Serves 6–12

This is an excellent choice for a casual summer's lunch. Alternatively, include with a selection of antipasto dishes.

200 g dried brown beans (or use 2 cups cooked or tinned beans), rinsed, then soaked several hours in water
1 tablespoon olive oil
several fresh sage leaves
50 ml extra virgin olive oil
1 tablespoon red wine vinegar
freshly ground black pepper to taste
salt
1 small red onion, finely chopped and soaked for an hour in cold water
185 g tin tuna fish in oil
juice of 1 lemon
1 tablespoon small capers
1 tablespoon coarsely chopped parsley, plus a few sprigs for garnishing

Transfer the beans to a large saucepan, pour in enough water to cover them generously, then add the olive oil and sage leaves. Bring to a gentle boil, partially covered, then turn to low and cook gently until barely tender. This will take between 20 and 60 minutes; be careful not to overcook. Drain and cool.

In a bowl mix the extra virgin olive oil with the red wine vinegar, black pepper, ½ teaspoon salt and the drained onion. Add the beans and toss well.

Tip the tuna into a bowl, pour over the lemon juice, sprinkle with a little salt and add the capers and parsley. Toss carefully, keeping the tuna in large flakes. The beans and tuna can now sit happily for an hour or two at room temperature before serving. (Or longer, refrigerated.)

At serving time, toss the beans again, spoon them into a bowl with all the dressing and mound the tuna on top. Pour over the tuna juices, decorate with a sprig of parsley and serve.

❖
Potatomania

Along with my olive oil and garlic addiction comes a heavy potato dependency. If I go more than a few hours (well, maybe a few days) without any, I suffer terrible withdrawal symptoms (chomping of jaws, simulating potato-munching and rooting in the vegetable patch hoping to unearth some left-behind spuds).

At first I tried to scatter the colossal number of potato recipes throughout the book in an effort to disguise the real truth (this is not a potato book, is it?) but in the end common sense prevailed. You'll find them not only in this section, but in most others too, blatantly clumped together. Enjoy them!

❖

RÖSTI

RÖSTI WITH HAM AND ONION

SPECIAL STUFFED SPUDS

'KITCHEN SINK' POTATOES

POTATO AND GRUYÈRE GRATIN

❖

RÖSTI

....

Serves 2 with salad as a light meal, or 3 as a vegetable accompaniment

These Swiss potato pancakes are a potatoholic's dream. Make sure you use old potatoes, as new ones don't contain enough starch to hold the rösti together. The process of wringing out the grated potatoes ensures that excess starch, which could make the rösti gummy, is extracted. Serve with other dishes which do not require last-minute cooking or fiddling.

300 g old potatoes (approx. 2 medium ones)
2 tablespoons oil
40 g butter
salt

Peel the potatoes, then immediately grate them coarsely by hand. Use your hands to wring out as much starch as possible.

Smear a shallow, 18–20 cm, sloping-sided pan with a little oil (use a cast-iron, copper, stainless steel or teflon-coated pan) and set it over a medium-high heat. Allow the pan to get quite hot, but not smoking-hot.

Drop in half the butter and swirl the pan until the butter melts and foams, then put in the grated potato. Spread it into a round shape, neatening the edges, then pat the surface lightly to knock out excess air.

Cook the rösti for about 5 minutes, shaking the pan from time to time to ensure it doesn't stick, or until it is a good golden-brown. Flip it over; or slide it onto a plate, cover with a second plate, invert and slip it back into the pan. Drop in several small pieces of butter around the sides of the pan. As the butter melts, allow it to run under the rösti. Sprinkle with salt and cook for about 5 minutes, or until a good golden-brown on the base. Turn out onto a heated serving plate, cut into wedges and serve immediately.

RÖSTI WITH HAM AND ONION

Serves 2 as a main course, or 3–4 as a brunch dish

Once you've mastered Potato Rösti try this more scrumptious version with ham and onion.

300 g old potatoes (approx. 2 medium ones)
1 medium onion, finely sliced
50 g ham off the bone, chopped
2 tablespoons oil
40 g butter
salt

Peel the potatoes, then immediately grate them coarsely by hand. Use your hands to wring out as much starch as possible. Quickly mix the potatoes, onion and ham together.

Heat the oil in the pan (see preceding recipe) over a medium-high heat until hot but not smoking. Drop in half the butter and swirl the pan until the butter melts and foams. Put in the potato mixture. Spread it into a round shape, neatening the edges, then pat the surface lightly to knock out excess air. Cook the rösti for about 5 minutes, shaking the pan from time to time to ensure it isn't catching, or until it is a good golden-brown. Slide the rösti onto a plate.

If the pan is dryish, drop in a little more butter and heat until it is hot. Cover the rösti with another plate, invert it and slide it back into the pan. Sprinkle lightly with salt and cook for another 6–7 minutes, or until golden and crisp. Turn out onto a heated serving plate, cut into wedges and serve immediately.

SPECIAL STUFFED SPUDS

....

Serves 4–6

These jacket-baked potatoes, filled with layers of creamy mashed potatoes, sautéed mushrooms, poached eggs and mornay sauce, then crowned with a ruffle of piped potato purée, are a vegetable-eater's dream (the ham is optional). They are amazing to look at, nutritious, and delicious too! The one drawback lies in their making; although not difficult to make they do require time.

6 large potatoes
salt
100 g mushrooms, sliced (or pre-cooked mushrooms)
knob of butter
generous tablespoon plain flour
50 ml stock
100 g ham (or cooked chicken), sliced (optional)

Mornay sauce
knob of butter (= 1 tablespoon butter)
generous tablespoon plain flour
125 ml milk
salt
15 g grated Parmesan cheese

6 small eggs, poached or lightly boiled for 5 minutes, then
  shelled
knob of butter
4 tablespoons hot milk
25 g grated Parmesan cheese

Scrub the potatoes, but do not peel them. Roll them in salt while they are still wet, then place them immediately on an oven rack in an oven preheated to 200 °C. Cook for about 1½ hours, or until tender.

Meanwhile, sauté the mushrooms in a small pan in the butter. Dust over the flour, add the stock and bring to the boil, stirring. If you are using ham or chicken, add it now. Mix all together and set aside.

Next make the mornay sauce. Melt the butter in a small saucepan, then take it off the heat and add the flour. Stir in the

116

milk and return the pan to a medium-high heat. Stir constantly until boiling, lower the heat and cook for another minute. Add a few pinches of salt and the Parmesan cheese. Turn the heat off, cover the pan and set aside.

Poach or soft-boil the eggs just before the potatoes are cooked. Remove the potatoes from the oven, cut a cap off lengthwise and carefully scoop out the pulp. Put the pulp into a warm bowl and mash thoroughly. Add a knob of butter, ¼ teaspoon salt and the hot milk to form a purée.

Sit the potatoes in a shallow oven dish and put a spoonful of the mushroom mixture in the bottom of each potato. Pat the eggs dry with kitchen paper, then sit one in each potato.

If the mornay sauce is gluggy, rewarm it gently, then carefully coat each egg with it. Spoon on the potato purée, or pipe it on using a piping bag fitted with a large rose pipe. (Ensure the filling is well covered with the purée.) Sprinkle over a little grated Parmesan cheese and brown the potatoes under the grill or reheat them in an oven preheated to 200 °C for 10–15 minutes. Serve immediately.

Piping

Various designs can be piped. Usually the piping bag and nozzle are held in an upright position, with one hand gently squeezing the mixture in the bag while the index finger of the other hand guides the nozzle. If both hands are on the bag, vision is restricted. If the bag and nozzle are held on a slant instead of vertically, the result will be designs that topple over (instead of designs which stand erect).

An instance where a toppling effect is called for is in the piping of a curling rope used as a border. For this, the bag is held on a definite slant.

Filling a Piping Bag

Filling a piping bag so that it doesn't ooze the filling out over the top and over your hands is easily done.

Drop the chosen nozzle into the bag. Grasp the bag in one hand, nozzle pointing down, and fold over the top third of the bag. With the other hand scrape up the mixture for piping, using a rubber scraper, and lower it into the bag, scraping the mixture on the sides of the bag as you withdraw it. Continue filling the bag until it is about half to three-quarters full (or approximately up to the folded edge). Unfold the top of the bag and squeeze the mixture down towards the nozzle, ensuring none squelches up on the clean part of the bag. If you want to 'top up' the bag, fold the top third of the bag down again and repeat.

Comments and Grizzles about Potatoes

Most of us know that potatoes will turn green if exposed to the light and that the green part is mildly 'poisonous'. However, you would have to eat a lot to make you sick and probably a whole field of green potatoes to die ... But, if you can avoid 'greening' so much the better.

I'm totally against pre-washed potatoes. They sit, exposed to the light, often fluorescent, sweating in plastic bags. They rot quickly and often taste sour.

Remember the old days when potatoes were sold in heavy sacks? That was for a very good reason. The dirt protected the potatoes, keeping the external nutrients intact and protecting them from the light. The heavy sack also kept out the light, protected against changes in temperature and, most importantly, let the air pass through, preventing rotting.

When I grew up we always bought potatoes this way and they lasted for ages. The potatoes at the bottom of the sack were just as healthy as the ones at the top had been when the sack was purchased.

'KITCHEN SINK' POTATOES

Serves 6

These are so called because the first time I made them I put in just about everything within reach — bar the kitchen sink! If you're a 'vego' leave out the bacon and add a diced red or green pepper instead.

6 large potatoes, scrubbed
salt
225 g bacon (or 1 red or green pepper, cored and diced)
200 g grated Cheddar cheese (approx. 2½ cups)
1 very small onion, finely chopped
2 stalks celery, finely sliced
2 large tomatoes, diced
plenty of freshly ground black pepper
1 tablespoon finely chopped parsley
¼ teaspoon dried oregano, crumbled
½ cup milk
50 g butter

Sprinkle the wet potatoes with a little salt and sit them on a rack in an oven preheated to 200 °C. Cook for about 1½ hours, or until tender. Meanwhile put the bacon in a shallow oven dish under the potatoes and cook it until it is crisp. Remove to a board and chop coarsely.

In a large bowl mix 1½ cups Cheddar cheese with the onion, celery, tomatoes, black pepper, parsley and oregano. Mix in the bacon or the red or green pepper if used.

Transfer the potatoes from the oven to a board. Put the milk in a saucepan and heat it until it is hot (don't boil). Split the potatoes in half lengthwise, scoop out the pulp and place it in a large bowl. Mash thoroughly, adding ½ teaspoon salt, the hot milk and butter.

Add the filling ingredients, blend together, then pile them back into the potato shells. Sit these in a shallow roasting tin and sprinkle the rest of the cheese over them. Put them back in the oven for about 15 minutes, or until the tops brown lightly. Serve immediately.

Potato Purée

Ever wondered how to get a fluffy, light potato purée? Start by peeling the potatoes and cutting them into smallish, even-size cubes; this way they will cook quickly and evenly and not become water-logged.

Put the potatoes in a large saucepan and cover them generously with cold water. Add some salt, then boil gently until tender. Drain well and return to the saucepan. Place the saucepan back over the heat for 30 seconds (without the lid); this drives off any clinging moisture, making the potatoes drier and improving the flavour (be careful not to scorch them though, or the flavour will be ruined).

Mash with a hand masher or pass through a mouli-légumes; processing makes them heavy and sticky. Heat a small amount of milk until just under boiling point (use as much as necessary to make a soft purée). Add to the purée by degrees, along with a knob of butter, beating well with a wooden spoon; hot milk makes the purée fluffy, cold milk added to a starchy vegetable makes it tacky and gluey. Hot milk also stops the purée turning greyish, and, of course, keeps the purée hot. Beating it by hand introduces air and keeps the purée light.

Check the seasoning, add salt, beat it in, then taste and continue adding more salt until the purée has a real potato flavour. It should taste delicious.

The purée is best served immediately, but if you do have to hold it for a time don't keep it over heat; it will collapse, turn watery and grey, lose its goodness and good taste. Better to remove it from the heat, pour a little hot milk over the surface to prevent it drying out, and leave it to cool. Reheat over a gentle heat, beating with a wooden spoon, adding more hot milk if necessary.

POTATO AND GRUYÈRE GRATIN

Serves 4–6

Cheese is not usually included in the classic Gratin Dauphinois, a dish from the mountainous province of Dauphiné in France. But it provides a mild, nutty flavour, adds to the creaminess and makes the dish substantial enough to constitute a casual winter supper. Team it up with an interesting leafy salad.

1 kg potatoes, peeled
knob of butter
¾ teaspoon salt
freshly ground black pepper to taste
freshly grated nutmeg
70 g Gruyère cheese, grated
1 large clove garlic, crushed
300 ml cream

Slice the potatoes very thinly. Generously butter a smallish, heavy-based oven dish, then put in a layer of potatoes in concentric circles (reserve the neatest slices of potatoes for the top). Sprinkle over a little salt (use a teaspoon, not wet fingers), grind over a little black pepper and grate over a little nutmeg. Continue layering the ingredients, putting half the Gruyère cheese in the central layer. Arrange the top layer of potatoes neatly.

Mix the crushed garlic with the cream and pour it over the potatoes. Season with the last of the salt and a little more black pepper and nutmeg, then scatter over the remaining cheese. Dot with butter and cover with a lid.

Bake in an oven preheated to 180 °C for 15 minutes. Remove the lid and continue baking for a good hour, or until the potatoes are tender, but still creamy, and the topping is crusty. Serve hot.

Simple But Scrumptious

Don't you just love the title of this section? It's how I wish every recipe to be.

You can rattle up most of the following recipes at short notice, or, at least, without possessing any great culinary skills.

SORREL AND AVOCADO SALAD
WITH HOT BACON DRESSING

SWEET CORN PEPPER BAKE

MUFFINS WITH CHIVE BUTTER

ASPARAGUS AND HAM
THINGUMMY

BAKED BUTTERNUT WITH THYME

TACOS WITH AVOCADO
AND BACON

AVOCADO AND BACON
SANDWICHES

VEGETABLE KEBABS
ON THE BARBIE

SORREL AND AVOCADO SALAD
WITH HOT BACON DRESSING

Serves 4

This little number is bound to tickle your fancy (that's if you eat bacon of course!). Present it as a savoury luncheon dish, with fresh bread and a bottle of well-chilled, local Gewürztraminer or Riesling. Top it off with a selection of New Zealand cheeses.

½ small red onion (optional)
225 g rindless, streaky bacon
1 large bunch (approx. 150 g) sorrel leaves
1 buttercrunch lettuce
5 tablespoons olive oil
¼ teaspoon salt
freshly ground black pepper to taste
2 tablespoons red wine vinegar
1 large avocado, peeled and sliced

If you are using the onion, prepare it first. Peel it, leaving the root end intact (it helps hold the slices together once they are sliced). Cut it in half through the root end; set aside one half for another recipe. Cut the onion half into slivers, ensuring each sliver has a little of the root attached. Put them into a bowl of ice-cold water and soak for 30 minutes. Drain and pat dry with kitchen paper.

Place the bacon in a large, heated frypan. Cook over a low-medium heat until the fat starts to run, then increase the heat slightly and cook the bacon to a crisp. Tilt the pan to drain the fat, then transfer the bacon to a board. Chop it coarsely.

Meanwhile, wash the sorrel leaves, discarding any large stalks. Dry, then tear them into bite-size pieces. Wash and dry the buttercrunch and put it into a large bowl with the sorrel leaves. Scatter over the dried red onion slivers, if you are using them, and the chopped, hot bacon.

Add the olive oil, salt and black pepper to the bacon fat in the pan. Reheat, then pour in the red wine vinegar when hot (be careful, it sizzles and steams). Remove the pan from the heat and pour the sizzling contents over the salad. Toss it quickly, then top with the avocado slices. Toss gently and serve immediately.

SWEET CORN PEPPER BAKE

Serves 6

This makes a good brunch or lunch dish, especially when it is teamed with crisp bacon and buttery muffins (chive butter recipe follows).

1 medium onion, finely chopped
2 red peppers, cored, deseeded and coarsely chopped
knob of butter plus extra for greasing the dish and dotting the surface
*   of the 'bake'*
2 x 310 g tins cream-style sweet corn
¼ teaspoon salt
freshly ground black pepper to taste
pinch of chilli powder, or to taste
6 rounded tablespoons fresh soft breadcrumbs
1 egg

Put the onion and red peppers in a saucepan with a knob of butter, cover with a lid and cook slowly for about 12 minutes, until they are soft. Add the sweet corn, salt, black pepper and chilli powder. Stir through half the breadcrumbs, then mix in the egg. Turn into a buttered shallow ovenproof dish (approx. 20 cm in diameter).

Sprinkle over the remaining breadcrumbs, dot the surface with butter and bake for about 35–40 minutes in an oven preheated to 200°C.

The 'bake' can be prepared 1–2 hours before cooking, but it is best served hot, immediately after cooking.

MUFFINS WITH CHIVE BUTTER

This is a simple way of producing crisp, buttery muffins.

6 plain muffins
6 tablespoons soft butter
2 tablespoons snipped chives

Heat the oven to 200°C. Put the muffins on the oven rack and cook them for about 12 minutes, or until they are very crisp, turning once or twice. Remove from the oven, split each muffin in half horizontally and cool.

Blend the butter and chives together in a small bowl. Spread this generously on the cool muffins, then serve immediately.

ASPARAGUS AND HAM THINGUMMY

Serves 4

This little 'thingummy' is excellent for brunch, with scrambled eggs.

500–700 g asparagus, trimmed and washed well
salt
2 knobs of butter
75 g ham off the bone, diced
2 tablespoons snipped chives
freshly ground black pepper to taste
2 tablespoons freshly grated Parmesan cheese

Plunge the asparagus into a saucepan of salted, boiling water and cook uncovered for 2–7 minutes (depending on how crunchy or tender you like them). Drain.

Five minutes before serving time, heat a large frypan over a medium heat and drop in the butter. While it is sizzling, add the ham and cook for 1–2 minutes, stirring often. Then add the asparagus and chives. Cook for a few minutes, turning often, and add the black pepper.

When the asparagus is heated through, turn them into a heated serving dish, scatter the Parmesan cheese over and serve immediately.

BAKED BUTTERNUT WITH THYME

Serves 3–4 as a supper dish, or 6 as a vegetable accompaniment

In this dish the sweetness of the butternut is concentrated by baking. But the cheese makes the dish quite rich, and even though the tomatoes help balance it out, it is wise to serve a tangy green salad as an accompaniment.

1 medium butternut pumpkin
knob of butter, plus extra for greasing
freshly ground black pepper to taste
½ teaspoon salt
1 teaspoon finely chopped fresh thyme (or use a few pinches of dried thyme)
4 large tomatoes, skinned
2 cups grated tasty Cheddar cheese

Cut the pumpkin in half lengthwise. Butter an ovenproof dish and place the pumpkin in it, cut side down. Bake for 40–60 minutes in an oven preheated to 200°C, or until tender when pierced with a fine skewer. Remove it from the oven and leave to cool for 10 minutes.

Turn the pumpkin halves over with a fish slice and scoop out the seeds and discard. Carefully scoop out the flesh, leaving a thin layer of flesh next to the skin. Mix the pumpkin flesh in a bowl with the butter, seasonings and thyme. Blend in the tomatoes and one cup of Cheddar cheese. Pile this mixture back into the pumpkin halves and sprinkle the rest of the cheese over them. Place under a preheated grill and cook until bubbling and golden. Serve hot.

TACOS WITH AVOCADO AND BACON

Makes 6 tacos

The following three recipes contain that wonderful combination: rich, buttery avocados and crisp bacon.

225 g bacon
1–2 avocados
¼ teaspoon salt
1 teaspoon lemon or lime juice
1 small chilli, deseeded and finely chopped (or use ½ teaspoon chilli paste)
1 large tomato, finely diced
6 taco shells
3 leaves crisp lettuce, shredded
2 spring onions, finely sliced
12 black olives, halved, stoned and chopped
1½ cups grated Cheddar cheese

Lay the bacon in a roasting tin and bake it in an oven preheated to 180°C, turning occasionally, until it is crisp. Remove it from the dish, drain briefly on kitchen paper, then chop coarsely.

Cut open the avocados, extract the stones and scoop out the flesh. Put the flesh in a bowl, sprinkle over the salt and lime or lemon juice. Add the chilli and tomato. Fold quickly together, but don't beat the mixture to a purée.

Warm the taco shells in the oven for a few minutes to soften them (don't leave them too long or they will become brittle). Fill them in this order: shredded lettuce, spring onions, black olives, avocado mixture, bacon and Cheddar cheese.

If you like, spoon in a little homemade spicy tomato chutney (see recipe, page 279) or chilli tomato sauce before putting on the bacon and cheese.

AVOCADO AND BACON SANDWICHES

The following sandwich makes a great snack when you want something hot and savoury.

Per sandwich:
1 rasher of bacon, fried till crisp
2 slices wholegrain bread, toasted and buttered
about ⅓ avocado, sliced (1 avocado should be sufficient for 3
*   sandwiches)*
a few squirts lemon or lime juice
salt
freshly ground black pepper
1 spring onion, finely sliced or a few slices of red onion (optional)
2 lettuce leaves, washed and dried

Lay the bacon on one piece of hot toast and top with the slices of avocado. Squeeze on a little lemon or lime juice, sprinkle lightly with salt and grind on black pepper to taste. Scatter the onion over, if you are using it, and cover with the lettuce leaves. Top with another slice of toast. Serve immediately.

For a richer version, spread the top piece of toast with a little homemade mayonnaise.

VEGETABLE KEBABS ON THE BARBIE

Serves 6

Ever wondered what to serve non-meat eaters at a barbecue? Their own satay, of course, made with vegetables.

Marinade
⅓ cup dry white wine
¼ cup peanut oil
¼ cup lime juice
¼ cup lemon juice
1 teaspoon salt
freshly ground black pepper to taste
1 teaspoon finely chopped tarragon or lemon thyme
1 clove garlic, finely crushed

Vegetables
15 small pickling onions
5 peppers of assorted hues, cored, deseeded and cut into small chunks
2 smallish green zucchini and 2 smallish yellow zucchini (or 4 green ones), trimmed and cut into small chunks
12 button mushrooms, washed and dried
25–30 small cherry tomatoes

Mix all the marinade ingredients together in a large, shallow dish.

Place the unpeeled onions in a small saucepan and cover with cold water. Bring to the boil and cook, uncovered, for 7 minutes. Drain. When cool, remove the peel and trim the roots.

Place all the prepared vegetables in the marinade and leave them at room temperature, covered, for 2 hours.

Meanwhile, soak bamboo skewers in water for 30 minutes. Skewer the cherry tomatoes, five to a skewer, then skewer the remaining vegetables, alternating the ingredients and pushing them close together.

Cook the mixed vegetable kebabs over hot coals on the barbecue (or on the hot plate), basting with marinade from time to time, until they are crisp and brown. Cook the tomatoes over a very high heat for a few seconds a side, to char the skin, then serve immediately.

Something More Substantial

Rice, dried beans and starch vegetables can all be put to good use to make a meal more bulky and filling.

The following recipes are all a good choice to use as the central dish of a main course.

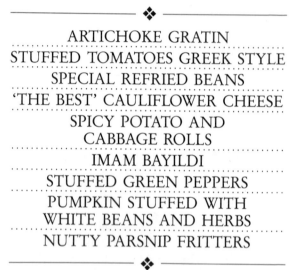

ARTICHOKE GRATIN
STUFFED TOMATOES GREEK STYLE
SPECIAL REFRIED BEANS
'THE BEST' CAULIFLOWER CHEESE
SPICY POTATO AND
CABBAGE ROLLS
IMAM BAYILDI
STUFFED GREEN PEPPERS
PUMPKIN STUFFED WITH
WHITE BEANS AND HERBS
NUTTY PARSNIP FRITTERS

ARTICHOKE GRATIN

Serves 4

This makes a very tasty, although rich, luncheon or supper dish. It can be assembled several hours in advance, then quickly reheated in the oven when required. For a change, and to make it more substantial, make 3–4 depressions on the top of the gratin and break in fresh eggs. Cook for 15 minutes or until the egg whites are set.

4 artichokes
juice of 1 lemon mixed with 2 litres cold water
¼ cup olive oil
6 spring onions, roughly chopped
150 g button mushrooms, sliced
scant ¼ teaspoon salt
freshly ground black pepper to taste
150 g ham, diced (optional)
¼ cup freshly grated Parmesan cheese
¼ cup fresh breadcrumbs
knob of butter

Trim the artichoke stalks, then cut off the top third of the artichokes and discard. Pull off about three-quarters of the remaining leaves until you reach the young, tender leaves. Spread open the leaves and scoop out any sharply pointed leaves and the choke (fibrous hairs). Use a knife to peel off any tough fibre from the stalks and artichoke bases. As the artichokes are prepared, plunge them into the mixed lemon juice and water. When all are ready, shake them free of water, cut each into four, then cut the quarters into slivers.

Heat the olive oil in a large frypan over a medium heat, add the artichokes and cook for about 20 minutes, turning often. Lower the heat and add the spring onions and mushrooms. Cook for 5 minutes, stirring often. Season with the salt and black pepper, then stir in the ham, if used. Turn into a shallow ovenproof dish.

Mix the Parmesan cheese and breadcrumbs together in a small bowl, then sprinkle over the artichokes. Dot with the butter and bake in an oven preheated to 200 °C for about 15 minutes, or until crisp on top.

STUFFED TOMATOES GREEK STYLE

Serves 6 as a luncheon dish or 12 as an accompanying vegetable

In Greece, and surrounding countries, rice is a popular stuffing for vegetables, and understandably so; it's cheap, making food more substantial at little extra cost, and it has the ability to absorb flavours, resulting in great taste.

12 large, ripe but firm tomatoes (choose tomatoes that will sit flat and not topple over)
salt
1 tablespoon castor sugar
freshly ground black pepper
½ cup olive oil, plus a little extra
1 large onion, finely chopped
1 cup short-grain rice, washed under running water and drained
2 tablespoons pinenuts
½ cup currants
1 tablespoon finely chopped mint
1 tablespoon finely chopped parsley
1 tablespoon dried breadcrumbs

Wash the tomatoes and cut a thin slice off each from the stem end. Set the slices aside to use as caps. Use a small teaspoon to scoop out the tomato pulp and seeds, and drain it in a small sieve set over a bowl. Leave it to drain for 5 minutes.

Sprinkle the insides of the tomatoes with a little salt and castor sugar, then grind some black pepper over them. Sit the tomatoes in an oiled baking dish, preferably one in which they fit snugly.

Pour off the watery liquid from the drained tomato pulp, then rub the pulp through the sieve and set it aside.

Heat the olive oil in a large frypan over a gentle heat. Add the onion and cook until it is transparent. Tip in the drained rice and fry for 1–2 minutes. Add the pinenuts, currants, mint, parsley, ½ teaspoon salt and some black pepper. Stir well, then blend in ½ cup tomato pulp and 1 cup water.

Cover and cook gently for 10 minutes, or until the rice is half cooked. Spoon the mixture into the prepared tomatoes (don't over-fill them) and top with the reserved slices. Sprinkle over the breadcrumbs and drizzle a little oil over them. Pour ½ cup of the reserved tomato pulp around the peppers, then bake for about

30 minutes in an oven preheated to 180°C. If the tomato pulp dries up during cooking, add a little more. Serve warm or at room temperature.

Ideas for Pita Bread

Fresh pita bread requires no doctoring, of course, but there are several things you can do with it.

- Eat it fresh, as stated.
- Warm it for about 3 minutes in a gentle oven.
- Toast it, whole or halved, in a moderate oven until crisp (good to use as a 'dunker').
- Freeze it and rewarm in a warm oven till soft, or till crisp.
- Split it and brush with garlic/herb/spice butter and bake till crunchy (store airtight when cool; if thin pita bread is used, split and well toasted, it will keep several days airtight); excellent just as a nibble, or as a 'dunker'.
- Use as a mock pizza base. Split and spread with tomato sauce, then top with diced ham/chopped salami/diced peppers/stoned olives/stuffed olives/anchovies/chopped herbs and top with grated Cheddar or mozzarella cheese. Bake for about 10 minutes till crisp and serve as a snack, as a light meal for children, or as party food.

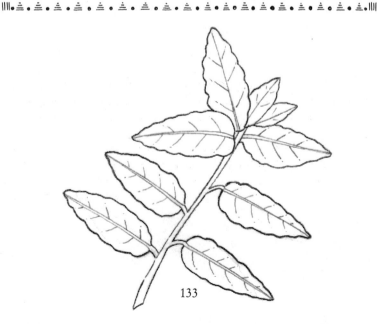

SPECIAL REFRIED BEANS

Serves 6–8

Here's a good dish to remember when easy-to-prepare, substantial and warming food is required. Accompanied by the Pineapple and Pepper Salad (page 239) and some crusty pita pockets, it makes an inviting and balanced meal.

2 tablespoons oil
1 large onion, finely chopped
750 g prime-quality minced beef
450 g tin refried beans
440 g tin pinto beans (or use red kidney beans)
2 teaspoons salt
3 tablespoons hot pepper sauce, or chilli sauce
250 ml jar (approx.) 'Red Jalapeno sauce', or hot taco sauce
1 cup finely grated Cheddar cheese
1 ripe but firm avocado
juice of ½ lemon
1 tablespoon finely chopped fresh coriander, or substitute mint
freshly ground black pepper to taste
½ cup sour cream (optional)
½ lettuce, finely shredded
a little extra red pepper sauce
½ cup plump black olives, drained
fresh coriander leaves to garnish (optional)

Heat a large frypan over a medium heat and add the oil. When it is hot add the onion and fry, stirring often, until it is lightly golden. Increase the heat to high, then add the beef and fry quickly, breaking up the meat with a fork, until the pinkness disappears. Tilt the pan, then leave the meat to drain for 10 minutes. Pour off the fatty liquid.

Spread the refried beans on the base of a heavy-based casserole with a spatula, then bury the pinto beans amongst the 'refrieds'. Add the salt and the hot pepper or chilli sauce to the meat, then spoon it over the beans. Pour on the 'Red Jalapeno' or hot taco sauce. Sprinkle over the Cheddar cheese.

The dish can be assembled to this point a day in advance; cover and refrigerate when cool, but bring it to room temperature before cooking. Bake in an oven preheated to 200°C for about 30 minutes, or until bubbling on top.

Meanwhile, peel the avocado and mash the flesh with the lemon juice and chopped coriander, plus ¼ teaspoon salt and some black pepper. Beat the sour cream with a wooden spoon until it is smooth.

When the beef and bean dish is ready, remove it from the oven and let it stand for 5 minutes at room temperature. Top with the chopped lettuce and spoon a little red pepper sauce in the centre. Spoon dollops of sour cream and mashed avocado around the outside of the sauce and decorate it with the olives and coriander leaves. Serve immediately.

Coriander

A feathery herb with an oily, grassy, citrus taste, it is used extensively in Asia, the Middle East and South America. It is often referred to as Chinese parsley. It is also used in Mexico and South America, where it is known as cilantro.

Coriander grows easily in the garden and, if picked with its long roots intact, placed in a container of water, covered with a plastic bag, and refrigerated, it will continue to grow for some time.

The seeds have an intoxicating lemon fragrance, but it is best to grind them as required as the heady aroma quickly dissipates.

135

'THE BEST' CAULIFLOWER CHEESE

Serves 6–8

Over the years, cauliflower cheese has remained one of my favourite dishes. This version, much more elaborate than the 'cauli and cheese sauce' I grew up with, is a treat to eat. Try it as a main course (serves 6), served with jacket potatoes or jacket kumaras and a salad.

Cheese sauce
20 g butter (= large knob of butter)
2 level tablespoons (20 g) plain flour
300 ml milk
¼ teaspoon salt
25 g finely grated Gruyère cheese

1 medium cauliflower, washed and trimmed into florets

Crisp crumbs
3 tablespoons butter (approx. 45 g) plus a little extra for greasing the bowl
1 cup fresh breadcrumbs
few pinches of salt
good grinding of black pepper
2 tablespoons freshly grated Parmesan cheese
1 tablespoon finely chopped parsley

First prepare the sauce. Melt the butter in a small saucepan, then remove the pan from the heat and add the flour. Blend well, then add the milk a third at a time, stirring well. Return the sauce to the heat, blend in the salt and stir constantly until it is boiling. Cook for 2 minutes, stirring, then remove it from the heat and beat in the Gruyère cheese. (If you want to make the sauce ahead of time, see instructions for storing it, in the recipe for Mornay Sauce, page 285).

Plunge the cauliflower florets into a saucepan of boiling salted water and cook for 6 minutes. Drain, refresh with cold water, leave to drain again, then wrap in kitchen paper to absorb clinging moisture.

Butter a small china basin of about 1 litre capacity. Put in the cauliflower florets, placing the stems pointing inwards and pressing them tightly together. Dribble about 3 tablespoons of the sauce over the stems as you layer up the cauliflower. Cover it with a small plate or saucer and put a weight on top.

Ten minutes before serving, tilt the bowl and drain off any accumulated liquid, then place the covered bowl in a hot oven to warm through. Gently heat the sauce (don't boil or it may go stringy). Invert the heated cauliflower onto a heated plate and spoon over the hot sauce. Scatter over the crisp crumbs (instructions follow) and serve immediately.

Crisp crumbs

Heat a large frypan and drop in the butter. When it is sizzling, add the breadcrumbs and cook over a medium heat, tossing often, until the crumbs are crisp and golden. Turn into a bowl and blend in a few pinches of salt, a good grinding of black pepper, the Parmesan cheese and parsley. The crumbs will stay crisp for a few hours if they are left uncovered and stored at room temperature.

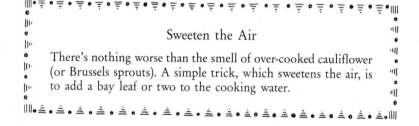

Sweeten the Air

There's nothing worse than the smell of over-cooked cauliflower (or Brussels sprouts). A simple trick, which sweetens the air, is to add a bay leaf or two to the cooking water.

SPICY POTATO AND CABBAGE ROLLS

Makes approx. 30 rolls; serves 6 as a main course or more if served with other vegetables

These make a tasty, savoury, all-vegetable main course, but be warned, there are several stages to the recipe, the bulk of which should be carried out long before dinner is required. Finishing off is then a simple matter of heating through.

1 large green or Savoy cabbage
½ teaspoon salt
3 tablespoons peanut oil

Filling
1 kg potatoes, peeled
salt
3 large onions, peeled and finely sliced
8 tablespoons peanut oil
2 tablespoons whole fennel seeds
2 tablespoons cumin seeds
2 teaspoons garam masala
2 tablespoons strained lemon juice
½ teaspoon ground cayenne pepper

Sauce
½ cup natural unsweetened yoghurt
2 tablespoons lemon juice
1 tablespoon finely chopped mint

Remove the core and any tough outer leaves from the cabbage. Wash it well. Choose a deep saucepan, fill it three-quarters full with water and bring to the boil. Add the salt and immerse the cabbage, core down. Hold it under the water with a large wooden spoon until the water reboils and cook it, uncovered, for 3 minutes (the cabbage should be in the water for a total of 6 minutes). Carefully lift the cabbage out of the water (this is easiest done with a carving fork) and place it in a colander. Rinse with cold water and when they are cool enough to handle, separate the leaves.

Return the leaves to the boiling water in batches, cooking them until they are wilted and reasonably tender. As they are cooked, dunk them into a bowl of cold water, then drain them in a colander. When all are done, pour more cold water over them

138

and leave them to drain in the colander, shaking them occasionally. Use scissors to snip the stems from the leaves, splitting the large leaves into two pieces. Lay them on kitchen paper and leave to dry.

Meanwhile, make the filling. If the potatoes are large, cut them in half. Place them in a saucepan and cover with cold water. Salt lightly, then bring them to the boil and cook until very tender. Drain, then chop them roughly into cubes.

In a large, heavy-based frypan, sauté the onions in 6 tablespoons peanut oil over a medium heat until they are a good golden brown. This will take about 20 minutes; stir occasionally, especially during the latter stages of cooking. Add the fennel seeds and cumin seeds and continue cooking for 2–3 minutes. Add the last 2 tablespoons of the oil and the cubed potatoes. Blend the ingredients together, mashing lightly with the back of a spoon. Add the garam masala, 2 teaspoons salt, the lemon juice and cayenne pepper. Continue cooking for a few more minutes, scraping the mixture from the sides of the pan with a metal spoon, until it is well amalgamated. Allow to cool.

Place a small mound of filling on one end of a cabbage leaf and roll it up tightly, ensuring the filling is enclosed. Repeat with the remaining leaves and filling. When all are ready, heat about 3 tablespoons peanut oil in a heavy-based frypan and when it is hot add some of the cabbage rolls. Fry them briefly, turning with tongs, until lightly browned. Remove to a plate and brown the rest of the cabbage rolls.

Return the browned rolls to the frypan, packing them in tightly. Add a scant ¼ cup water, cover the pan with a lid, and cook over a lowish heat for about 25 minutes, adding more water if it evaporates.

Serve with yoghurt sauce or a side dish like Cucumber with Sultanas and Yoghurt, page 247.

Sauce
Blend all the ingredients together in a small bowl and serve.

IMAM BAYILDI

....

Serves 4

The origin of this mouth-watering dish is highly controversial; the Greeks claim it as theirs, but the Turks, who can lay claim to the word Imam, state just as fiercely that the dish originated in Turkey. The story, told by both, goes something like this: A Turkish/Greek priest, called an Imam, nearly fainted, or did faint (depends on the story-teller), when he was served this dish. Hence the name, fainting priest. Whether he fainted because the dish smelled and looked so good, or because of how much garlic or olive oil was used in the making of it, is just another point to make Greek and Turkish blood boil. Whatever . . . it makes a superb main course, but it is also good cut into tiny morsels and served as a 'mezze' (nibble). Like me, it's always better after a little siesta, so try and make it a day before serving; store it covered and refrigerated, but bring it to room temperature before serving.

4 medium eggplants
salt
100 ml olive oil
2 large onions, thinly sliced
2 large cloves garlic, crushed
400 g tin Italian tomatoes, mashed
2 tablespoons coarsely chopped parsley (preferably flat-leaf parsley)
freshly ground black pepper to taste
½ teaspoon sugar
juice of 1 lemon
½ cup water

Cut the stems off the eggplants, then peel off strips of the skin lengthwise, leaving alternate strips of skin and flesh. Sprinkle well with salt and leave to drain for an hour in a colander.

Heat ¼ cup olive oil in a large frypan set over a low heat. Add the onions. Cover the pan and cook them gently for 10 minutes, or until they are soft. Add the garlic and cook for a further 2 minutes, then add the Italian tomatoes, parsley, black pepper and ½ teaspoon salt. Cook uncovered for 10 minutes, then set aside.

Heat the remaining olive oil in a deep, heavy-based saucepan over a medium-high heat (this helps confine the splattering). Pat the eggplants dry with kitchen paper, then lower them carefully into the hot oil. Fry quickly, turning with tongs, until they are evenly browned. Transfer to a plate and cool briefly.

Cut a slit in the eggplants, taking care not to cut right the way through, and force them open to form a cavity. Spoon some of the stuffing inside the cavities, then sit the eggplants in a shallow, ovenproof dish (choose one in which they fit snugly). Spoon the rest of the tomato mixture on top.

Mix the sugar, lemon juice and water together and pour this around the eggplants. Cover the dish with a lid or a double thickness of tinfoil and bake for 45–60 minutes or until tender. Remove the lid or foil and bake in an oven preheated to 180°C for 10–15 minutes more, until the juices are reduced and syrupy. Transfer to a dish, pour the juices over, then allow to cool to room temperature before serving.

Curly Versus Flat Leaf

The leaves of regular parsley curl up slightly, whereas the leaves of 'flat-leaf' parsley, as the name suggests, do not. Both can be tricky to grow from seed, but once the plants are established some plants should be encouraged to go to seed to ensure new growth.

The two types are interchangeable, but flat-leaf parsley has a slightly less bitter taste (that's not to say it's sweeter), with a fresher, grassy aroma and taste (it's reminiscent of freshly mown grass). If available, use it in Mediterranean dishes. Neither type freezes well.

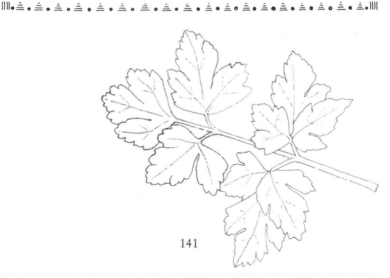

STUFFED GREEN PEPPERS

Serves 4 as a main course, or 8 as a vegetable accompaniment

This dish of peppers is sort of Greekish in origin. It makes delicious eating. Be sure to choose fat, squat peppers that can stand upright in the cooking dish. The peppers are equally good at room temperature or hot, and don't seem to object to a day or two reposing in the refrigerator; cover them, keep them chilled but bring them to room temperature before serving.

1 cup long-grain rice
150 ml olive oil
2 onions, finely chopped
¼ cup currants
¼ cup pinenuts
¾ teaspooon salt
plenty of freshly ground black pepper
2 tablespoons finely chopped mint
2 tablespoons finely chopped parsley
2 medium tomatoes, skinned and diced
400 ml cold water
8 large squat peppers of assorted hues
½ cup fresh breadcrumbs

First prepare the rice. Tip it into a sieve and wash it well under running water until the water runs clear. Tip it into a bowl, cover with cold water and soak for an hour, then drain in a sieve.

Put 100 ml of the olive oil in a frypan and add the onions. Cook over a medium heat until they are soft and transparent. Add the rice, stir to coat in the oil, then cook for 1–2 minutes, stirring. Add the currants, pinenuts, salt, black pepper, mint and parsley. Stir well, then add the tomatoes and water. Bring to the boil, stirring, then turn the heat to low. Cook gently until the rice is half tender (about 10 minutes), stirring often.

Meanwhile prepare the peppers. Carefully cut around the stalks and remove these with the core and seeds. Trim the stalk tops and set aside. Pack the rice mixture into the hollow peppers, filling them three-quarters full, put the tops back on, and place them in an oiled dish. Brush each pepper generously with oil, drizzle the rest of the oil over them and sprinkle over the breadcrumbs. Cook for about 45 minutes in an oven preheated to 180°C.

PUMPKIN STUFFED WITH
WHITE BEANS AND HERBS

Serves 6

This is an excellent choice for a vegetable main course.

*½ cup dried white beans (or use black-eyed beans) or 1 cup tinned
beans, rinsed and drained
1 buttercup pumpkin weighing about 1.5 kg
salt
freshly ground black pepper to taste
small knob of butter
1 teaspoon roughly chopped garlic
2 tomatoes, skinned and diced
¾ cup fresh breadcrumbs
½ cup grated Cheddar cheese
1 teaspoon finely chopped rosemary
1 tablespoon finely chopped parsley (keep a little aside for garnishing)*

Place the beans in a bowl and cover with water. Leave to soak
until plumped (about 4 hours). Drain, place in a saucepan and
cover generously with cold water. Bring to the boil, partially cover
with a lid and cook gently for an hour or until nearly tender.
Drain.

Wash the outside of the pumpkin well, then slice a cap off the
stalk end to make a 'lid'. Do this carefully, using a large sharp
knife, on a clean, dry surface. Scoop out and discard the pumpkin
seeds and pith. Sprinkle ½ teaspoon salt inside the pumpkin, grind
over some black pepper, then drop in the butter and garlic. Replace
the lid of the pumpkin and sit it in a shallow, ovenproof dish.
Bake for about an hour, or until nearly tender, in an oven
preheated to 200°C.

Meanwhile, in a bowl, mix the beans, tomatoes, breadcrumbs,
Cheddar cheese, rosemary, parsley, ¾ teaspoon salt and a little
freshly ground black pepper.

Remove the pumpkin from the oven, lift off the lid, letting
the steam escape away from your face. Fill it with the bean mixture.
Put the lid back on and return it to the oven for a further 30
minutes. Transfer to a serving plate, and slice the pumpkin into
wedges at the table.

NUTTY PARSNIP FRITTERS

Serves 6

Parsnips have a sweet, nutty flavour, which is emphasised here
by the inclusion of fresh creamy walnuts or pinenuts. Try these
fritters for a casual winter or luncheon dish, accompanied by a
spinach salad and a crisp, biting white wine; it makes an interesting
meal.

75 g freshly shelled walnuts, or pinenuts
1 kg parsnips, peeled
salt
75 g butter
2 large eggs
2 level tablespoons plain flour
¼ cup milk
freshly ground black pepper to taste
oil for deep-frying

Put the walnuts or pinenuts into a shallow, ovenproof dish. Toast
in an oven, preheated to 170°C, for about 10 minutes, or until
they are lightly golden. Cool. (If using walnuts, peel off as much
skin as possible.)

Cut the parsnips into wedges, discarding any woody cores. Put
them in a large saucepan, cover with cold water, salt lightly and
bring to the boil. Cook gently, partially covered with a lid, until
tender. Drain.

The fritter mixture is quickly made in a food processor.
(Alternatively, pass the parsnips through a mouli-légumes and beat
in the remaining ingredients with a wooden spoon.) Transfer the
parsnips to the bowl of the processor, fitted with a chopping blade,
and process until puréed, adding the butter in large knobs through
the feed tube while the machine is going. When the mixture is
totally smooth, drop the eggs in through the feed tube, one at
a time, with the machine still going. Add ¾ teaspoon salt and
the flour, and lastly the milk. Blend briefly. Transfer to a bowl,
grind on black pepper to taste and stir the nuts through. If
required, the mixture can be prepared about an hour ahead to
this point.

Heat a large heavy-based saucepan with frying oil (a saucepan
with a 3.5–4 litre capacity will need about 1.5 litres of oil) over

144

a medium-high heat (or use a deep fryer). When the oil is hot, drop in 'blobs' of the mixture using two teaspoons (use one spoon to scrape the mixture off the other). Flip them over once or twice during cooking and cook until they are deep golden brown. Lift them out with a slotted spoon and drain briefly on crumpled brown paper (or kitchen paper). Sprinkle lightly with salt and serve immediately.

Once the frying is finished, put the lid on the saucepan to confine the frying odours.

Improve Your Nuts

Many of the nuts sold in this country are rancid, but they can be improved by toasting; it dries off some of the rancid oils and develops a nuttier flavour. It also improves the keeping qualities.

Spread the nuts (pinenuts, almonds, etc.) on a shallow dish and toast in an oven preheated to 180 °C, for 7–10 minutes, until lightly golden. Cool, then store airtight until required.

Hazelnuts, unless absolutely fresh, are always improved by toasting. Toast the nuts until the skin bursts open and the nuts develop a golden colour, visible through the burst skins. Tip them into an old cloth, bundle them up and rub vigorously; this should release the skins. Hazelnuts attract weevils — be sure to check them before purchase. Do not buy them if they are crumbling or obviously gnawed. Storing fresh, untoasted nuts in the freezer, in a sealed bag, will also prolong their life; thaw 5 minutes before using.

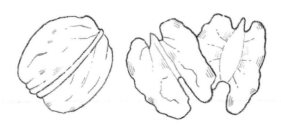

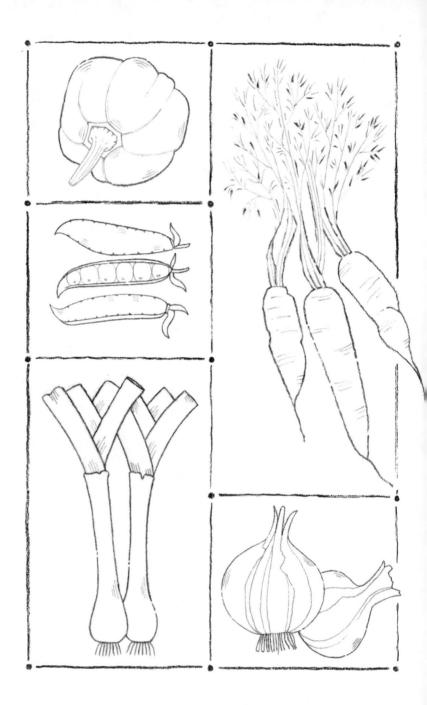

ESCORTING VEGETABLES

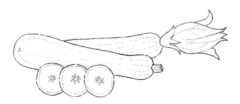

How many times have you heard it said or thought it? 'Vegetables can make or break a meal.'

When their role is to offer contrast of colour, texture or taste, or to harmonise with or enhance flavours in another dish (or dishes), that is exactly what vegetables should do. Even when they are well cooked, boiled carrots, peas and mashed potatoes, although serviceable, are plain boring served two nights on the trot (once a month is once too often for me!) and badly cooked or over-cooked vegetables add little nutritionally, texturally or taste-wise. The escorting vegetables, the dishes you 'peg on' to the main dish, are the perfect vehicle to introduce a little pizazz into your meals.

When you are planning a meal, consider first the main dish (whether it is meat-based or not is immaterial). Is it firm-textured or juicy, self-saucing or not, spicy or fresh-tasting, crisp, crunchy, creamy or soft, steamed, fried, baked or grilled? Then you can decide on the complements. For instance, spicy dishes work well with something neutral like rice and something 'cooling' dressed with yoghurt. A roast chicken with gravy is reasonably rich; don't serve it with a creamy, rich potato dish like Gratin Dauphinoise. Reserve the gratin to be a 'star' all on its own, teamed up with a salad. It's best to balance the chicken's richness with steamed vegetables or offset it with a tangy salad, perhaps a fruity one. Crêpes are softish, so they work well with a textured salad or one with the surprise crunch of croûtons. And so on and so forth.

If you want to construct a meal from vegetable dishes without a pivotal or main dish, choose dishes that will work together in harmony. Offset something crunchy with a soft purée, something fried or rich with a steamed or braised vegetable, soft-textured foods with something crisp.

Don't have all the dishes based on starch (too filling), or all the dishes containing raw foods, or more than one oil-based dressing (sometimes you can get away with this if the dishes are balanced in other areas) or more than one cream-enriched or sauced dish. And don't have everything reeking of garlic or tossed in butter. Remember, contrast is the key.

QUICKIES

GOOD DISHES FOR WINTER

SPIRITED ACCOMPANIMENTS

A BUNCH OF OLD FAVOURITES

A FEW CLASSICS

RINGING THE CHANGES

Quickies

No doubt this will soon become the most well-thumbed section in the book. But do glance around, because there are heaps of other simple, quick dishes throughout this book.

❖

MUSHROOMS IN THE WOK

HOT BUTTERED CUCUMBER

ZUCCHINI WITH
NOISETTE BUTTER

LEEKS WITH WHITE WINE
AND GARLIC

RED PEPPERED CABBAGE

GREEN BEANS WITH NUTMEG

GINGERED BROCCOLI

SAUTÉED ZUCCHINI

BAKED BUTTERCUP WITH
ROSEMARY AND GARLIC

CRISPY CRUMBED EGGPLANT

CHINESE BRAISED GREENS

❖

MUSHROOMS IN THE WOK

Serves 4

This is an excellent way to cook button mushrooms, keeping them juicy, while developing a nutty, toasty flavour. For a quite different result finish off the cooking by splashing in a little red wine vinegar.

few drops of peanut oil
large knob of butter
300 g button mushrooms, wiped (or wash and dry if the mushrooms feel gritty)
freshly ground black pepper to taste
¼ teaspoon salt
1 tablespoon red wine vinegar (optional)

Lightly oil the wok, then set it over a medium-high heat until hot and just starting to haze. Drop in the butter, swirl the wok and tip in the mushrooms. Stir-fry over quite a hot heat until they are lightly browned and cooked to your liking. (The trick is to have the wok hot, but not so hot that the butter and mushrooms burn.) Grind on some black pepper, sprinkle on the salt, toss a few more times, then tip into a heated serving dish. Serve immediately.

If you wish to finish off with red wine vinegar, season as described, then increase the heat to high. Just when it looks as if the mushrooms will burn, throw in the vinegar, which should steam and practically evaporate. Stir once or twice, then serve as above.

HOT BUTTERED CUCUMBER

Serves 4–6

Never heard of hot cucumber? You better believe it! This is *good*. It stays green and crisp and juicy and teams perfectly with delicate dishes, particularly fish like salmon. It is also good as an alternative to zucchini.

1 slim telegraph cucumber, washed
large knob of butter
few pinches of salt
plenty of freshly ground black pepper
1–2 tablespoons snipped chives (optional)

Leave the skin on the cucumber. Trim the ends and cut it into four long strips, then into chunks.

Heat a large frypan over a low-medium heat and drop in the butter. Add the cucumber while the butter is sizzling and stir-fry for a few minutes. Sprinkle on the salt and grind over black pepper. Continue cooking, stirring often, until the cucumber is hot (be careful not to let it fry). Sprinkle over the chives, toss and serve.

ZUCCHINI WITH NOISETTE BUTTER

Serves 4

This is a tasty way with zucchini.

600 g zucchini
knob of butter
1 tablespoon olive oil
½ teaspoon salt
freshly ground black pepper to taste
1 teaspoon freshly chopped marjoram (or ½ teaspoon dried marjoram)

Slice the zucchini into chunks on the diagonal. Lay the slices on kitchen paper and cover with another piece of kitchen paper. Leave until dry (this can be done 1–2 hours before cooking them).

Heat the butter and olive oil in a large frypan over a medium heat. Add the zucchini and allow them to brown on all sides (turn with tongs). Sprinkle on the salt, grind over a little black pepper and scatter the marjoram over. Tilt the pan and transfer the zucchini to a heated serving dish with a slotted spoon. Serve immediately.

Borage Brings the Bees

It's true . . . well, the borage flowers bring the bees. The borage plant blossoms so willingly and so generously that it's a good idea to put at least one in the vegetable garden, particularly near zucchini, to bring the bees.

... And the Leaves

Use the leaves in tortellini or ravioli. Wash well, cook, drain and chop, and mix them with ricotta cheese, nutmeg, black pepper, salt, cooked and softened onion and garlic and Parmesan cheese.

... And the Flowers

Pretty blue and pink borage flowers look quite delightful floating on top of soups and punches or on top of salads. They have a mild, cucumber taste. Pick the flowers, pull off the hairy green bit, then soak them briefly in water. Drain on kitchen paper and use.

Gremolada

Traditionally served on top of the Italian dish, Ossobuco, Gremolada makes an admirable topping for tomato-based dishes, butter or green beans, cauliflower, new potatoes, broccoli, carrots, etc ... the scope is endless.

2 tablespoons finely grated lemon rind
2 tablespoons finely chopped parsley (you could change this to
  lemon thyme for a change, or a herb of your choice)
1 large clove garlic, finely chopped

Mix the ingredients together in a small bowl. Keep covered until required.

The Gremolada is best used within 2–3 hours of making. Sprinkle it over hot vegetables (the warmth draws out the flavours) and serve hot or at room temperature.

LEEKS WITH WHITE WINE AND GARLIC

Serves 6

This is a flavoursome treatment for leeks. They are blanched ahead of time, then, when required, the cooking is finished off in a fusion of wine, garlic and olive oil.

6 medium leeks, trimmed and washed well
salt
3 tablespoons extra virgin olive oil
3 tablespoons dry white wine
1 large clove garlic, crushed
1 bay leaf
freshly ground black pepper to taste

Slice the leeks on the diagonal, into bands about 1.5 cm wide. Bring a large saucepan of water to the boil, salt lightly, then plunge in the leeks. Bring to the boil, uncovered, then cook gently, stirring from time to time, for 3 minutes. Drain them in a colander, refresh with plenty of cold water, shake well, then leave to drain again. The leeks can be prepared to this point 1–2 hours before required; keep them at room temperature.

When you are ready to finish the leeks, put the extra virgin olive oil, white wine, garlic, bay leaf, black pepper and ¼ teaspoon salt into a large frypan. Bring to the boil, turn the heat to medium, shake the pan, then tip in the leeks. Cook them gently for a few minutes, tossing often, until tender. Turn into a heated dish and serve.

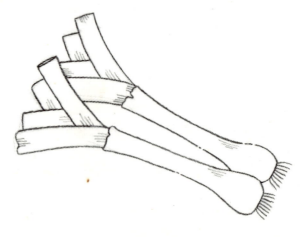

RED PEPPERED CABBAGE

Serves 6

This dish is a revelation to many people, as it is crisp and crunchy, juicy and sweet!

30 g butter
1 small onion, finely chopped
1 red pepper, cored and finely sliced
1 small cabbage
½ teaspoon salt
freshly ground black pepper to taste
1 teaspoon finely chopped marjoram or oregano (or ½ teaspoon dried marjoram or oregano)

Melt the butter in a large saucepan over a gentle heat and add the onion and red pepper. Cover with a lid and cook gently for about 10 minutes, or until tender.

Meanwhile, prepare the cabbage by splitting it in half and cutting out the core. Shred finely and add to the pan. Toss well and add salt, black pepper and the chosen herb. Continue cooking, tossing constantly, until the cabbage just starts to wilt (about 4 minutes). Immediately tip it into a heated dish and serve.

Refreshing

This means 'to rinse with water'. Vegetables are refreshed with a cup or two of cold water after blanching or cooking, to halt the cooking process, to remove strong flavours or rinse off scum, and to help keep the colour of the vegetables. The vegetables may be served immediately, or reheated gently by tossing in a pan with a knob of butter and a grinding of black pepper (or a little garlic or herb butter, or in a little stock).

Starchy foods, like pasta and rice, are refreshed to rinse off any clinging starch, but warm water should be used as cold water makes the starch tacky.

GREEN BEANS WITH NUTMEG

Serves 4

A few grates of fresh nutmeg works wonders with green beans. Try these with garlicky roasted beef.

500 g green beans, topped, tailed and halved
salt
large knob of butter
fresh nutmeg for grating
freshly ground black pepper to taste

Plunge the beans into a saucepan of boiling, salted water and cook uncovered for 2–7 minutes, or until crisp-tender. Drain and refresh with cold water, then leave to drain.

Melt the butter in a large saucepan over a low-medium heat, add the beans, then grate over a little nutmeg to taste. Grind over black pepper and sprinkle on a little salt. Toss frequently until the beans are piping hot, taking care not to let them fry.

Tip into a heated dish, using a scraper to remove all the spicy butter from the pan, and serve immediately.

Hot Beans

Green beans don't keep their heat for long after cooking (dense vegetables do, watery ones don't) so serve them immediately after draining.

Also, remember the higher the water content of a vegetable (for example beans and mushrooms) the more salt required to draw out the flavours.

Cooking Green Vegetables

Vegetables that grow above the ground have been exposed to light and the changes in the weather and don't need such cosseted cooking.

They are plunged into boiling, salted water, which shortens the cooking time, ensuring they can be cooked until tender, yet maintain structure and flavour without becoming water-logged.

The vegetables are cooked with the lid off, at a gentle boil (a fierce boil could cause vegetables with a delicate structure to disintegrate). Cooking greens, such as beans and broccoli, with the lid on can cause the vegetables to discolour. Vegetable acids, which would normally be driven off in the steam, sit on the inside of the lid, dripping back into the vegetables, causing discolouration and often an unpleasant odour or taste.

To halt the cooking process (particularly useful if the vegetables are not to be served hot but are to be used in a salad), splash a cup or two of cold water over them (this is called 'refreshing'). It also helps maintain a good green colour.

If you want to 'refresh' the vegetables to keep the fresh colour, but you want to serve them hot, return them to the dry saucepan after refreshing, with a knob of butter and a grind of black pepper and heat gently until hot (be careful not to fry them).

Steaming Vegetables

Less nutrients are lost when vegetables are cooked above, rather than in, boiling water. Steaming also preserves more of the flavour and structure of the vegetables. This is particularly noticeable with new potatoes, when they are to be used in a salad.

However, green vegetables, such as beans and broccoli, are better boiled, because steaming causes them to lose their bright, appealing colour.

GINGERED BROCCOLI

Serves 6

This is a good way with broccoli — fast, crisp and fresh — and particularly useful when you want an accompanying vegetable that is not rich.

700–800 g broccoli, trimmed into florets
salt
1 tablespoon oil
knob of fresh ginger (about 2 tablespoons), peeled and finely chopped
¼ cup water
1 tablespoon soy sauce
1 tablespoon dry sherry
1 teaspoon raw sugar

Place the broccoli in a metal colander or steaming basket and set it over a small saucepan of boiling water. Salt lightly, cover with a lid and steam for 4–5 minutes, or until tender. Lift out the colander or steaming basket and refresh the broccoli with plenty of cold water. Leave it to drain (this can be done in advance).

About 5 minutes before serving time, heat a large frypan and add the oil. When it is hot add the ginger and stir-fry for about 2 minutes, then add the broccoli. Cook for 1 minute, tossing gently, then add the previously mixed water, soy sauce, sherry and raw sugar. Cook, stirring often, for 1–2 minutes, until the broccoli is heated through. Transfer to a heated serving dish and serve immediately.

Lovely Zucchini Flowers

Ever wondered what to do with those lovely zucchini blossoms which don't turn into vegetables but instead grow on a long stalk? (These are the ones the bees didn't call on.)

Apart from the Italian treatment of dunking them in batter and

SAUTÉED ZUCCHINI

Serves 6

This is a simple, light summer dish which is good to make when zucchini are plentiful and cheap.

2 tablespoons olive oil
6 zucchini, washed, dried and sliced thickly on the diagonal
3 spring onions, trimmed and cut into short lengths
2 large cloves garlic, crushed
2 large tomatoes, skinned and diced
¼ teaspoon salt
freshly ground black pepper to taste

Heat the olive oil in a large frypan over a medium heat and when hot add the zucchini. Toss immediately in the oil, then loosely drape a piece of kitchen paper on the surface to absorb splatters (or use a splatter screen). Fry for about 5 minutes, until the zucchini are partially browned, stirring often and replacing the paper if necessary. Transfer them with a slotted spoon to a bowl.

Turn the heat down a little and add the spring onions and garlic. Fry gently for 1–2 minutes until the spring onions wilt — do not overcook, or the spring onions will lose their green colour. Add the tomatoes, salt and black pepper and continue cooking gently for about 10 minutes. Return the zucchini to the pan, heat them through, then transfer to a serving bowl. This is good hot or at room temperature.

shallow-frying them in oil (they can be stuffed first with anchovies or herby mixtures), they make an exquisite frittata. Pick the flowers and remove the pistils if preferred. Shake, rinse and soak the flowers in water briefly, then shake, dry and chop. Add them to the beaten egg and cheese mixture and pour this onto cooked onions and zucchini.

BAKED BUTTERCUP WITH ROSEMARY AND GARLIC

Serves 6

Here's something really tasty, taking no more than 5 minutes to prepare.

1 medium buttercup pumpkin, scrubbed
knob of soft butter
1 teaspoon finely chopped fresh rosemary
2–3 cloves garlic, crushed
1 teaspoon salt
plenty of freshly ground black pepper

With a large sharp knife carefully slice a cap off the pumpkin. Scoop out the seeds and any loose fibre and discard these. Spread the butter over the insides of the pumpkin, then scatter the rosemary over. Drop in the garlic, then season the insides of the pumpkin with salt and black pepper. Replace the cap and sit the pumpkin in a shallow ovenproof dish.

Add 1 cup water to the dish and bake the pumpkin in an oven preheated to 200 °C for about an hour or until tender. If the water dries up, add a little more (it creates steam, helping to keep the pumpkin moist during cooking).

Carefully transfer the pumpkin to a heated serving dish, then serve, sliced into wedges.

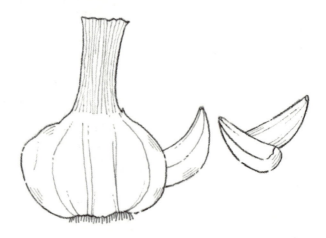

CRISPY CRUMBED EGGPLANT

Serves 2–3

Coating slices of eggplant in breadcrumbs before frying them creates a delicious result; crispy on the outside and creamy in the centre. Serve this as a simple supper dish, with a salad and bread and maybe a spoonful or two of pickle or chutney on the side. Otherwise include it in Mediterranean or Middle Eastern menus. The only problem you might encounter in making it is this: any crumbs that fall off the first batch of eggplant slices can start to burn before the second batch of slices is cooked. I suggest using the minimum amount of oil and wiping out the pan between batches.

1 large eggplant (or 2 medium ones)
salt
1 egg
½ cup fine dry breadcrumbs
¼–½ cup oil

Slice the eggplant into rounds 0.50–0.75 cm thick. Sprinkle with salt and leave them to drain in a colander for 40 minutes. Pat dry with kitchen paper. Beat the egg with ¼ teaspoon salt and coat the slices with it. Let the excess egg drip off, then cover with breadcrumbs and pat on. As the slices are prepared lay them on a dry surface.

Heat ¼ cup oil in a large frypan over a low-medium heat and, when it is hot, lower in several slices of eggplant. Cook until they are a deep golden colour, turn carefully and cook the second side. Lift out with a slotted spatula and drain briefly on crumpled kitchen paper. Sprinkle lightly with salt. Repeat with the remaining slices, and serve hot.

CHINESE BRAISED GREENS

Serves 6

This is quick-cooking and crunchy and goes well not only with Chinese food but also with other spiced foods, particularly rice.

2 Chinese cabbages (bok choy), weighing about 750 g in total
2 tablespoons peanut oil
2 cloves garlic, crushed
1 tablespoon grated fresh ginger
½ cup light stock or water
1 tablespoon oyster sauce (optional)
1 teaspoon soy sauce
1 teaspoon cornflour mixed with 1 tablespoon water
1 teaspoon sesame oil

Prepare the cabbages by trimming off the roots and shaving off most of the greenery (it is usually tough and bitter). Wash well, then chop the white ribs into large chunks.

Set the wok over a medium-high heat and add the peanut oil. Swirl to coat the wok with the oil and when hottish put in the garlic and ginger. Stir-fry briefly until it is fragrant and lightly browned. Add the cabbage and stir-fry for 2–3 minutes.

Add the stock or water, the oyster sauce if used, and the soy sauce. Cover and simmer gently for about 5 minutes or until the green parts have softened slightly, but the white ribs are still crisp-tender. Pour in the cornflour and water mixture and stir for about 1 minute until the juices have thickened. Sprinkle over the sesame oil, toss lightly, then transfer to a heated serving dish. Serve immediately.

Good Dishes for Winter

When you think about it, it's very silly hankering after out-of-season vegetables. Invariably they are imported and expensive, the quality is dubious, and, no doubt, they have been sprayed with chemicals on arrival in the country.

So in the dark depths of winter don't lust after asparagus or peas, peppers and zucchini; instead be experimental with the season's offerings, enjoying them at their best and cheapest.

❖

BRUSSELS SPROUTS WITH CREAM
'LIVELY' LEEKS
CRISPY TURNIPS
GINGERED CARROTS
AND TURNIPS
CRISPY CRUMBED SPROUTS
STUFFED GEM SQUASH
SWEET AND SOUR LEEKS
WITH RAISINS
BEETROOT WITH CAPERS
JULIENNE OF PARSNIPS
BRUSSELS SPROUTS
WITH CROÛTONS
BRAISED LEEKS WITH
PARMESAN CHEESE

❖

BRUSSELS SPROUTS WITH CREAM

Serves 4

The thought of badly cooked Brussels sprouts sends a shiver up my spine. But cooked until just fork-tender and swathed in an aromatic, cream coating they are elevated to dinner-party status.

500 g young Brussels sprouts
salt
150 ml cream
freshly ground black pepper to taste
freshly grated nutmeg to taste

Trim the Brussels sprouts and remove any damaged leaves. Cut a shallow cross on the base of each. Wash well. Plunge them into a saucepan of boiling, lightly salted water and cook uncovered for 6–10 minutes, or until crunch-tender (or cook to your liking). Drain and refresh with plenty of cold water, shake well and leave them until thoroughly drained.

Put the cream in a saucepan and reduce it by half over a medium heat. Grind in black pepper and grate in some nutmeg. Add the Brussels sprouts, shake well and simmer gently for a few minutes until they are heated through. Turn into a heated vegetable dish and serve immediately.

Take a Leaf from This Book

Instead of preparing and serving Brussels sprouts in the conventional way, why not break them apart and cook and present them as single leaves? (particularly good with mature sprouts).

Trim the sprouts, then carefully peel away the leaves. Discard the cores. Rinse, then cook for 3–4 minutes in salted boiling water. Drain and refresh. Heat a little butter in a wok or frypan over a low heat. Stir-fry until the leaves are hot and crisp-tender. Season with salt and black pepper and one of the following: a squeeze of orange or lemon juice, a little grated orange or lemon peel, a good grating of nutmeg, or a little finely chopped thyme or lemon thyme.

'LIVELY' LEEKS

Serves 6

When leeks are plentiful and inexpensive, inject a bit of zing into your meal with 'lively' leeks.

6 medium leeks
¼ cup olive oil
3 large cloves garlic, crushed
1 tablespoon soft brown sugar
freshly ground black pepper to taste
¼ teaspoon salt
1 tablespoon tomato purée dissolved in 1 tablespoon hot water
2 tablespoons lemon juice

Use a large knife to cut off the tips of the leeks, then shave off any tough parts, or remove any coarse, outer leaves. Trim off the roots, and cut each leek in two lengthwise. Rinse thoroughly under running cold water, shake them dry, then cut into short lengths.

Heat the olive oil in a large saucepan over a low-medium heat and add the garlic. Cook gently, stirring, until it is a pale gold colour, then add the brown sugar. Cook for a few minutes until syrupy, then add the leeks. Stir well and grind over the black pepper and add the salt. Mix the diluted tomato purée with the lemon juice and pour this over the leeks. Stir well, then cover with a lid and cook gently, stirring occasionally, for about 15 minutes, or until tender. Serve hot.

Cutting a Cross

Some of the old methods are the best. Cutting a cross on the base of Brussels sprouts, for instance, does serve a purpose. It allows the boiling water to enter the base of the sprouts, the most dense part, ensuring it is cooked by the time the rest of the leaves are.

This is particularly helpful with more mature sprouts, which can become soggy on the outside before the centre is tender. Young, even-sized sprouts do not usually require cutting.

CRISPY TURNIPS

Serves 6

I once read, and am inclined to agree with, the following statement:
'Turnips are at their best when tiny, or at least no bigger than
an egg. When they're double the size of an egg they're only fit
for the pigs.'

800 g small, white turnips, peeled (if egg-size, cut into quarters)
salt
1 tablespoon oil
60 g butter
1 medium onion, finely chopped
4 tablespoons fresh breadcrumbs
freshly ground black pepper to taste
1 tablespoon finely chopped parsley

Put the turnips in a saucepan, cover with cold water, salt lightly
and bring to the boil. Boil for 1 minute, then drain. Dry off on
kitchen paper.

Put the oil and two-thirds of the butter in a frypan and set
over a medium heat. When sizzling, add the onion and cook fairly
quickly, stirring often, for about 10 minutes, or until lightly
browned (take care not to let it burn). Add the breadcrumbs and
the remaining butter, season with ¼ teaspoon salt and some black
pepper. Cook, tossing often, until crisp, then add the turnips to
the pan and cook for 5 minutes, or until heated through. Blend
in the parsley, then turn into a heated serving dish (include all
the crispy bits). Serve immediately.

GINGERED CARROTS AND TURNIPS

Serves 4–6

Fresh ginger makes its presence known in this simple dish of carrots and turnips. Try it teamed with lamb, or to offset rich meat or vegetable dishes. Alternatively, substitute coriander for the mint or parsley and serve it with Asian-style dishes.

3 young turnips, peeled and cut into julienne
salt
3 carrots, peeled and cut into julienne
knob of butter
1 teaspoon very finely chopped, then 'mashed' (mash with the
*   blade of a knife) fresh ginger*
1 clove garlic, crushed
freshly ground black pepper to taste
1 level teaspoon brown sugar
1 tablespoon finely chopped parsley or mint

Put the turnips in a saucepan, cover with cold water, salt lightly and bring to the boil. Drain and refresh with cold water. Repeat the process with the carrots, but cook for 1–2 minutes after bringing them to the boil. Drain and refresh.

Just before the vegetables are required, heat a large frypan over a medium heat and drop in the butter. When it sizzles, add the ginger and garlic and cook for 1–2 minutes, stirring often. Add the turnips and carrots, toss well and grind over black pepper. Add ½ teaspoon salt and the brown sugar, and continue cooking until the vegetables are heated through, taking care not to let them catch or fry. Stir through the parsley or mint, turn into a heated dish and serve immediately.

CRISPY CRUMBED SPROUTS

Serves 4

Remember this recipe in mid-winter when you are bored with using the season's vegetables in the same ways. This is colourful, crispy and scrumptious. It would make an ideal accompaniment to a good potato purée and either a sauced vegetable or meat dish.

3 tablespoons olive oil
1 onion, roughly sliced
1 clove garlic, crushed
400 g tin Italian tomatoes, drained
1 teaspoon fresh marjoram or ½ teaspoon crumbled dried
 marjoram
¼ teaspoon salt
freshly ground black pepper to taste
500 g Brussels sprouts

Toasted crumbs
large knob of butter
¾ cup fresh breadcrumbs

Put the olive oil, onion and garlic in a saucepan, set over a medium heat and cook gently, stirring often, until a light golden colour. Add the tomatoes and break them up with a wooden spoon. Cook uncovered, stirring occasionally, for 15 minutes, then add the marjoram, salt and black pepper. The sauce can be prepared several hours in advance if required; cool, cover and refrigerate.

Trim the Brussels sprouts and remove any damaged leaves. Cut a shallow cross on the base of each. Wash well. Plunge them into a saucepan of boiling, lightly salted water and cook uncovered for 6–10 minutes, or until crunch-tender (or done to your liking). Drain and refresh with plenty of cold water, shake well and leave to drain. The sprouts can be cooked 1–2 hours before required; leave them at room temperature.

Just prior to serving, cut the Brussels sprouts into quarters and reheat the sauce. Tip the sprouts into the sauce, stir well and heat through gently. (Take care to heat the mixture only or the sprouts will lose their crunch.)

Transfer to a heated serving dish and sprinkle over the toasted crumbs. Serve immediately.

Toasted crumbs

Heat a small frypan over a medium heat and drop in the butter. Add the crumbs while it is foaming and cook, tossing often, until they are a light golden brown (be careful not to burn them). Transfer to a plate. Use within 2 hours.

STUFFED GEM SQUASH

Serves 4

Gem squash are small, orange-coloured and orange-shaped squash, with a delicate sweet flavour. They can be split in half and roasted, cooked and used as containers for pumpkin or vegetable soups, or stuffed with herby, spicy or cheesy crumb mixtures.

2 gem squash, split in half and deseeded
salt
freshly ground black pepper to taste
¼ cup fresh breadcrumbs
¼ cup grated Cheddar cheese
1 large slice ham, finely diced
2 tablespoons finely grated Parmesan cheese
knob of butter

Sit the squash in a small ovenproof dish, sprinkle over a little salt and grind over a little black pepper. Mix the breadcrumbs, Cheddar cheese and ham together in a small bowl.

Spoon this into the squash, sprinkle over the Parmesan cheese and dot the tops with butter. Bake in an oven preheated to 180 °C for about 45 minutes, or until the squash are tender.

SWEET AND SOUR LEEKS WITH RAISINS

Serves 4

Here is yet another variation on the sweet and sour theme, this time using raisins to sweeten.

3 medium leeks
2 tablespoons oil
1 tablespoon lemon juice
2 tablespoons tomato purée
¼ cup water
½ teaspoon salt
freshly ground black pepper to taste
2 tablespoons raisins

Use a large knife to cut off the tips of the leaves of the leeks, then shave off any tough parts, or remove any coarse outer leaves. Trim off the roots, cut each leek in two lengthwise, then rinse thoroughly under running water. Shake dry, then slice them into short lengths.

Put the leeks in a saucepan with the oil, lemon juice, tomato purée, water, salt and black pepper. Cover with a lid and quickly bring to the boil. Immediately turn the heat to low and simmer for 5 minutes. Add the raisins. Continue cooking for about 10 minutes more, stirring occasionally, or until tender. Serve hottish or at room temperature.

BEETROOT WITH CAPERS

Serves 4–6

Hot beetroot makes a superb vegetable, tossed in butter and herbs, or a tangy dressing. This recipe is one of my 'cheats', using tinned beetroot.

850 g tin whole baby beetroot, drained (or 12–15 fresh baby
* beetroots, prepared and cooked as in Baby Beetroot Salad,*
* page 252)*
large knob of butter
½ teaspoon salt
freshly ground black pepper to taste
½ teaspoon castor sugar
grated rind of 1 lemon
1 rounded tablespoon capers, drained
juice of ½ lemon
1 tablespoon snipped chives
1 tablespoon chopped parsley

First prepare the beetroot.
   Melt the butter in a large saucepan over a medium heat. When it is foaming add the beetroot, salt, black pepper, castor sugar and lemon rind. Shake the pan frequently until the beetroot are hot. Add the capers, lemon juice, chives and parsley and cook for 1 minute. Tip into a heated dish and serve immediately.

JULIENNE OF PARSNIPS

Serves 4–6

I consider it a great shame that many of the cheaper, more readily available, vegetables are often ignored. Take parsnips, for example. They make an excellent soup, are interesting when spiced or curried, and, even more simply, they are delicious when cooked with seasonings and a jot or two of butter. Try the following recipe with a roast of beef in winter and serve a big, peppery Shiraz red wine. It's a winning combination.

500 g parsnips, peeled
salt
good knob of butter
freshly ground black pepper to taste
1 tablespoon snipped chives, or finely chopped parsley

Cut the parsnips into even, thin matchstick shapes (julienne), discarding any woody cores. Place in a saucepan, cover with cold water, salt lightly and bring to the boil. Simmer for 2 minutes, drain and rinse with warm water and drain again. Place in a saucepan with butter, plenty of black pepper and a few pinches of salt. Cover and cook over a very gentle heat until done to your liking (5–10 minutes). Stir through the chives or parsley and serve at once.

Julienne

This means to cut ingredients, usually vegetables, but sometimes fruit or meats, into thin sticks, rather like matchsticks. Use a sharp knife, trim any rough edges, then cut into thin blocks and then into strips.

BRUSSELS SPROUTS WITH CROÛTONS

Serves 6

Here's another interesting way with an often badly cooked vegetable.

800–900 g even-sized Brussels sprouts
3 thick slices grainy bread, crusts removed
¼ cup frying oil
salt
large knob of butter
3 spring onions, finely sliced
1 clove garlic, crushed
freshly ground black pepper to taste
1 teaspoon lemon juice

Trim the Brussels sprouts and remove any damaged leaves. Cut a shallow cross on the base of each. Wash well.

Cut the bread into small cubes and heat the oil in a large frypan. When the oil is hot, tip in the bread cubes, toss with a slotted spoon and fry, turning once or twice, until a pale gold colour. Remove with a slotted spoon and drain on crumpled kitchen paper. Sprinkle a little salt over them. When cool, store in an airtight container until serving time (not only to keep them crisp but to stop you nibbling at them!).

Bring a large saucepan of water to the boil, salt well, then plunge in the sprouts. Cook, uncovered, for 6–10 minutes (depends on their size and your preference). Drain and refresh with plenty of cold water, then drain again. Cut into halves or quarters.

Heat the butter in a large frypan, add the spring onions and garlic and cook gently for a few minutes until wilted and a pale gold colour. Set aside until serving time.

Five minutes before serving time, reheat the frypan with the spring onions and garlic and add the sprouts. Sprinkle lightly with salt and grind over plenty of black pepper. Toss over the heat until heated through, then pour the lemon juice over them. Transfer to a heated dish, stir through the croûtons and serve immediately.

BRAISED LEEKS WITH PARMESAN CHEESE

....

Serves 4

These tender leeks, topped with Parmesan cheese, make a delicious accompaniment to simple pan-fried, or crumbed and shallow-fried meats. Alternatively, forget the meat and serve them with a dish of sautéed mushrooms, or Mushrooms with Marsala (page 216) and a creamy potato or parsnip purée. Finish the meal with a spinach salad.

4 leeks
2 large knobs of butter
⅓ cup water
¼ teaspoon salt
plenty of freshly ground black pepper
½ cup freshly grated Parmesan cheese

Use a large knife to trim the tips of the leaves off the leeks. Remove any coarse or tough leaves, then trim the roots. Cut each leek in two lengthwise, then rinse them thoroughly under running water.

Trim the leeks to fit a large frypan. Sit them in the pan, in one layer. Dot with butter, pour on the water, sprinkle with salt and grind over a little black pepper. Cover and cook gently for about 20 minutes, turning once or twice, or until the leeks are tender. Remove the lid and allow the liquid to evaporate and the leeks to brown a little. Transfer them to a heated serving plate, scatter the Parmesan cheese over and serve immediately.

❖

Spirited Accompaniments

There's nothing like a bit of chilli-heat to liven up a dish, or a few freshly ground spices to add interest to a meal. Some of these dishes are quite hottish, some are just pleasantly spiced but a few others kick like a mule (you'll have fun discovering which do what!).

❖

CHICK-PEAS 'N CHILLI

SPICY FRIED POTATOES

CURRIED CAULIFLOWER
AND POTATO

SPICED PUMPKIN PURÉE

EGGPLANT WITH SPICES
AND CORIANDER

NOT ROGER'S DHAL

SWEET AND SOUR VEGETABLES

JEAN'S BEANS

❖

CHICK-PEAS 'N CHILLI

Serves 6

If you like spicy, rather than searingly hot food, this dish is just what the doctor ordered. Serve it with Asian-style dishes, or with a yoghurt-based vegetable dish and pita pockets.

225 g dried chick-peas
½ teaspoon turmeric
1 fresh red chillli, split in two
10 cardamom pods
1 teaspoon cumin seeds
2 teaspoons coriander seeds
1 teaspoon chilli powder
1 teaspoon salt
3 tablespoons oil
1 medium onion, finely chopped
3 cloves garlic, crushed
1 tablespoon coarsely grated fresh ginger
1 small piece cinnamon stick
2 large tomatoes, skinned and diced
2 tablespoons chopped coriander leaves

Wash the chick-peas, place them in a bowl, cover generously with cold water and leave to soak for several hours or overnight. Drain, rinse, then put them in a saucepan with the turmeric and split chilli. Cover generously with cold water, bring to the boil, then simmer gently for about an hour, or until tender. Drain, reserving 1 cup of the cooking liquid.

Meanwhile, prepare the spice mixture. Split open the cardamom pods and extract the seeds. Grind them with the cumin and coriander seeds, then stir in the chilli powder and salt.

Heat the oil in a large frypan over a medium heat and add the onion, garlic and ginger. Sauté gently until golden, stirring often, then tip in the spice mixture. Add the cinnamon stick and stir-fry for 2 minutes. Blend through the diced tomatoes, then cook gently until pulpy.

Add the drained chick-peas and the cup of reserved cooking liquid. Partially cover the pan and cook gently until the liquid has thickened. Blend in the coriander and serve hot or at room temperature.

SPICY FRIED POTATOES

Serves 4

Another yummy way with potatoes!

60 g butter
1 kg potatoes, peeled, cut into large cubes and dried in a cloth
4 cloves garlic, crushed
1 teaspoon chilli powder
1 teaspoon ground cumin
1 teaspoon turmeric
1 teaspoon salt
plenty of freshly ground black pepper
1 large red pepper, cored, deseeded and diced
2 tomatoes, skinned, cored and diced
¾ cup water
¼ cup unsweetened yoghurt
1 tablespoon finely chopped mint

Heat a large frypan over a medium heat and drop in the butter
(an electric frypan works well). Allow it to melt, then add the
potatoes. Toss these in the butter and fry until crisp and golden
(takes about 40 minutes), turning often.

Add the garlic, spices and salt, black pepper and red pepper
and cook for 5 minutes, stirring. Blend in the tomatoes, cook
for 1 minute, then pour in the water. Cover with a lid and cook
for 12–15 minutes, or until the potatoes are tender.

Meanwhile, mix the yoghurt and mint together. Transfer the
potatoes to a serving dish and drizzle over the minty yoghurt.
These are good served hot or at room temperature.

CURRIED CAULIFLOWER AND POTATO

Serves 8

This is one of my favourite spicy dishes; unlike most other cauliflower dishes, it fills the kitchen with a tantalising fragrance. It's not expensive to make either, and it feeds a good number. And it's one of those dishes which is as good cold as it is hot. Serve with other Indian dishes (it's particularly good with yoghurt-based dishes and juicy sambals).

50 g butter
500 g potatoes, peeled and cubed
½ cup vegetable oil
1 teaspoon black mustard seeds
1 onion, finely chopped
1 teaspoon lemon juice
1 teaspoon ground coriander seeds
1 teaspoon ground cumin
¾ teaspoon ground turmeric
½ teaspoon cayenne
½ teaspoon paprika
2 tomatoes, peeled and diced
2 tablespoons chopped fresh coriander (substitute mint if not available)
1 tablespoon grated fresh ginger
1 teaspoon salt
1 large cauliflower, washed and broken into florets

Melt the butter in a large frypan (I find a large electric frypan easiest to use). Add the potatoes and fry until they are tender and lightly browned. Transfer the potatoes to a plate. Wipe out the pan and add the vegetable oil. When hot, but before it starts smoking, add the mustard seeds. Cover with the lid and shake the pan constantly until they pop.

Slip in the onion and brown it lightly. Reduce the heat and add the lemon juice, ground coriander, cumin, turmeric, cayenne and paprika. Blend well, then add the tomatoes, fresh coriander, ginger and salt. If the mixture seems a little dry, add a tablespoon or so of water.

Add the cauliflower and potatoes and turn them to coat in the spices. Reduce heat to low and cover tightly. Cook for 15 minutes, or until the cauliflower is well impregnated with the spice mixture and crunch-tender, stirring occasionally. Transfer to a serving dish and serve hot or warmish.

SPICED PUMPKIN PURÉE

Serves 4–6

The freshness of lemon and the hint of spice magically transform the pumpkin into an extremely moreish dish.

1 kg butternut or grey pumpkin, peeled, deseeded and cut into large
    chunks
salt
freshly ground black pepper to taste
small knob of butter
grated rind of 1 lemon
few grates of fresh nutmeg

Position the pieces of pumpkin in a metal colander, or steaming basket, over a saucepan of boiling water. Sprinkle over a little salt. Cover with a lid or double thickness of tinfoil and steam for about 15 minutes, or until tender. Remove the colander or steaming basket from the saucepan and allow the pumpkin to cool.

Dry the pumpkin off on kitchen paper, then either mash it with a vegetable masher or pass it through a sieve. Alternatively, work very briefly in a food processor (over-processing will make the purée watery).

Turn the pumpkin purée into a saucepan and beat in salt and black pepper to taste, the butter, lemon rind and a few grates of nutmeg. Cover and set aside until required. (If you are making the purée more than 3 hours in advance it is best to refrigerate it once cool.)

At serving time, reheat the purée carefully over a low heat, stirring often. Spoon it into a heated dish and serve hot.

EGGPLANT WITH SPICES AND CORIANDER

Serves 6

This dish always receives rave reviews by lovers of spicy foods. The softish, creamy, chilli-hot mixture is ideal with rice and other Indian dishes.

1 large eggplant
salt
3 tablespoons oil
1 teaspoon black mustard seeds
1 medium onion, finely chopped
1 hot red chilli, split in two, deseeded and finely chopped
1 teaspoon garam masala
½ teaspoon chilli powder
1 large tomato, skinned and finely chopped
¼ cup water
¾ cup plain unsweetened yoghurt
2 tablespoons finely chopped fresh coriander

Cut the eggplant into large cubes, put it in a colander and sprinkle generously with salt. Leave it to drain for 40 minutes. When ready to cook, pat the eggplant cubes dry with kitchen paper.

Heat the oil in a large saucepan, over a medium heat, and add the mustard seeds. Cover with a lid and shake the pan until they pop. Lift off the lid and quickly drop in the onion and chilli. Put the lid back on and cook gently until soft. Add the garam masala and chilli powder and fry for 1–2 minutes, stirring, then drop in the eggplant cubes. Toss gently until the eggplant cubes are well coated in the spice mixture. Fry for a few minutes, then stir in the tomato, 1 teaspoon of salt and the water.

Cover with a lid and cook gently, for about 25–30 minutes, until the eggplant is very soft. Mash to a purée, then leave to cool. Before serving, stir in the yoghurt and coriander leaves. Serve hottish, warm or chilled.

NOT ROGER'S DHAL

Serves 6–8

Roger, a good friend of mine, makes superb dhal. Whenever I serve this dhal to our close friends they ask hopefully, 'Is this Roger's dhal?' I always reply, 'No, it's not Roger's dhal,' and the name seems to have stuck. (They all agree, though, that this dhal is not bad!)

250 g red lentils
1½ teaspoons coriander seeds
1½ teaspoons cumin seeds
3 tablespoons oil or ghee
2 onions, sliced
2 tablespoons chopped garlic
1 teaspoon chilli powder
½ teaspoon ground ginger
½ teaspoon ground turmeric
¼ teaspoon salt
1 tablespoon lemon juice

Wash the lentils thoroughly in a sieve under running cold water until the water runs clear. Leave to soak in a bowl of cold water for 30 minutes. Drain.

Grind the coriander and cumin seeds and set aside. Heat the oil or ghee in a large saucepan, over a low-medium heat. Add the onions and fry until golden. Add the garlic, chilli powder, ginger and turmeric. Fry for 1 minute more, then add the drained lentils. Turn to coat in the spices, then add 3 cups of hot water and bring to the boil.

Cover the pan, turn heat to low and cook gently for 30 minutes. Remove the lid, stir in the salt and cook for about 20 minutes, or until the mixture is porridge-like. Stir often during the last minutes of cooking to prevent it sticking. Stir in the lemon juice and cool. Serve warmish or at room temperature.

SWEET AND SOUR VEGETABLES

Serves 6

These vegetables are colourful, crispy and tangy-sweet to eat. Serve with Chinese-style dishes, or with rich foods that need toning down.

¼ teaspoon salt
1 large onion, peeled (leave root on) and cut into wedges
2 carrots, sliced thinly on the diagonal
2 sticks celery, sliced on the diagonal
3 peppers, red, yellow or green, cored, deseeded and cut into thick strips
100 g snow peas, topped and tailed, or 100 g asparagus, trimmed, soaked and cut into short lengths
4 tablespoons white vinegar
50 ml chicken stock or water
4 tablespoons brown sugar
1 tablespoon cornflour
1 tablespoon soy sauce

Bring a large saucepan of water to the boil over a high heat and add the salt. Drop in the onion and cook uncovered for 2 minutes. Carefully lower in the carrots, celery, peppers and, if you are using it, the asparagus. Cook for 3 minutes, drop in the snow peas, stir vigorously, then drain. Refresh with cold water and leave to drain. The vegetables can be blanched 1–2 hours before serving time if required.

Rinse out the pan and put in the white vinegar, stock or water and brown sugar. Set over a low heat and stir until the sugar is dissolved. Mix the cornflour and soy sauce with a tablespoon of water and pour this into the vinegar mixture, stirring. Bring to a gentle boil, stirring, then add the vegetables. Cook gently, turning often with a spoon, for several minutes, or until they are heated through. Tip into a heated serving dish and serve immediately.

JEAN'S BEANS

Serves 6

Although these beans take a bit of work, it's worth it. They're nicely hot and spicy, so serve them with some kind of 'cooler', or sambals and rice.

750 g fresh green beans, topped and tailed
salt
1 medium onion, chopped
3 cloves garlic, roughly chopped
small knob of fresh ginger, peeled and roughly chopped
1 medium tomato, skinned, cored and chopped
½ teaspoon ground turmeric
6 tablespoons oil
2 teaspoons freshly ground coriander seeds
1 teaspoon freshly ground cumin seeds
½ teaspoon black mustard seeds
1 teaspoon whole cumin seeds
½ hot fresh green chilli, deseeded and finely chopped (or to taste)
2 teaspoons lemon juice

Plunge the beans into a saucepan of lightly salted boiling water and cook uncovered for 3–4 minutes. Drain, refresh with cold water and drain again.

Blend the onion, garlic, ginger, tomato and turmeric in a blender or food processor until they are mixed to a paste.

Heat 4 tablespoons of the oil over a low-medium heat in a roomy saucepan. Add the onion paste. Fry for about 5 minutes, stirring often. Add the ground coriander and cumin seeds and fry for a few more minutes. Turn off the heat.

In a frypan, heat the remaining 2 tablespoons oil over a medium heat. Add the black mustard and cumin seeds. Shake the pan occasionally, and when the mustard seeds begin to pop add the chopped chilli. Cook for 1 minute, then add to the onion mixture.

Add the prepared beans and toss to coat them in the mixture. Turn heat to low, add ½ teaspoon salt and the lemon juice. Cook uncovered, stirring often, until the beans are crisp-tender or done to your liking. If the beans start to stick, add a little water. Transfer to a serving plate and serve hot or at room temperature.

A Bunch of Old Favourites

Like a book of favourite poems, favourite recipes can never be completely forgotten; they just tend to get buried under more recent 'finds'. But like anything that you're truly comfortable with in life, it's nice to trot them out occasionally.

These are some which have stood the test of time with me.

CRISPY PARSNIP BAKE

Serves 6

This is an excellent winter dish; inexpensive, substantial, sweet, creamy and crisp!

900 g parsnips, peeled
1 large kumara, peeled and diced
1 large potato, peeled and diced
salt
butter
¼ cup cream
1 egg, lightly beaten
few grates of fresh nutmeg
freshly ground black pepper to taste
½ cup fresh breadcrumbs

Cut the parsnips into chunks, discarding any woody cores, and put them into a large saucepan with the kumara and potato. Cover with cold water, salt well and bring to the boil. Cook until tender, drain, return to the saucepan and put back on the heat for 1–2 minutes, to drive off clinging water.

Mash or process the vegetables, then beat in 2 knobs of butter, the cream, beaten egg, ¼ teaspoon salt, the nutmeg and black pepper. Blend until smooth.

Pile the mixture into a shallow, buttered, ovenproof dish, smooth the top, then scatter over the breadcrumbs. Dot the top with butter. The dish may be prepared several hours ahead to this point; refrigerate it when cool, but bring it to room temperature before baking.

Cook for 25–30 minutes in an oven preheated to 180 °C, or until crisp on top. Serve hot.

JULIENNE OF CELERY, CARROTS, PARSNIPS AND LEEKS

Serves 6

These vegetables, which virtually steam in their own juices, are delicious. I particularly enjoy their sweet flavour with lamb.

3 sticks celery, washed
2 large carrots, peeled
2 large parsnips, peeled
1 large leek, trimmed, split lengthwise and washed
2 knobs of butter
½ teaspoon salt
freshly ground black pepper to taste
1 tablespoon finely chopped parsley

Cut all the vegetables into fine julienne (small strips a little thicker than a match). First trim the vegetables, then cut them into matchstick lengths, then into sticks (for carrots and parsnips cut into lengths, cut these into thin pieces, then cut these into strips).

Melt the butter in a large saucepan and add the vegetables. Sprinkle over salt and pepper, and add 1 tablespoon of water. Cover with a lid and cook gently for about 12 minutes, stirring occasionally, or until just tender. Toss the parsley through them and serve.

Surprisingly, any leftovers are just as good reheated the next day.

Cooking Root Vegetables

Root vegetables, or those which grow under the ground, usually have a firmer, denser structure than vegetables that grow above the ground, like beans and zucchini, which contain more water.

Root vegetables are usually cooked by being placed in a saucepan of cold, salted water, brought to the boil, then cooked with the lid on, or partially on.

This method is chosen as it is a gentle, controlled way of cooking, heating up slowly and allowing plenty of time for the heat to penetrate the denseness of the vegetables, and ensuring even

GREEN BEANS WITH TOMATO

Serves 6

Slowly cooked onions and tomatoes provide these beans with an agreeably sweet flavour.

large knob of butter
1 medium onion, finely chopped
3 large tomatoes, skinned and diced
¼ teaspoon salt
freshly ground black pepper to taste
450 g green beans, topped and tailed

Melt the butter in a large frypan and add the onion and 2 tablespoons water. Cover with a lid and cook very gently until tender. Remove the lid, increase the heat slightly and allow the onion to colour to a light gold. Add the tomatoes, salt and black pepper and cook gently for about 12 minutes, until pulpy.

Meanwhile, plunge the beans into a saucepan of gently boiling, salted water and cook uncovered for 5–8 minutes, or until cooked to your liking. Drain and refresh with cold water. Shake the beans well and add them to the tomato mixture. Turn to coat in the mixture, then allow to heat through. Turn into a heated serving dish and serve immediately.

cooking (fast boiling would soften the exterior long before the centre was cooked).

The lid stays on, or partially on, to trap in the steam and to prevent the water level from dropping. If the vegetables are not kept immersed in the water, they will cook unevenly. The exposed vegetables, for example potatoes, become dryish on the outside while still hard in the centre.

Sometimes the water (or stock) froths over if the lid is on, so it may be angled slightly to allow a little steam to escape.

When they are tender, drain the vegetables immediately.

BAKED HERBED TOMATOES

Serves 6

These deliciously sweet tomatoes fit into many menus. Their slight acidity is welcome with rich breakfast or brunch dishes, but they also work well with roasted meats and vegetarian meals.

6 medium tomatoes
salt
castor sugar
freshly ground black pepper
1 tablespoon finely chopped parsley
1 tablespoon snipped chives
large knob of butter

Cut the tomatoes in half through the 'equator' and sit cut-side facing up, in a shallow, ovenproof dish. Sprinkle each with a little salt and castor sugar and grind over a little black pepper. Scatter over the herbs, then distribute the butter, cut into tiny pieces, on top.

Cook in an oven preheated to 180°C for 15 minutes until the tomatoes are heated through and sizzling on top. (If they don't sizzle, pop them under the grill.) Do not overcook, nor keep them hot, as they will collapse. If you are not ready to serve them, remove them from the oven, cool and rewarm gently when required.

Don't Throw It Down the Sink

Remember that the water in which vegetables are cooked contains nutrients: don't throw it down the sink! Use it in vegetable soups, gravies and sauces. It will store, refrigerated, for 1–2 days.

PURÉE OF LEEKS AND POTATOES

Serves 4

This is so good it's hard to believe! It's the sort of thing I find myself dipping into, again and again (just to check on the seasoning of course!) whilst I complete any accompanying dishes.

2 medium leeks
2 knobs of butter
salt
freshly ground black pepper to taste
good few grates of fresh nutmeg
¼ cup dry white wine
500 g potatoes, peeled and cut into chunks
¼ cup cream
¼ cup milk
1 tablespoon snipped chives

Use a large knife to cut off the tips of the leaves of the leeks, then shave off any tough parts, or remove any coarse leaves. Trim off the roots, cut each leek in two lengthwise, then rinse them thoroughly under running water. Shake dry, then slice them finely.

Heat the butter in a frypan and put in the leeks. Cook for about 10 minutes until wilted (don't allow them to brown), then sprinkle over salt, black pepper and nutmeg. Mix together, then pour in the dry white wine. Bring to the boil, cover and cook very gently until tender.

Meanwhile boil the potatoes in salted water until tender. Drain and pass them through a mouli-légumes or mash to a purée with a potato masher.

Add the cream and milk to the leeks, heat them to boiling point, then beat in the potato purée. Allow this to heat through, then transfer it to a hot dish. Sprinkle with chives and serve immediately.

If the leeks are ready before the potato is sieved, take them off the heat, then, when the potatoes are ready, rewarm them carefully with the cream and milk.

If necessary, the dish can be cooked before required, and reheated gently; stir often to prevent sticking on the base of the pan.

COLOURFUL VEGETABLE STIR-FRY

Serves 6–8

Colour and crunch are the buzz words in this recipe. The stir-fry makes an excellent choice for entertaining, as all the vegetables can be blanched ahead of time, then quickly stir-fried until glazed and crunch-tender.

10 cups prepared vegetables (see below)
salt
3 tablespoons olive or peanut oil, or 50 g butter
freshly ground black pepper to taste
1 tablespoon finely chopped lemon thyme
1 tablespoon finely chopped parsley
2 tablespoons snipped chives

Choose a selection of 5 or 6 vegetables and blanch them according to the following times and methods:
asparagus, trimmed and cut into short lengths: 2–3 minutes
green or yellow zucchini, sliced on the diagonal: 45 seconds
snow peas, topped and tailed: 30 seconds
cauliflower or broccoli florets: 60–80 seconds
tiny Brussels sprouts, trimmed and cut with a cross at the stalk
    end: 3–5 minutes (depending on size)
green or yellow scallopini, root ends trimmed: 3–7 minutes
    (depending on size)
red, green or yellow peppers, cored and cut into chunks: 45 seconds
tiny turnips, trimmed but with a little greenery left on: 3–5
    minutes (depending on size)
tiny new potatoes, scrubbed: cooked until just tender, about 15
    minutes
button mushrooms, stalks trimmed: blanching not required
cherry tomatoes: blanching not required

The vegetables can be prepared up to 3 hours in advance. Cook each one separately in fresh, lightly salted boiling water. After blanching, drain, and immediately pour on 3–4 cups cold water to halt the cooking process and help set the colour. Drain well, then pat dry with kitchen paper. Lay them on a tray lined with a double thickness of kitchen paper, cover loosely with more kitchen paper and set aside until required; do not refrigerate.

When you are ready to cook, heat a wok over a medium-high heat and drop in the oil or butter. When it is hottish put in the mushrooms, if used, and stir-fry quickly for 5 minutes. If any liquid accumulates, pour it off before continuing. Tip in all the vegetables (apart from the cherry tomatoes, if used). Stir-fry for 5 minutes more, or until hot and crisp-tender. If you are using cherry tomatoes, add these now, along with salt to taste, plenty of freshly ground black pepper and the herbs. Toss them together, then tip onto a heated serving dish. Serve immediately.

If you are not using mushrooms, heat the oil or butter as described, then tip in all the vegetables, except the cherry tomatoes, and stir-fry for 5–7 minutes. Finish off as described.

SWEET PEPPERS AND POTATOES WITH ROSEMARY

Serves 6

An easy, yet delicious, filling, summer dish which is good hot, warmish or at room temperature (leftovers are just as good the next day).

1.5 kg new potatoes, peeled and cut into chunky 'fingers'
½ cup olive oil
1 teaspoon salt
freshly ground black pepper to taste
2 stalks fresh rosemary
5–6 large red and yellow peppers, cored, deseeded and cut into thick chunks

Put the potatoes, olive oil, salt, black pepper and rosemary stalks in a large roasting tin. Turn the potatoes with a large spoon to coat them with the oil and seasonings.

Cook for 30 minutes in an oven preheated to 200 °C, then add the peppers. Cook for an hour, turning often, or until the potatoes are crisp and the peppers glistening and lightly charred.

GREEK LEEKS

Serves 6

This is a good, flavoursome way with leeks — herby, tangy and olivey — which complements plainer foods like crumbed, fried meat, or roasted meats. For an all-vegetable meal, serve them with jacket potatoes or jacket kumaras, or rice, and one or two other vegetable dishes of your choice.

1 kg (5–6) leeks
3 tablespoons olive oil
4 medium tomatoes, skinned, cored and diced, or 1 cup tinned
*   Italian tomatoes, mashed*
freshly ground black pepper to taste
½ teaspoon salt
1 tablespoon lemon juice
1 large clove garlic, crushed
1 tablespoon chopped marjoram (or use 1 teaspoon dried marjoram)
½ cup black olives, stoned

Use a large knife to cut off the tips of the leeks, then shave off any tough parts or remove any coarse leaves. Trim off the roots, then cut each leek in two lengthwise. Rinse thoroughly under running water. Shake dry and slice thinly.

Put all the ingredients into a large saucepan, mix with a wooden spoon, then set over a medium heat. Cover with a lid and cook for about 12 minutes, or until nearly tender.

Remove the lid and cook for about 5 minutes, stirring often, or until the liquid has almost evaporated and the leeks are tender. Serve hot, warm or at room temperature.

How Much to Use?

Fresh herbs are bulkier than dried, and dried herbs are more concentrated. My advice when using dried herbs is to use half or slightly less than half the fresh quantity (i.e. 1 tablespoon finely chopped marjoram = ½ tablespoon dried marjoram, crumbled).

MIXED PEPPERS IN A PAN

Serves 6

Here's another way of cooking sweet peppers in a pan. Serve them with one or two salads, and some crusty bread, for a casual summer lunch or picnic.

6 peppers, of assorted hues
¼ cup olive oil
2 cloves garlic, roughly chopped
¼ teaspoon salt
plenty of freshly ground black pepper
1 tablespoon capers, drained
½ cup black olives, drained

Cut the peppers in half and discard the cores and seeds. Cut them into chunks. In a large frypan heat the olive oil over a medium-high heat and when hot drop in the peppers and garlic. Cook for about 10 minutes, stirring often, then turn heat to low, and cover with a lid. Cook for about 12–15 minutes, or until the peppers are tender, stirring occasionally.

Remove the lid, increase the heat to high and cook until the liquid is driven off and the peppers are slightly browned. Add the salt, black pepper, capers and olives. Serve hot or at room temperature.

Release Those Oils

Rubbing dried herbs in the palms of the hands not only breaks the herbs into smallish, manageable bits, but the warmth of the palms seems to draw out the oils, or remaining aromas of the herbs. Highly recommended (at least for the sniff value, if nothing else!).

MARY'S WAIHEKE SPUDS

Serves 4

The little island of Waiheke, just off Auckland's east coast, was the place of invention for these scrumptious potatoes, although Mary's inspiration is undeniably Greek.

2 smallish onions
6 cloves garlic, peeled
1 kg potatoes, peeled and cut into thick fat fingers (thumbs is probably
 a better description)
juice of 1 lemon
¼ teaspoon salt
freshly ground black pepper to taste
2 large sprigs fresh rosemary
75 ml olive oil

Peel the onions, leaving the root attached. Cut in half through the root, then into slim wedges. Put the onions, garlic and potatoes in a large, oiled roasting tin. Pour the lemon juice over, sprinkle with salt, grind on black pepper and add the rosemary sprigs. Drizzle with the olive oil.

Cook in an oven preheated to 200 °C for 1–1¼ hours, turning often, or until the potatoes are tender and lightly browned. Transfer to a serving bowl and serve hot.

A Few Classics

It's good to know that when you're tired of fiddling around and experimenting with recipes that don't quite live up to expectations, you can fall back on a few 'tried and true' classic combinations.

❖

POTATOES SAVOYARDE

BRAISED RED CABBAGE
AND APPLES

CREAMED PARSNIPS

BUTTERED JERUSALEM
ARTICHOKES

SWEET GARDEN PEAS

CHÂTEAU POTATOES

SAUTÉ POTATOES

ANNA POTATOES

ROAST POTATOES

BUTTERED FENNEL

STEAMED NEW POTATOES

ASPARAGUS WITH NOISETTE
BUTTER AND HERBS

BUTTERED BUTTER BEANS

PEAS 'BONNE FEMME' STYLE

NEW SEASON ASPARAGUS

GLAZED BABY TURNIPS

CREAMY SCALLOPED POTATOES

BUTTERED BROAD BEANS

❖

POTATOES SAVOYARDE

Serves 4

Remember this dish in winter when you want an unobtrusive potato dish to go with meat, something that can be 'bunged' in the oven and forgotten about. A word of warning — don't be generous with the cheese; 60 g provides a light creaminess, any more makes the dish unnecessarily rich.

900 g old potatoes, peeled
butter
60 g Gruyère cheese, grated
¾ teaspoon salt
freshly ground black pepper to taste
2 large cloves garlic, crushed
300 ml chicken or beef stock

Slice the potatoes very thinly and set aside a handful of the neatest slices for the top of the dish.

Generously butter a smallish, heavy-based casserole, or oven-proof dish, and arrange a layer of potatoes on the base. Scatter over a little Gruyère cheese, sprinkle on a little salt, grind over a little black pepper and dot with smidgins of crushed garlic. Continue forming the layers, finishing with a neatly arranged layer using the reserved potato slices, arranged in concentric circles.

Pour over the stock. Cover with a lid and bake in an oven preheated to 180°C for 15 minutes. Remove the lid and bake for an hour, or until the potatoes are tender and crisp on top.

BRAISED RED CABBAGE AND APPLES

Serves 6

In winter, when red cabbage and cooking apples are plentiful, this is an excellent choice; it is satisfying and inexpensive and makes an admirable partner for rich foods, particularly meat and game. And that's not all: it can be prepared ahead, served hot or at room temperature and it actually tastes better the day after making. (Store it covered and refrigerated for up to 5 days.)

1 large, firm red cabbage
large knob of butter
2 cooking apples (choose a tart, crunchy variety)
½ teaspoon salt
1 tablespoon castor sugar
1 tablespoon malt or white wine vinegar

Split the cabbage in half with a sharp knife. Slice out the core, discard the outer leaves, then wash the two halves under running water. Shake dry. Chop coarsely, then plunge the cabbage into a large saucepan of boiling water and cook uncovered for 2–3 minutes. Turn the cabbage in the water with a large spoon as it cooks. Drain.

Rub butter on the base of a heavy-based casserole or saucepan and add half the cabbage. Peel and core the apples, slice them finely and arrange them on top of the cabbage. Put in the rest of the cabbage, then sprinkle over the salt, castor sugar and vinegar. Cover with a tight-fitting lid and set on a medium heat.

When the cabbage is steaming and nearly boiling, turn the heat to low and cook very gently for 30 minutes. Quickly lift off the lid, letting clinging moisture drop onto the cabbage, turn the mixture with tongs and check the liquid level. If there is less than 2 tablespoons liquid, add 1–2 tablespoons of water (don't be tempted to flood the cabbage; provide just enough liquid to prevent it catching on the base of the pan). Cook for 30 minutes, or until soft and very tender. Serve hot or at room temperature.

An alternative cooking method is to cook the cabbage in an oven preheated to 170°C for about an hour.

CREAMED PARSNIPS

Serves 4–6

Do try these, for they have a wonderfully sweet, nutty flavour. Although they are particularly good with roasted meats, like beef or pork, these parsnips will be welcome whenever a soft, fluffy purée is called for, to act as a 'cushion' for sauced foods or gravy, or as a contrast to crisp, snappy vegetables or crisp-fried foods.

1 kg parsnips, peeled and trimmed
salt
large knob of butter
freshly ground black pepper to taste
approx. 200 ml milk, brought to boiling point
chopped parsley for garnishing (optional)

Cut the parsnips into slim wedges, discarding any woody cores. Put them in a large saucepan and cover with cold water. Sprinkle with salt, cover with a lid and bring to the boil. Cook at a gentle boil, partially covered with a lid, for about 12–15 minutes, or until very tender. Remove any scum that rises to the surface. Drain and rinse with 1–2 cups warm water. Then either use a mouli-légumes, placing only one or two pieces of parsnip under the press at every turn (this prevents a build up of parsnips around the edges of the mouli, which can quickly turn sticky) or purée the parsnips in a food processor.

Beat in the butter, 1 teaspoon of salt and a little black pepper. Beat in enough of the hot milk (150–200 ml) to make the purée light and creamy. (If you are using a food processor the whole operation can be carried out in the machine.)

Transfer the purée to a heated serving dish, sprinkle with parsley and serve hot.

If you wish, the parsnip purée can be prepared ahead and reheated over a low heat. Stir constantly, as the mixture is inclined to catch on the base of the pan. When reheating you may need to beat in a little extra hot milk, as the mixture tends to thicken a little on standing.

BUTTERED JERUSALEM ARTICHOKES

Serves 4

This makes an interesting alternative to potatoes.

1 kg large, even-shaped Jerusalem artichokes, scrubbed
1 tablespoon lemon juice
1 teaspoon salt
30 g butter
freshly ground black pepper to taste
1 tablespoon chopped parsley

Place the artichokes in a saucepan and cover with cold water. Add the lemon juice and salt. Cover and quickly bring to the boil. Immediately reduce the heat to low and cook, partially covered with a lid, until the artichokes are just tender (5–12 minutes, depending on the size). Drain in a colander, peel with a small sharp knife, and cut the artichokes into thinnish rounds. They may be prepared an hour or so ahead to this point.

When you are ready to finish them off, heat the butter in a large frypan and when sizzling add the sliced artichokes. Stir to coat in the butter and season well with salt and black pepper. Cook over a medium heat for 4–5 minutes, stirring often. When well heated through, lower the heat and stir in the parsley. Serve immediately.

If you prefer the artichokes crisper, fry them in the butter for 10–12 minutes, or until crisp. Transfer to a heated dish and serve immediately.

SWEET GARDEN PEAS

Serves 4–6

In my book nothing can beat tiny sweet green peas tossed with a little mint and fresh butter.

1 kg fresh green peas
½ teaspoon castor sugar (optional)
salt
2–3 sprigs fresh mint
knob of butter
freshly ground black pepper to taste

Remove the peas from their pods, rinse and shake dry (1 kg peas in the pod should yield about 3 cups shelled peas).

Put the peas in a saucepan, cover with cold water, add the castor sugar, if used, and sprinkle with a little salt. Add a sprig of mint, then bring to the boil. Cook gently, uncovered, for about 12 minutes, or until tender.

Drain, and discard the mint sprig. Return the peas to the cleaned pan and drop in the butter. Sprinkle lightly with salt, grind on a little black pepper and add a fresh sprig of mint. Set over a low heat until the butter melts, shaking the pan occasionally. Serve immediately.

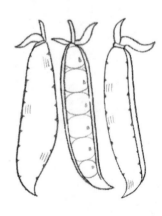

CHÂTEAU POTATOES

Serves 4

These potatoes develop a crisp golden outside, due to the bottom heat, but the lid traps in the steam, giving them soft, fluffy insides. The potatoes should be round, so they can roll in the dish when shaken, and therefore brown evenly.

1 kg potatoes (preferably new ones), peeled
60 g butter (yes, that's right! It's not a dish for dieters)
salt

Use a vegetable peeler to shape the potatoes into small rounds about double the size of a walnut. Dry them very well in a clean cloth.

Heat a heavy-based pan (cast-iron is ideal), large enough to take all the potatoes in one layer, and when it is hot, drop in the butter, which should sizzle immediately but mustn't burn. Add the potatoes and turn the heat to low. Spoon the butter over the potatoes, then cover tightly with a lid or double thickness of tinfoil. Cook slowly for about 40 minutes, shaking the pan from time to time to ensure they aren't sticking. The temperature is important; if it's too high the potatoes may catch and the butter burn. The potatoes should 'talk' to you, a gentle little sizzle, not great crackling sounds, and the odour should be that wonderful smell of gently frying butter with not a hint of burning.

Don't take off the lid during the first 30 minutes of cooking, or else the steam will escape. After 30 minutes you can have a peek. Remove the lid or tinfoil and scrape up any crunchy bits with a metal spoon. Sprinkle generously with salt, cover again and continue cooking until the potatoes are golden brown and tender.

SAUTÉ POTATOES

Serves 4

So many sins have been committed under the guise of 'sauté potatoes' that it's enough to make a serious cook weep. Potatoes thrown into hot fat and left to fry do not measure up. Sauté potatoes, sizzling and golden, swathed in crumbly buttery crusts, need your time and a certain amount of judgement.

1.5 kg old potatoes, peeled
salt
2 tablespoons light vegetable oil
50 g butter

Cut the potatoes into even-sized pieces, roughly the size of an egg. Put them in a saucepan, cover with cold water, salt lightly and bring to the boil. Cook gently until tender, then drain.

Heat a large, heavy-based frypan over a medium heat. Turn the hot potatoes on to a board and cut them into large chunks. Add the vegetable oil to the pan, swirl to coat the sides of the pan, then drop in the butter. Allow the butter to melt and sizzle, then add the potatoes. Immediately start tossing with a flat-bladed knife, tossing gently at 30–second intervals. Don't worry if the potatoes start to crumble; it's part of the character of the dish.

Continue cooking for about 15 minutes, tossing every minute, until the potatoes are crumbly, crisp and golden brown. Sprinkle with salt, then tip all the contents in the pan into a hot serving dish. Serve immediately.

ANNA POTATOES

Serves 4

This golden potato mould, rich with butter, is heaven for potatoholics.

1 kg old potatoes
60 g butter, softened
salt

Choose even-sized, cylindrical potatoes. Peel, keeping them round in shape, and slice very thinly.

Butter well a 20–cm diameter, heavy-based dish or frypan (if using a frypan it must have an ovenproof handle). Cover the base of the pan with overlapping slices of the potato, starting the first ring either around the outside edge of the pan, or in the centre. Place the second ring, with the slices overlapping in the opposite direction, so that the entire base of the pan is covered with potatoes. Remember that this layer of potatoes will be uppermost when the potatoes are turned out. Sprinkle lightly with salt and dot with butter, taking care not to dislodge the slices. Continue layering the ingredients until the dish is full (use more potatoes and butter if necessary).

Put on a tight-fitting lid, or cover with a double thickness of tinfoil, pressed securely around the dish. Put it on an element set on a low-medium heat and cook for about 20 minutes, to allow the base of the dish to brown. Take care with the heat; the potatoes should only just be audibly sizzling, no more, or they may catch and burn.

Transfer the dish or frypan to an oven preheated to 180 °C and cook for a further 20–30 minutes. Remove from the oven and stand for 5 minutes. Lift off the lid or tinfoil, then carefully loosen the potatoes from the side of the dish. Cover with a heated serving plate, invert, and lift off the cooking dish or frypan. Serve immediately.

ROAST POTATOES

Partially cooking old potatoes in water (parboiling) before roasting in hot oil produces super-crisp, crunchy 'roasties'. Older potatoes are best, as the high starch content gives a fluffier inside. Choose potatoes of an even size to ensure they will cook through at the same time. If neatness is desired, the potatoes can be shaped into ovals with a potato peeler to give them a uniform look, before parboiling.

Peel the potatoes, then put them in a saucepan. Salt lightly and bring to the boil. (Use about 1.5 kg potatoes for 6–8 people.)

Meanwhile, heat a roasting tin in a hot oven with 6 tablespoons (90 ml) of vegetable oil.

Cook the potatoes, uncovered, for 5 minutes, then drain well. As soon as the potatoes are cool enough to handle, scratch them all over with a fork. This makes a rough layer that crumbles and crispens well.

When the oil is very hot and just starting to haze, remove the tin from the oven. Put in the potatoes, in one layer (if the potatoes are too crowded, sitting one on top of the other, moisture will be trapped in and they won't brown).

Cook for about 1¼–1½ hours, in an oven preheated to 200 °C, turning them from time to time. Sprinkle with salt during the last 15 minutes. When they are crisp and crunchy, transfer them to a plate lined with kitchen paper. Drain briefly, then move them to a heated serving plate. Serve immediately.

BUTTERED FENNEL

Serves 4

This simple treatment for fennel is one of the best. Serve it with cheese-sauced or cheese-flavoured dishes, or with fish.

4 slim young fennel bulbs
salt
juice of ½ lemon
large knob of butter
1 tablespoon finely chopped fennel leaves (optional)
freshly ground black pepper to taste

Prepare the fennel by trimming away the root end and removing stems and any bruised or coarse parts. Wash well. Plunge into a saucepan of boiling, lightly salted water, add the lemon juice and cook, uncovered, at a gentle boil for 15–20 minutes, or until tender. (Check with a skewer; be careful not to overcook them.)

Drain, refresh the fennel with a cup of cold water, shake out the excess water and drain for 1–2 minutes.

Return the fennel to the pan with the butter, set it over a low heat and allow it to heat through until it is very lightly browned. Sprinkle on the chopped fennel, grind over black pepper, then tip it into a heated serving dish. Serve immediately.

STEAMED NEW POTATOES

Serves 6

I'm not just a potato fan, I'm an addict! I adore tiny new potatoes steamed until just tender (I prefer them steamed as more flavour is lost in boiling), tossed with butter and mint.

1 kg small new potatoes, scrubbed
½ teaspoon salt
2 tablespoons coarsely chopped mint
large knob of butter
freshly ground black pepper to taste
1 tablespoon finely snipped chives (optional)

Position the potatoes in a metal colander or steaming basket over a saucepan of boiling water (the colander or steaming basket should nearly fit inside the pan). Sprinkle over a little salt and half the mint. Cover tightly with a lid or double thickness of tinfoil, and steam until tender over vigorously boiling water.

Allow 12–15 minutes for small, freshly dug potatoes but up to 30 minutes for large ones. (Test by inserting a flat-bladed knife through a potato; it should pass through without resistance. Be careful not to overcook, because the potatoes will burst.)

When they are ready, lift out the potatoes with tongs and place in a heated serving dish. Dot with the butter, grind over black pepper and scatter over the remaining mint. If you like a mild, sweet onion flavour toss through a tablespoon of snipped chives. Serve immediately.

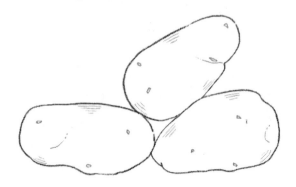

ASPARAGUS WITH NOISETTE BUTTER AND HERBS

· ·

Serves 6

At the beginning of the asparagus season, when you're dead keen to eat them, simple treatments like the following are all that is called for. Leave the difficult sauces, stuffings, soups and savouries for the end of the asparagus season when imagination is needed to avoid repetition.

700 g asparagus, trimmed and soaked
salt
50 g butter
juice of 1 lemon
1 tablespoon finely chopped herbs (choose from parsley, chives, chervil,
 tarragon, basil, marjoram, oregano, lemon thyme, or a mixture
 of any)

Plunge the asparagus into a saucepan of salted boiling water and cook uncovered for 2–7 minutes (depends on the thickness of the asparagus and how crunchy you like them). Drain, then pile onto a heated plate.

Meanwhile, make the noisette butter. Heat a large, heavy-based frypan over a high heat. Drop in the butter, let it melt, then allow it to turn a light nut-brown. (Be careful not to let it burn, but make sure it does change from predominantly yellow to brown, to ensure a nutty flavour.)

Have the lemon juice and herbs already mixed, and the moment the butter has turned brown pour them in. The contents will steam up immediately, so be prepared for that to happen. Swirl the pan and pour the contents over the asparagus. Serve immediately.

This dish can be served as an accompanying vegetable, but it is also good as a finger-licking starter (serves 4), using fat, plump asparagus. Serve on individual plates and eat with the fingers, dunking the spears into the savoury butter (very yummy!).

BUTTERED BUTTER BEANS

Serves 4

Buttery beans, fragrant with herbs, are one of summer's delights.

500 g yellow butter or 'wax' beans, topped, tailed and strings removed
salt
2 large knobs of butter
1 tablespoon finely chopped parsley
1 tablespoon snipped chives
1 tablespoon finely chopped tarragon (optional)
freshly ground black pepper to taste

Plunge the beans into a saucepan of well-salted, boiling water.
Cook uncovered for about 10 minutes, or until just tender. Drain.
   Melt the butter in the cleaned-out saucepan and add the herbs.
Return the beans to the pan, grind over black pepper, then toss
over a gentle heat until hot and fragrant (be careful not to fry
them). Turn into a heated serving dish and serve immediately.

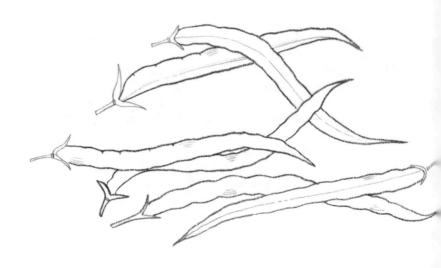

PEAS 'BONNE FEMME' STYLE

....

Serves 4–6

This French country treatment for peas is so delicious that it even tastes quite good when made with frozen peas. Serve with a simple roast chicken and steamed new potatoes. For a vegetable meal, omit the bacon in this recipe and serve with Green Beans with Nutmeg (page 156), steamed, jacket, or roast potatoes and Baked Buttercup with Rosemary and Garlic (page 160).

1 kg fresh green peas (should yield about 3 cups shelled peas)
large knob of butter
3 rashers streaky bacon, cut into thin strips
10–12 spring onions, trimmed and cut into short lengths
¼ teaspoon salt
freshly ground black pepper to taste
few grates of fresh nutmeg
1 level tablespoon plain flour
150 ml water
heart of a small lettuce, shredded

Remove the peas from their pods, rinse and shake dry.

Put the butter in a saucepan, set over a medium-high heat and when sizzling add the bacon. Cook until lightly coloured, stirring occasionally, then add the spring onions. Cook for 5 minutes.

Lower the heat, add the salt, black pepper and nutmeg, sprinkle on the flour, mix it in, then blend in the water. Bring to the boil, then add the lettuce and peas. Return to the boil, then turn the heat to low, cover with a lid and cook for 15–20 minutes, or until tender. (If a lot of liquid accumulates during cooking, lift off the lid and cook quickly until tender.) Serve immediately.

NEW SEASON ASPARAGUS

Serves 6

For me there can be nothing more simple and delicious than plump asparagus, swathed in just-melted fresh butter ... well, yes, perhaps there is — the above generously dusted with freshly grated Parmesan cheese! When purchasing the asparagus, choose spears of an even size, so they can cook evenly, and store them, refrigerated, with the cut stems immersed in a little water and the tips loosely covered with a clean plastic bag.

850 g even-sized asparagus
salt
small knob of butter
freshly ground black pepper to taste

Snap off or trim the woody ends of the asparagus. Wash well under running water, then soak the tips in cold water for 15 minutes to dislodge any grit. Remove them from the water, shake, then plunge them into a saucepan of lightly salted, boiling water. Cook uncovered for 2–7 minutes (depends on the thickness and how crisp-tender you like them). Drain carefully, turn them into a hot dish, dot with butter and grind over a little black pepper. Serve immediately.

Ring the changes by adding a little crushed garlic to the butter, or by sprinkling with ½ cup freshly grated Parmesan cheese (or use both garlic and Parmesan cheese).

GLAZED BABY TURNIPS

Serves 4

This is a simple treatment, best suited to tiny turnips. They emerge crisp and sweet, bathed in a shiny glaze. If you like, add a little finely chopped parsley, chervil or snipped chives.

500 g baby turnips
salt
knob of butter
1½ tablespoons castor sugar
freshly ground black pepper to taste

Trim and peel the turnips. Leave them whole if very small (smaller than an egg) or cut into even-sized chunks if larger. Place them in a saucepan and cover with cold water. Salt lightly and bring to the boil, then cook gently for 2 minutes. Drain. The turnips may be prepared 1–2 hours ahead to this point.

Melt the butter in a saucepan over a medium heat. Add the castor sugar and turnips. Toss well, sprinkle over a little salt and grind over black pepper to taste. Cook for several minutes, uncovered, shaking the pan from time to time, until the turnips are covered with a very shiny glaze. Serve hot.

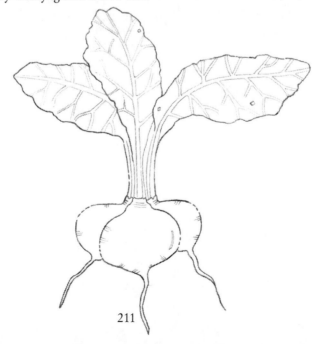

CREAMY SCALLOPED POTATOES

Serves 6

Here's a simplified, less rich, version of the recipe Potato and Gruyère Gratin, page 121.

1 kg potatoes, peeled
large knob of butter
¾ teaspoon salt
freshly grated nutmeg
300 ml cream

Slice the potatoes very thinly. Generously butter a smallish, heavy-based oven dish. Put in a layer of potatoes (reserve the neatest slices for the top) in concentric circles. Sprinkle over a little salt, using a teaspoon, and grate over a little nutmeg. Continue layering the dish until all the potatoes are used, arranging the top layer neatly.

Pour over the cream and dot with butter. Cover with a tight-fitting lid and bake for 30 minutes in an oven preheated to 180°C. Remove the lid and continue cooking for about 45 minutes, or until the potatoes are tender but still creamy and the top is crusty.

If the cream evaporates before this point, and the potatoes seem a little dry, add a few tablespoons light stock or water. Serve hot.

BUTTERED BROAD BEANS

Serves 4

Young broad beans are best for this recipe. If the beans are mature and the outer shell is tough, flick them off and discard them after blanching. This greatly reduces the quantity, but at least they will be edible.

1 generous kg young broad beans
salt
knob of butter
freshly ground black pepper to taste
1 tablespoon of any of the following herbs, or a combination of two:
    coarsely chopped parsley; snipped chives; chopped savory; chopped
    chervil; chopped thyme

Remove the beans from the pods, place them in a saucepan and cover with cold water. Salt lightly, bring to the boil, then boil gently until just tender (5–15 minutes, depending on the maturity of the beans). Drain, rinse with warm water and drain again. This can be done 1–2 hours before finishing them off.

Heat the butter in the cleaned-out saucepan, add the beans and warm through. Sprinkle on a little salt, grind over black pepper then add the herb, or herbs. Toss gently, then tip the beans into a heated serving dish. Serve immediately.

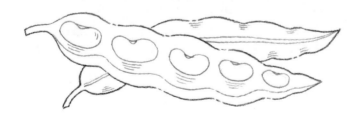

Ringing the Changes

And last, but not least, the 'weird and wonderful'. Sweet, hot, sour, spiced or fruity, grilled, braised or sautéed, these are all worth a shot.

SWEET AND SOUR PUMPKIN

MUSHROOMS WITH MARSALA

PINEAPPLE STUFFED PEPPERS

SAUTÉED WITLOOF

BRAISED WITLOOF

CURRIED PARSNIP PURÉE

BRUSSELS SPROUTS WITH SIZZLED
BACON AND PINENUTS

ZUCCHINI WITH RAISINS
AND PINENUTS

EGGPLANTS WITH
MINT AND LEMON

BUTTER BEANS WITH
GREEN PEPPER AND TOMATO

SPICED BAKED YAMS WITH
APPLES AND PRUNES

SWEET AND SOUR PUMPKIN

Serves 4–6

After noting my enthusiasm for pumpkin-filled tortelli, my sister-in-law, Isanna, whipped up this tasty treat one day. Given the sweet and sour treatment, and cooked with plenty of garlic, with which it shares a great affinity, pumpkin really comes into its own; the addition of a little chopped mint is optional.

1 kg firm fleshed pumpkin, peeled and seeds removed
100 ml olive oil
6 cloves garlic, finely chopped
scant tablespoon castor sugar
¼ teaspoon salt
3 tablespoons white wine vinegar
1 tablespoon finely chopped mint (optional)
freshly ground black pepper to taste

Cut the pumpkin into small slices about 1–2 cm thick. Wash and pat dry with kitchen paper.

Heat the olive oil in a large frypan, carefully lower in the pumpkin slices and brown them on all sides over a medium-high heat (this will take 15–20 minutes). Cover with a lid, lower the heat and cook for about 15 minutes, or until tender. Lift the pumpkin out with tongs and place it in a bowl.

Increase the heat under the pan and add the garlic. Fry until a pale nut-brown in colour, stirring often. Add the castor sugar and salt, and pour in the white wine vinegar. Stir until the sugar dissolves.

Return the pumpkin to the pan, add the mint if you are using it, and carefully turn the pumpkin in the glaze. Grind over black pepper. Tip all the contents of the pan into a serving bowl and allow to cool. Serve at room temperature.

MUSHROOMS WITH MARSALA

Serves 8

Marsala imparts an aromatic spicy-sweetness to foods and easily forms a syrupy glaze. Try these mushrooms with dishes flavoured with Parmesan cheese, either vegetable or meat.

1 tablespoon olive oil
large knob of butter
750 g button mushrooms, wiped clean and trimmed
salt to taste
plenty of freshly ground black pepper
125 ml Marsala

Heat the olive oil in a large frypan over a medium-high heat and drop in the butter. Add the mushrooms and stir to coat them in the oil and butter. Cook for about 5 minutes, stirring often, until the mushrooms are lightly browned and 'squeaky'. Sprinkle on a good ¼ teaspoon salt and grind over a little black pepper. Increase the heat and pour in the Marsala.

Cook for several minutes more, tossing often, until the mushrooms are tender. Transfer to a serving bowl using a slotted spoon. Reduce the liquid remaining in the frypan until it is syrupy, then pour it over the mushrooms. Serve hot or at room temperature.

Warming Stuff

It's a good idea to have a bottle of Marsala, the fortified red wine from Sicily, on hand. Like sherry, it does not go off after opening, so it can be utilised and enjoyed over a long period.

Marsala goes particularly well with garlicky or Parmesan cheesy things; it can be flamed, served as an aperitif, or as a dessert wine. It adds an incomparable flavour, and provides a syrupiness which gives pan juices a sauce-like consistency.

And a little glass of it, warmed in the hands and consumed around a warm winter fire, sure brings a rosy glow to the cheeks!

PINEAPPLE STUFFED PEPPERS

Serves 4

Water chestnuts give a surprise crunch to these juicy, tasty peppers.

4 large green peppers
1 onion, finely chopped
butter
12 tinned water chestnuts, roughly chopped
440 g tin pineapple pieces in natural juice, drained and roughly
  chopped
few pinches of salt
freshly ground black pepper to taste
¾ cup fresh breadcrumbs

Put the green peppers directly on a rack in an oven preheated to 220°C. Cook for about 20 minutes, turning once or twice, until they are lightly charred (don't overcook them or they will become too soft). Rinse off any blackened peel under running water. Cut the peppers in half lengthwise, carefully scoop out the seeds and remove any membranes. Leave them to drain upside-down on a chopping board.

Place the onion in a small saucepan with a knob of butter, cover with a lid and cook until it is soft. Transfer to a bowl, then add 2 knobs of butter to the pan and set aside. Add the water chestnuts, pineapple pieces, salt and black pepper and half the breadcrumbs to the onion. Mix well.

Melt the butter in the pan and drizzle a little on the base of a shallow ovenproof dish.

Stuff the peppers with the filling and lay them in the buttered dish. Scatter over the remaining breadcrumbs. Drizzle with the butter, then bake in an oven, preheated to 200°C, for about 20 minutes, or until the breadcrumbs on top are crisp. Serve hot.

SAUTÉED WITLOOF

Serves 4–6

This is an unusual treatment for witloof (you'll either love it or hate it) which goes well with ham or smoked ham dishes.

6 witloof
salt
juice of 1 lemon
large knob of butter
freshly ground black pepper to taste
1 tablespoon finely chopped parsley

Trim and wash the witloof and discard any damaged leaves. Gouge out the core at the base of each witloof cone, then put the witloof in a pot of cold salted water. Squeeze in the lemon juice, then put the pot on an element set on high and bring to the boil, uncovered. Boil for 3 minutes, drain, and when cool shake out as much water as possible from the witloof. Cut into rounds.

Heat a large frypan over a medium heat and drop in the butter. When it is sizzling add the witloof and sauté for several minutes until it is a pale gold colour. Grind over black pepper, sprinkle on the parsley and serve immediately.

BRAISED WITLOOF

Serves 4

Witloof is a versatile vegetable. Cooked this way it takes on a good flavour, not dissimilar to globe artichokes. It is particularly good teamed with crisp, crunchy food, where its juicy succulence makes a fine contrast.

6–8 witloof
large knob of butter
strained juice of ½ lemon
½ teaspoon salt dissolved in 1 tablespoon warm water
freshly ground black pepper to taste
1 tablespoon finely chopped parsley

Trim and wash the witloof and discard any damaged leaves. Gouge out the core at the base of each witloof cone, then put the witloof in a pot of cold salted water. Squeeze in the lemon juice, then put the pot on an element set on high and bring to the boil, uncovered. Boil for 3 minutes, drain, and when cool shake out as much water as possible from the witloof. Cut into rounds.

Heat a large frypan over a medium heat and drop in the butter. When it is sizzling add the witloof and sauté for several minutes until it is a pale gold colour. Grind over black pepper, sprinkle on the parsley and serve immediately.

CURRIED PARSNIP PURÉE

Serves 6

A teaspoon or two of curry powder enhances the naturally sweet flavour of parsnips.

1 kg parsnips, peeled and trimmed
salt
50 g butter, cut into small pieces
1–2 teaspoons fresh curry powder
freshly ground black pepper to taste
good grating of fresh nutmeg
a little finely chopped parsley, mint or coriander for garnishing

Cut the parsnips into wedges, put them in a saucepan and cover with cold water. Salt lightly, bring to the boil, then turn the heat to low and simmer gently until tender. Drain. Either push the parsnips through a mouli-légumes, or use a food processor for a quick, smooth result.

Blend in the butter first, then the curry powder, black pepper, nutmeg and ¾ teaspoon salt. Transfer to a heated serving bowl and sprinkle over a little of the chosen herb.

If required, the purée can be made in advance and gently reheated at serving time.

BRUSSELS SPROUTS WITH SIZZLED BACON AND PINENUTS

Serves 4

Forget those water-logged sprouts of your childhood — this recipe transports them to new culinary heights. The bacon and spring onions make them sweet and savoury and the pinenuts provide nuttiness and crunch.

500 g smallish Brussels sprouts
salt
knob of butter
200 g bacon, derinded and finely chopped
6 spring onions, roughly chopped
freshly ground black pepper to taste
2 tablespoons pinenuts

Trim the Brussels sprouts and cut a cross on the base of each. Wash them well. Boil in lightly salted water (or steam) until 'crunch-tender' (no longer like bullets, but not in any way squishy). Drain very well and cut into quarters.

Meanwhile, put the butter in a medium-sized saucepan and add the bacon. Cover the pan and cook over a medium heat until the bacon starts to sizzle and turn crisp, stirring occasionally. Add the spring onions and cook, covered, for a few minutes. Grind over black pepper and add the pinenuts. Stir well with a metal spoon, cover and cook for another 5 minutes. Remove the pan from the heat, add 1 tablespoon water, then cover with the lid again. This will lift the crunchy sediment from the base of the pan.

The dish can be prepared an hour ahead to this point; keep both the sprouts and bacon mix at room temperature.

Five minutes before it is required, reheat the bacon and spring onion mix, add the quartered Brussels sprouts and warm gently, uncovered and stirring often, until heated through.

ZUCCHINI WITH RAISINS AND PINENUTS

Serves 4–6

The inclusion of raisins and pinenuts in this Sicilian dish shows an Arabic influence. It goes very nicely with crumbed, crisp-fried 'schnitzels' of pork or veal, or with a fresh, crisp salad and pita bread.

3 tablespoons plump raisins
3 tablespoons white wine vinegar
3 tablespoons pinenuts
⅓ cup olive oil
1 large onion, finely chopped
2 large cloves garlic, crushed
750 g zucchini
½ teaspoon salt
freshly ground black pepper to taste

Tip the raisins into a small container and pour on the white wine vinegar. Leave them to soak while preparing the other ingredients.

Heat a heavy-based frypan over a medium heat and tip in the pinenuts. Dry-fry for several minutes, tossing often, until they are lightly golden. Set aside.

Heat the olive oil in a large saucepan over a gentle heat and add the onion. Cook gently for 10–12 minutes or until the onion is soft and just turning pale gold. Add the garlic and fry, stirring often, for 2 minutes.

Meanwhile, cut each zucchini into 4–5 large chunks, cutting them on the diagonal, and add them to the pan. Fry gently, stirring often, for 3–4 minutes. Add the salt, black pepper, raisins and vinegar. Cook gently, uncovered, for 3–10 minutes, until the zucchini are done to your liking. Add the pinenuts, toss well and serve immediately.

Although this dish is delicious cold, the vinegar tends to leach the colour from the zucchini. If you don't mind that, and we certainly don't in our household, the dish will happily fit into any Mediterranean menu, where most of the food is served at room temperature. I think the flavours are even better the day after making. (Store covered and refrigerated, but bring it to room temperature before serving.)

EGGPLANTS WITH MINT AND LEMON

Serves 6

This is delicious teamed with barbecued lamb dishes and, although cooked in oil, the lemon and mint keep the richness in check.

2–3 eggplants (should weigh 600–700 g in total)
salt
4 tablespoons olive oil
3 cloves garlic, finely chopped
freshly ground black pepper to taste
1 teaspoon lemon juice
1 tablespoon finely chopped parsley
1 tablespoon finely chopped mint

Cut the eggplants into large cubes, put them in a colander and sprinkle generously with salt. Leave them to drain for 40 minutes. When ready to cook, pat the cubes dry with kitchen paper. Heat 3 tablespoons of the olive oil over a medium-high heat in a large, deep frypan. When the oil is hazing add the eggplant cubes, stir them to coat in the oil, then cook, stirring often, until the oil is absorbed and the eggplant cubes are partially browned.

Add the garlic and 1 tablespoon oil, season with ¼ teaspoon salt and a good grinding of black pepper. Turn the heat to low and cover with a lid. Cook gently, stirring often, for about 10 minutes, or until tender. Pour on the lemon juice and blend through the herbs. Serve at room temperature.

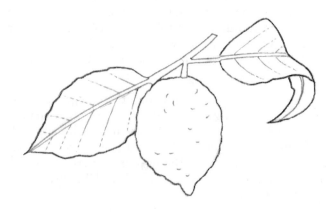

BUTTER BEANS WITH GREEN PEPPER AND TOMATOES

Serves 4

The combination of ingredients used in this recipe bring a Mediterranean flavour to butter beans.

3 tablespoons olive oil
1 medium onion, finely sliced
1 large clove garlic, crushed
1 large green pepper
½ cup (approx. 400 g tin) Italian tinned tomatoes, mashed
¼ teaspoon salt
freshly ground black pepper to taste
500 g butter beans

Put the olive oil into a pan and add the onion and garlic. Cover and cook very gently for about 10 minutes or until softish.

If the green pepper is fleshy, peel off the outside skin with a vegetable peeler (the skin of 'fleshy' peppers tends to separate during cooking), then remove the core and seeds. Slice thinly and add it to the onion along with the tomatoes, salt and pepper.

Cover and cook gently for about 12 minutes, or until the mixture thickens like a sauce. (Be careful not to let it catch on the base of the pan.) Tip in the butter beans, toss them to coat with the mixture, then add ¼ cup of water.

Cover the pan and cook gently for about 20 minutes. If there is not much liquid left after this time, and the beans are not tender, add a little more water. Continue cooking until the butter beans are very tender. Serve hot.

The butter beans can be cooked ahead of time, cooled, then reheated carefully.

SPICED BAKED YAMS WITH APPLES AND PRUNES

Serves 4–8

This makes an excellent accompaniment to roast pork. Teamed up with a green vegetable, like Brussels sprouts, it makes an admirable winter repast.

700 g small pink yams, scrubbed to remove grit
salt
2 cooking apples
large knob of butter (use some to grease the baking dish)
¼ teaspoon ground cinnamon
few pinches of ground cloves
½ cup finely chopped, pitted prunes
¼ cup light brown sugar
½ cup fresh breadcrumbs
¼ cup melted butter

Put the yams in a vegetable colander, or steaming basket, and sit this over a saucepan filled with a small amount of boiling water. Sprinkle lightly with salt, cover tightly with a lid and steam for 15 minutes, or until the yams are cooked through (a skewer should just pass through, finding a hint of resistance). Remove the lid and lift the colander or steaming basket off the saucepan. When the yams are cool enough to handle, slice them into thin rounds.

Meanwhile, peel the apples, discard the cores and cut the flesh into smallish chunks. Put the knob of butter in a small pan, and add the apples. Cover with a lid and cook very gently until they are soft and puréed, stirring occasionally. Blend in the cinnamon, cloves, prunes and brown sugar.

Butter well a shallow gratin dish, about 20 cm in diameter, and lay in the sliced yams. Sprinkle lightly with salt, then cover with the apple purée. Cover with the breadcrumbs, patting them on, then drizzle over the melted butter. Bake in an oven preheated to 180°C for about 30 minutes, until crisp and golden.

If you are serving this dish with roast pork, the oven will be set at a higher temperature. Therefore bake the yams on the shelf below the pork for 25 minutes only.

SALADS

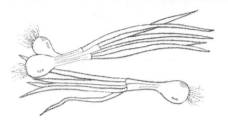

Years ago the 'great New Zealand salad' consisted of chopped lettuce, sliced cucumber and tomato, dressed with either malt vinegar, salt and ground black pepper, or sickly-sweet mock mayonnaise. Thank goodness times have changed!

These days a 'salad' can be green or otherwise, hot, warmish, cold or chilled, creamy, tangy or fruity, herby, or garlicky, and, best of all, interesting.

In this section you'll find regular salad items, such as those mentioned above, and the unusual, dressed with different oils and vinegars, flecked with herbs, jazzed up with olives, capers, green peppercorns and nuts, or pepped up with ginger, chillies and spices.

There are salads to serve at the beginning of a meal, others that are best as an accompaniment, or as a palate cleanser after the main course; yet others can form the basis of a light meal, served with good bread and followed by cheese and fruit.

❖

SPRING SALADS

SUMMERY SALADS

FRUITY SALADS

WINTER SALADS

PEPPED-UP SALADS

❖

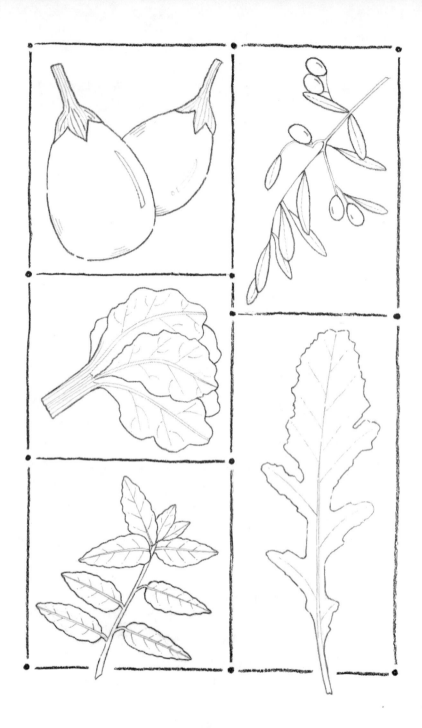

❖

Spring Salads

Ah, springtime! Now is the time to indulge your asparagus/artichoke/green pea/broad bean (or whatever) fantasy. Don't hold back — eat heaps of them while you can!

❖

ARTICHOKE AND FENNEL SALAD
BROAD BEAN SALAD
SUNKIST SALAD
SPRING SALAD BOWL
AVOCADO AND TOMATO SALAD
POTATO AND ASPARAGUS SALAD

❖

ARTICHOKE AND FENNEL SALAD

Serves 6–8

Combining new artichokes and fennel bulb might sound odd, but it makes an excellent mix. The result is nutty and earthy with plenty of crunch. Be sure to use small, young artichokes as they are marinated only, not cooked. Try it after a pasta meal.

⅓ cup extra virgin olive oil
grated rind of 1 lemon
1 tablespoon lemon juice
⅓ cup freshly squeezed orange juice
¾ teaspoon salt
freshly ground black pepper to taste
2 young artichokes
1 litre water mixed with the juice of 1 lemon
1 fennel bulb
1 tablespoon chopped marjoram (or use ½ teaspoon dried marjoram)

Put the extra virgin olive oil, lemon rind, lemon juice, orange juice, salt and black pepper in a medium-sized bowl. Whisk together until well blended.

Trim and prepare the artichokes as described in the recipe Artichoke Frittata, page 80. After soaking in the acidulated water, shake them well, then cut into wafer-thin slices. Place them in the bowl with the dressing, toss well, then leave to marinate for 1–2 hours.

Prepare the fennel by trimming away the root end, and removing the stems and bruised parts. Slice into thin slivers and add to the artichokes along with the marjoram. Toss well and chill for 1–2 hours before serving.

Acidulated Water

This is water to which lemon juice or vinegar has been added. Food is held in acidulated water to prevent discolouration, for example artichokes after trimming.

BROAD BEAN SALAD

Serves 4

This salad is a special spring treat. Be sure to use young beans.

1 generous kg fresh, young broad beans
salt
2 tablespoons extra virgin olive oil
1 teaspoon lemon juice
dab of French mustard
1 large clove garlic, crushed (optional)
2 tablespoons mixed herbs (choose from savory, basil, chives, thyme
  and parsley)
freshly ground black pepper to taste

Remove the beans from the pods, rinse them and place in a saucepan. Cover with cold water, salt lightly and bring to the boil. Cook gently, uncovered, until just tender (5–10 minutes, depending on the maturity of the beans). Drain and rinse again with warm water, then drain again. Tip on to a piece of kitchen paper and pat dry.

In a large bowl whisk the extra virgin olive oil, lemon juice, mustard, garlic (if used), herbs, a few pinches of salt and some black pepper. Add the warm beans and toss well. Serve at room temperature.

Broad Bean Salad Variations

Like mint and fresh peas, the herb savory complements broad beans. The warm clove-like taste of basil is also good. If you only have a handful of beans, turn them into a salad mixed with other spring treats, such as asparagus (briefly blanch the asparagus and cut into short lengths), or mix with cherry tomatoes, black olives and feta cheese and toss with a garlicky dressing.

Alternatively, omit the herbs and garlic and add the segments of two juicy oranges along with a plain vinaigrette. Teamed with glazed ham it is quite superb.

SUNKIST SALAD

Serves 4–6

Bright nasturtium flowers give this salad a splash of sunny colour. The leaves are also used, adding a pleasant pepperiness. Just be sure to pick flowers and leaves from a home garden or an area where chemical sprays have not been used.

2 tablespoons plump raisins
1½ tablespoons red wine vinegar
1 clove garlic, crushed
1 tablespoon capers, drained
¼ teaspoon salt
freshly ground black pepper to taste
4 tablespoons extra virgin olive oil
12 very small nasturtium leaves
12 nasturtium flowers
1 buttercrunch lettuce
2 tablespoons fresh sunflower seeds (optional)

Put the raisins in a small saucepan with the red wine vinegar and a tablespoon of hot water. Cover with a lid and cook on a low heat for 5–7 minutes, then set aside, covered, for 1–2 hours.

Mix the garlic, capers, salt and pepper into the raisins and vinegar, then whisk the oil into this mixture.

Remove the stalks from the nasturtium leaves and flowers, rinse them carefully under gently running water, then soak in a bowl of cold water.

Wash and dry the buttercrunch leaves, tear them into bite-size pieces, then put in a large bowl. Shake the nasturtium leaves dry and add them to the bowl.

Reblend the dressing and pour it over the salad. Toss well. Nestle the dried nasturtium flowers in the salad and sprinkle over the sunflower seeds if used. Serve immediately.

SPRING SALAD BOWL

Serves 6–8

If you're wanting a finer example of 'tossed salad', one with style and exquisite taste, look no further!

1 small curly red lettuce
a small handful lamb's lettuce (corn salad) or sorrel leaves
1 bunch curly endive leaves
1–2 'balls' radicchio
2 tablespoons coarsely chopped chervil
1½ tablespoons champagne vinegar (or use tarragon vinegar)
generous ¼ teaspoon salt
freshly ground black pepper to taste
6 tablespoons walnut oil

Prepare all the salad leaves by trimming, washing and drying. (If using sorrel remove any tough stalks.) Tear into bite-size pieces where appropriate and place them in a large salad bowl. Cover with plastic wrap and chill for 1–2 hours. Remove from the fridge and sprinkle over the chervil.

Mix the champagne vinegar, salt and black pepper together in a small bowl, then whisk in the walnut oil. Pour this over the salad, toss well and serve immediately.

Preparing Salad Greens

If you enjoy salads, get yourself a salad spinner. These usually work on a centrifugal system: a salad basket is spun around a bowl by a pull-handle and any water on the greens placed in the basket is spun out. It's an excellent method for drying washed salad greens and herbs, causing little damage.

The old Italian trick of bundling the salad items, etc. in a clean cloth and shaking it vigorously out the window is 'kinda quaint', but bruises the leaves beyond repair.

Once the leaves are dried they can be kept crisp by putting them into a plastic bag and chilling them in the fridge for an hour, or several hours, but it is best not to tear the greens into bite-size pieces until assembling the salad.

AVOCADO AND TOMATO SALAD

Serves 4

Have you ever looked for something interesting to serve along-side smoked fish during the warmer months? This delightful combination of sun-ripened tomatoes and avocados, doused with a lemony dressing, is just perfect.

1 large, juicy lemon
3 large tomatoes, skinned, cored and cut into chunks
¼ teaspoon salt
freshly ground black pepper to taste
2 tablespoons olive oil or peanut oil
pinch of castor sugar
1 tablespoon snipped chives
2 large, ripe but firm avocados

Grate the rind from the lemon and set it aside. Peel the lemon with a small serrated knife, removing all the pith with the peel. Hold the whole, peeled lemon in one hand, and make a cut on either side of each segment to free it from the 'membrane', so the segments will slip out. Cut each segment in half and put them in a bowl with the tomato chunks.

Squeeze the juice from the membrane into a small bowl and add the grated lemon rind, the salt, black pepper, olive or peanut oil, castor sugar and chives. Whisk well and add to the bowl, then pour the contents over the lemon segments and tomato chunks. Toss well.

Cut the avocados in half, extract the stones, then peel. Cut into chunks, lay them on top of the salad and toss very gently. Serve immediately.

POTATO AND ASPARAGUS SALAD

Serves 6

Don't miss trying this salad when the asparagus season comes around.

1 kg new potatoes, scrubbed
salt
1½ tablespoons white wine vinegar
freshly ground black pepper to taste
2 cloves garlic, crushed
100 ml extra virgin olive oil
grated rind of 1 orange
2 tablespoons finely chopped herbs (mint, parsley, marjoram)
350 g asparagus, trimmed and soaked briefly

Sit the potatoes in a steaming basket or metal colander and set it over a saucepan of boiling water. Sprinkle with salt, cover with a lid or tinfoil, set over a medium-high heat and steam for 20–30 minutes, or until tender. Lift off the lid and remove the steaming basket from the saucepan.

In a small bowl blend the white wine vinegar, ½ teaspoon salt, black pepper and garlic, then whisk in the extra virgin olive oil. Pour off about one quarter of the dressing into a larger bowl and add the grated orange rind to it. Set this aside for the asparagus.

Add the herbs to the small bowl of dressing and set it aside for the potatoes.

Slice the potatoes while they are still warm and arrange them in a ring on a large shallow dish. Pour the herby dressing over them.

Plunge the asparagus into a saucepan of salted, boiling water and cook uncovered for 2–7 minutes, or until crisp-tender. Drain and refresh with cold water. Drain briefly, then pat dry with kitchen paper. Cut the asparagus into short lengths, and tip them into the bowl of orange-flavoured dressing. Toss well, then pile this into the centre of the potato salad. Serve either warmish or at room temperature.

Summery Salads

Here's an interesting collection of summer-time salads, some of which are served warmish or at room temperature, and others that are best after a brief spell in the refrigerator.

❖

SUMMER CORN SALAD

QUICK CHICK-PEA AND
CORIANDER SALAD

HOT POTATO SALAD WITH
PIMENTO-STUFFED OLIVES

'GREEK' SALAD

PINEAPPLE AND PEPPER SALAD

POTATO AND BASIL SALAD

WARM POTATO SALAD WITH
WHITE WINE DRESSING

NEW POTATO AND GARLIC SALAD

MUSHROOM SALAD WITH
GREEN PEPPERCORNS

CONFETTI SALAD

CUCUMBER AND FETA SALAD

CUCUMBER WITH SULTANAS
AND YOGHURT

WHITE BEAN AND TOMATO SALAD

GINGERED PEPPERS AND
SNOW PEAS

❖

SUMMER CORN SALAD

Serves 8

In the height of summer when corn, tomatoes, basil and avocados are at their peak, why not combine them and make this unusual salad.

3–4 fresh corn cobs, or 2 x 420 g tins whole kernel corn, drained
6 medium tomatoes, skinned
1 small red onion, sliced into rings (optional)
1½ tablespoons white wine vinegar
2 tablespoons finely chopped basil
¼ teaspoon salt
plenty of freshly ground black pepper
75 ml olive oil
1–2 ripe but firm avocados

If you are using fresh corn, cook the cobs in unsalted water for about 12 minutes, or until tender. Drain and leave until cool enough to handle. Use a sharp knife to slice the kernels from the cobs.

Halve the tomatoes, cut out the cores and cut into wedges. Transfer them to a large bowl and add the corn and red onion if used. Toss well.

In a small bowl blend the white wine vinegar, basil, salt and black pepper. Whisk in the olive oil. Pour this over the salad and toss again. Cover and chill for 2–3 hours.

Peel the avocados, extract the stones and cut the flesh into large cubes or slices. Add to the salad, toss very gently and serve immediately.

QUICK CHICK-PEA AND CORIANDER SALAD

Serves 6

This simple-to-make salad has a particularly summery feel about it, especially if a yellow pepper rather than a red one is used. Although it can be eaten as soon as it is made, a 'rest' of 24 hours in the refrigerator won't do any harm.

50 ml olive oil
1½ tablespoons lemon juice
rounded ¼ teaspoon salt
freshly ground black pepper to taste
1 large clove garlic, crushed
2 x 300 g tins chick-peas, drained, rinsed and drained well (or use 2 cups cooked, drained chick-peas)
1 yellow or red pepper, cored, deseeded and sliced thinly into short lengths
2 tablespoons finely chopped fresh coriander

Whisk the olive oil, lemon juice, salt, black pepper and garlic together in a bowl. Add the chick-peas, sliced pepper and coriander. Toss well and serve.

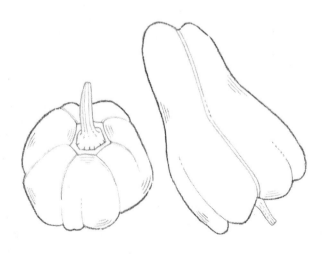

HOT POTATO SALAD WITH PIMENTO-STUFFED OLIVES

Serves 6

Although the name of this recipe indicates it is served hot, this salad is equally good served at room temperature.

1 kg small new potatoes, scrubbed
salt
6 rashers bacon, finely chopped
1 tablespoon olive oil
freshly ground black pepper to taste
1 teaspoon finely chopped marjoram (or use ½ teaspoon dried marjoram)
1 cup pimento-stuffed olives, rinsed and drained

Position the potatoes in a metal colander or steaming basket over a saucepan of boiling water. (The colander or basket should nearly fit inside the pot.) Sprinkle over a little salt, and cover tightly with a lid (or double thickness of tinfoil). Steam over vigorously boiling water until the potatoes are nearly tender.

Meanwhile, cook the bacon in a heated, lightly oiled frypan set over medium heat. Cook until crisp, then transfer to a piece of kitchen paper to drain, leaving any fat in the pan. Take the pan off the heat, transfer the bacon to a board, and set the pan aside. When the bacon has cooled, chop it coarsely.

Remove the colander or basket from the saucepan and turn the potatoes onto a chopping board. Chop roughly.

Reheat the pan with the bacon fat, add the olive oil, and when hot, tip in the potatoes. Add ½ teaspoon salt, black pepper and the marjoram. Fry for about 5 minutes, or until piping hot. Spoon the olives through, then transfer the contents to a serving dish. Scatter the cooked bacon over and serve.

'GREEK' SALAD

Serves at least 6

A salad in Greece is not made to a formula; it consists of whatever is available at the time. The following version is fresh and summery and well suited to 'al fresco' eating.

1 small red onion
1 telegraph cucumber, cut into wedges (if the skin is tough or bitter
remove it)
3 large ripe tomatoes, cut into wedges
1 green pepper, cored and deseeded and cut into strips
½ cup Kalamata olives, drained
few pinches of salt
few pinches of dried oregano
freshly ground black pepper to taste
4 tablespoons olive oil, plus little extra for top of salad
1 tablespoon red wine vinegar
100 g feta cheese

Slice the red onion into thin rings, then soak them in a bowl of cold water for about an hour. Drain and pat dry. Put the cucumber, tomatoes, green pepper and olives into a large salad bowl, and scatter over the onion rings. Sprinkle over a little salt and oregano, then grind on some black pepper to taste. Pour on the olive oil and red wine vinegar, then toss well together. Top with the slab of feta, sprinkle with a little oregano and drizzle over a little more oil. Serve immediately.

PINEAPPLE AND PEPPER SALAD

Serves 6–8

Juicy, tangy, but sweet, describes this colourful salad. It's particularly good with spicy or fiery hot foods. And you won't be struck off the 'good cooks' register if you use tinned pineapple in place of fresh.

1 fresh pineapple
3 red peppers, cored, deseeded and cut into thinnish strips
1 green pepper, prepared as the red peppers
1 large clove garlic, crushed
¼ teaspoon salt
freshly ground black pepper to taste
¼ cup white wine vinegar
½ cup salad oil

Split the pineapple in half and use a curved grapefruit knife to lever out the flesh. Cut the centre core away and discard, then chop the remaining flesh into bite-size pieces. Place in a bowl with any juice.

Add the prepared red and green peppers to the pineapple.

Put the garlic, salt, black pepper and white wine vinegar in a bowl and whisk in the salad oil. Pour it over the pineapple and peppers. Toss well, cover with a lid and chill for at least an hour before serving.

POTATO AND BASIL SALAD

Serves 6

When basil is plentiful, buy a bag of 'waxy' salad potatoes (new ones, not old starchy potatoes) and combine the two. Served warm, this salad is lip-smacking good, particularly with tomato-olive-zucchini combinations.

900 g 'waxy' new potatoes (choose even-sized ones)
salt
4 tablespoons extra virgin olive oil
1 teaspoon white wine vinegar
dab of Dijon-style mustard
2 tablespoons finely chopped basil

Scrub the potatoes, then position them in a metal colander or steaming basket over a saucepan of boiling water (the colander or steaming basket should nearly fit inside the pan). Sprinkle generously with salt and cover tightly with a lid or double thickness of tinfoil. Steam over vigorously boiling water until tender. Allow 12–15 minutes for small potatoes, but up to 30 minutes for large ones. Test by inserting a flat-bladed knife into a potato; it should pass through with just a hint of resistance.

Lift the colander or steaming basket off the saucepan, and peel the potatoes as soon as they are cool enough to handle. Slice into rounds and arrange in a large, shallow serving dish.

In a bowl blend the extra virgin olive oil, white wine vinegar, mustard and basil together with a generous ½ teaspoon salt. Drizzle this over the salad. Toss very gently and serve warm.

WARM POTATO SALAD WITH WHITE WINE DRESSING

....

Serves 6

This is an interesting variation on the preceding recipe.

1 kg small new potatoes, scrubbed
salt
3 tablespoons olive oil or peanut oil
1 large clove garlic, crushed
¼ teaspoon Dijon-style mustard
plenty of freshly ground black pepper
3 tablespoons dry white wine
1 small red onion, finely sliced into rings

Sit the potatoes in a steaming basket or metal colander and set it over a saucepan of boiling water. Sprinkle with salt, cover with a lid or tinfoil, set over a medium-high heat and steam for 20–30 minutes, or until tender. Lift off the lid and remove the steaming basket from the saucepan.

In a large bowl mix the olive or peanut oil, garlic, mustard, ½ teaspoon salt and some black pepper together. Pour in the dry white wine and blend well.

Cut the potatoes in halves or quarters and add to the dressing while they are still hot. Scatter the onion over them and toss well together. Keep at room temperature, tossing often, until ready to serve. The salad is at its best while still warm.

NEW POTATO AND GARLIC SALAD

Serves 6

Like the preceding two recipes, this delicious salad makes the most of 'waxy' salad potatoes, this time using capers.

900 g 'waxy' new potatoes
salt
¼ cup extra virgin olive oil
freshly ground black pepper to taste
1 teaspoon wine vinegar
dab of French mustard
2 tablespoons finely chopped basil (or flat-leaf parsley)
1 tablespoon capers, drained (chop if large)
2 cloves garlic, very finely chopped

Position the potatoes in a metal colander or steaming basket over a saucepan of boiling water (the colander or steaming basket should nearly fit inside the pot). Sprinkle over a little salt, then cover tightly with a lid or tinfoil. Steam until tender over vigorously boiling water, allowing 12–15 minutes for small, freshly dug potatoes, but up to 30 minutes for large ones. Test by inserting a flat-bladed knife into a potato; it should pass through with just a little resistance. When just tender, lift the colander or steaming basket off the pan and peel the potatoes as soon as they are cool enough to handle. Slice into rounds or cut into cubes, and arrange in a shallow dish.

Make the dressing by whisking the extra virgin olive oil, ½ teaspoon salt, black pepper, wine vinegar and mustard together. Add the basil, capers and garlic and whisk well. Spoon the dressing over the salad, and serve it warmish.

MUSHROOM SALAD WITH GREEN PEPPERCORNS

....

Serves 6–8

Full of fresh herbs and green peppercorns, this recipe makes an ideal summer salad.

500 g very fresh white button mushrooms, wiped with a damp cloth
grated rind of 1 lemon
75 ml lemon juice
75 ml extra virgin olive oil
1 teaspoon salt
plenty of freshly ground black pepper
1 rounded teaspoon drained green peppercorns
1 tablespoon coarsely chopped parsley
1 tablespoon finely chopped fresh thyme
1 tablespoon finely chopped fresh marjoram, or 1 tablespoon snipped
  chives

Trim the stalks of the mushrooms if necessary, then slice them thinly. Place in a bowl.

Whisk the lemon rind, lemon juice, extra virgin olive oil, salt and black pepper together in a bowl. Blend in the green peppercorns and herbs, then pour the dressing over the mushrooms. Toss well, and leave to marinate for 1–2 hours, tossing occasionally. Before serving, toss well and transfer to a serving bowl.

Although the salad is at its best while the mushrooms are still a little bit crunchy, it can be made up to 24 hours in advance. Cover and keep it chilled, and serve cold.

White Mushrooms

If you want an attractive white mushroom salad, one with clear juices, not browny black, use lemon juice in the dressing instead of vinegar; lemon juice has the effect of keeping everything clean, clear and white.

'Salt to Taste'

The amount of salt required in an oil-based dressing is often not stated. The recipe will probably read 'salt to taste' and that's because it depends on the type and quality of oil used.

The heavier oils, like olive oil, peanut oil and walnut oil, require more salt than light oils, such as safflower oil and canola oil. Oils also differ from brand to brand.

Get Rid of the Oil Slick

Although an oil-based dressing may 'taste' of the oil used (for example, olivey or fruity if made from olive oil, or nutty if made from a nut oil) it should never actually taste 'oily' or greasy.

Salt, with its slight abrasiveness, has the effect of cutting through the oil texture in a dressing (as well as flavouring the food, of course). To illustrate this, smear a little oil on your palms, then rub them together. They will feel smooth and slippery. Now sprinkle on a little salt and rub them together again. You'll notice the salt's abrasiveness and how it gets rid of the slippery feeling. Imagine this on your palate.

Add salt to the dressing by degrees, say 2–3 pinches. Whisk it in, let it settle a few minutes, then whisk again. Dip a small teaspoon into the dressing (or your finger) and taste. It should be smooth, but it shouldn't leave your mouth coated in oil. If you have over-salted the dressing, dilute with more oil and readjust the acid content.

CONFETTI SALAD

Serves 6

A pretty salad dotted with yellow and red cherry tomatoes. Try it after a main course dish of pasta.

1 'ball' radicchio (or use red lettuce), trimmed
1 buttercrunch lettuce
2 tablespoons finely chopped basil
2 tablespoons snipped chives
1 cup yellow or red cherry tomatoes, sliced in half
4 tablespoons extra virgin olive oil
1 teaspoon red wine vinegar
½ teaspoon salt
freshly ground black pepper to taste
½–1 teaspoon Dijon-style mustard
1 clove garlic, crushed

Wash and dry the radicchio (or red lettuce) and buttercrunch lettuce. Tear into bite-size pieces, then put them in a salad bowl. Cover with plastic wrap and refrigerate for 1–2 hours. Then remove the salad from the fridge and scatter over the herbs and cherry tomatoes.

Blend the extra virgin olive oil, red wine vinegar, salt, black pepper, mustard and garlic and pour over the salad. Toss well and serve immediately.

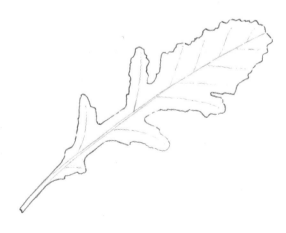

CUCUMBER AND FETA SALAD

Serves 6

This is a good warm-weather salad to serve with Greekish or
Middle Eastern dishes. Serve it well chilled.

1 large telegraph cucumber
¼ cup black olives, drained
2 tablespoons lemon juice
1 tablespoon finely chopped marjoram or oregano (or half quantity
*   of either dried herb)*
few pinches of salt
freshly ground black pepper to taste
3 tablespoons extra virgin olive oil
100 g feta cheese

Cut the cucumber in half lengthwise, then into thin half-circles.
Put it in a bowl with the black olives.

Put the lemon juice, chosen herb, salt and black pepper in a
bowl and whisk in the extra virgin olive oil.

Pour the dressing over the cucumber, toss well, then cover and
chill until serving time. Before serving, toss well and top with
the crumbled feta cheese.

Toasting Cumin Seeds

Toasting cumin seeds develops their wonderfully nutty spiciness.
Place them in a dry frypan and keep them over a medium heat
until lightly coloured and fragrant. Shake the pan occasionally.

Cool the seeds and grind to a powder in a small grinder. When
cool, store airtight until required. The ground spice should stay
fresh for several weeks.

CUCUMBER WITH SULTANAS AND YOGHURT

Serves 6–8

Chilled cucumber and yoghurt make a refreshing sambal (side-dish) to serve with spicy dishes. This one has sweet sultanas and cumin included.

1¾ cups (about 500 g) natural unsweetened yoghurt
½ cup plump sultanas
1 tablespoon finely chopped mint
½ teaspoon ground cumin
½ teaspoon salt
1 telegraph cucumber, sliced thinly

Line a small sieve with a piece of kitchen paper and rest it over a bowl. Pour in the yoghurt and leave it to drain for an hour. Carefully turn the yoghurt into a large bowl and blend in the sultanas, mint, cumin and salt. Fold in the cucumber. Cover and chill well before serving.

'Eat as They Grow'

Something which is essential to my happiness, is being able, at any time, to pick a salad from the garden. Contrary to how it might sound, it doesn't require a great deal of gardening.

I grow salad greens like cos lettuce, buttercrunch lettuce, rocket, curly endive and red-leaf lettuces, all of which can be picked as they grow. This not only encourages them to grow more sturdy and to produce more leaves, but stops them going to seed early (plenty of water also helps). The plants will last for several months in cooler weather.

Always pick the leaves from the outside, removing any damaged or browning ones to prevent rotting, and try to pick them when the sun is not shining on them, to minimise wilting. Wash and dry immediately, then crisp briefly, if necessary, in an untied plastic bag in the refrigerator.

WHITE BEAN AND TOMATO SALAD

Serves 8

This tasty, garlicky salad tastes even better the day after making. Serve it as part of a Mediterranean meal, or with pita pockets and a spinach salad for a tasty, light meal.

400 g dried baby lima beans, or small haricot beans (or 4 cups cooked or tinned beans, drained), rinsed then soaked for several hours in water
2 large tomatoes, skinned
½ cup olive oil
2 tablespoons red wine vinegar
generous teaspoon salt
plenty of freshly ground black pepper
1 large clove garlic, crushed
3 tablespoons chopped parsley (preferably flat-leafed parsley)
1 cup black olives, drained
1 red onion, very finely sliced

Transfer the beans to a large saucepan, pour in enough water to cover them generously, then put on the lid. Bring to the boil, skim off any 'scum', then transfer to an oven preheated to 170°C. Cook for about 30 minutes or until the beans are barely tender (be careful not to overcook as they quickly become mushy), stirring occasionally, and topping up with water if necessary.

Meanwhile, cut the tomatoes in half and flick out the seeds. Dice the flesh and set aside. Mix the olive oil, red wine vinegar, salt, black pepper, garlic, parsley, black olives, onion and tomatoes in a large bowl.

When the beans are ready, rinse with a little warm water and leave them to drain. Add them to the salad, mix well with a big spoon and leave to cool. Toss before serving.

GINGERED PEPPERS AND SNOW PEAS

Serves 4

Colourful, crisp and fresh-tasting, this salad is excellent with rich, creamy or mayonnaisy dishes, or with smoked fish.

1 large red pepper
1 large green pepper
1 large yellow pepper
salt
12 snow peas, topped and tailed
2 tablespoons salad oil
dash of sesame oil (optional)
knob of fresh ginger, coarsely grated then squeezed to extract juice
    (use the juice only)
1 tablespoon fresh lime juice
freshly ground black pepper

Prepare the peppers by halving them, removing the cores and seeds and cutting them into fine slivers. Bring a saucepan of water to the boil and add a few pinches of salt. Blanch the peppers, one colour at a time, by dropping them into boiling water and cooking for 1 minute only (don't cover the pan). Lift the peppers out of the water with a slotted spoon, place in a colander and run the cold tap over them until they feel cool. Shake them dry and drain on kitchen paper.

Do the same with the snow peas, but blanch them for 45 seconds only. The vegetables can be prepared 1–2 hours ahead; spread them on a tray lined with kitchen paper and drape with more kitchen paper.

In a small bowl mix the salad oil, sesame oil if used, ginger juice, lime juice, salt and black pepper to taste.

At serving time arrange the peppers, in their separate colours, on a large serving plate. Put the snow peas in the centre, then drizzle the dressing over everything and serve.

Fruity Salads

Fruit with vegetables, particularly in salads, offers a tangy or sweet taste, as well as introducing juiciness and splashes of colour.

❖

CABBAGE FRUIT SALAD

BABY BEETROOT SALAD

RADICCHIO AND ORANGE SALAD

WATERCRESS, SPINACH AND
GRAPEFRUIT SALAD

WINTER FRUIT SALAD

WITLOOF AND ORANGE SALAD
WITH CHIVES

PINEAPPLE AND CABBAGE SALAD

TANGY FRUIT SALAD

❖

CABBAGE FRUIT SALAD

....

Serves 4–6

Pinenuts, grapes and a creamy mint dressing turn cabbage into something very toothsome.

¼ cup pinenuts
½ small white cabbage
4 sticks celery, finely sliced
¼ cup sultanas (or raisins)
bunch of grapes (should yield about 1 cup once taken off the stalk), halved if large
3 red-skinned apples, washed (leave skin on unless tough)
1 tablespoon finely chopped parsley

Dressing
6 tablespoons peanut oil
2 tablespoons lemon juice
½ teaspoon salt
freshly ground black pepper to taste
3 tablespoons liquid cream
1 tablespoon finely chopped mint (optional)

Put the pinenuts in an ovenproof dish and toast them in an oven preheated to 180°C for about 7 minutes, or until a pale golden-brown. Allow to cool.

Remove the core and any tough leaves from the cabbage. Wash well, shake dry, then shred it finely. Place in a large bowl and add the celery, sultanas, grapes (pipped if preferred) and pinenuts.

Mix the peanut oil, lemon juice, salt and black pepper together, then beat in the cream and mint. Toss the dressing through the salad. Slice the apples and mix them in. Sprinkle over the parsley and serve immediately.

BABY BEETROOT SALAD

Serves 8

Now here's a good winter salad with plenty of taste and style. At a pinch it can be made with tinned whole beetroot, but as they contain a preserving acid, cut back the lime juice to 2 tablespoons. Marinating the beetroot in the lime dressing overnight cuts the sweetness and develops a good flavour, but the salad can be served as soon as it is assembled if need be.

10 small beetroot
3 tablespoons lime juice
4 tablespoons olive oil or peanut oil
¼ teaspoon salt
freshly ground black pepper to taste
6–8 smallish oranges
few pinches of finely chopped parsley

Trim excess stalks from the beetroot tops, but be sure not to nick the skin as the beetroot will bleed during cooking (likewise do not trim the tapering root). Wash them carefully, then put them in a large saucepan, cover with cold water, put on a lid and bring to the boil. Lower the heat and cook gently, partially covered, for about 1½ hours or until the beetroot are tender (top up the water from time to time if necessary).

Pour off the hot water, then let the cold tap run over the beetroot for a few minutes. Slip off the skins, stalks and roots. Drain on a plate, then slice them into rounds and place in a shallow dish.

Whisk the lime juice, olive or peanut oil, salt and black pepper together and pour over the beetroot. When cool, cover and refrigerate for up to 24 hours.

Prior to serving, slice off the peel and pith from the oranges using a small serrated knife and an exaggerated sawing movement. Slice the oranges into rounds, place them in a bowl, with any juice, and cover and refrigerate until required.

Arrange alternate slices of orange and beetroot in a shallow serving dish. Blend any orange juice with the lime marinade, then pour it over the salad. Sprinkle with parsley and serve.

RADICCHIO AND ORANGE SALAD

Serves 4

Here's a luscious winter salad, full of colour and flavour.

1 curly red lettuce
1–2 'balls' radicchio
2 juicy oranges
3 tablespoons orange juice
2 tablespoons extra virgin olive oil (the fruitier the better)
few good pinches of salt
good grinding of black pepper

Wash and dry the red lettuce and radicchio, then tear them into bite-size pieces and place in a plastic bag. Refrigerate for a few hours.

Prepare the oranges as described in 'Filleting Citrus Fruits', page 257. Squeeze the juice from the membranes and place 3 tablespoons of it in a small bowl. Whisk in the extra virgin olive oil, salt and black pepper.

At serving time put the radicchio and red lettuce into a salad bowl with the orange segments. Reblend the dressing, pour over the salad, toss together, then serve.

Why Waste the Leaves?

If you grow your own beetroot, don't waste the leaves. The young, tender leaves make delicious eating as a salad item, possessing a nutty, mildly pungent flavour and spectacular colourings.

Wash them well, dry and chop coarsely, discarding any tough stems, and add them to salads along with sprouts and nuts, for a health-packed salad.

The leaves can also be cooked. Blanch them briefly in lightly salted water, drain well and return to a cleaned pan with a small knob of butter. Reheat, tossing and serve hot.

WATERCRESS, SPINACH AND GRAPEFRUIT SALAD

Serves 4

This unusual combination is juicy and fresh and mildly peppery. It makes a perfect finish to a meal of game birds, such as quail or duck (it's delicious following a crispy-skinned honey-glazed duck for example), or as an accompaniment to smoked fish. It is also good after rich or fried foods.

1 large bunch spinach
1 large bunch watercress, washed and shaken dry
2 large grapefruit (use for the juice and rind as well)
1 tablespoon grapefruit juice
½ teaspoon finely grated grapefruit rind
1 tablespoon finely grated fresh ginger
scant ¼ teaspoon salt
pinch of castor sugar
freshly ground black pepper to taste
dab of Dijon-style mustard
2 tablespoons olive oil or peanut oil

Trim the stalks off the spinach, wash the leaves well, then dry them. Tear into bite-size pieces and place in a bowl. Slide watercress leaves off their stalks, dry in a cloth or salad spinner and mix with the spinach.

First grate a little rind off one of the grapefruit and set the rind aside. Peel the grapefruit with a serrated knife, removing all the white pith with the peel. Working over a sieve set over a bowl, hold the whole, peeled grapefruit in one hand, and make a cut on either side of each segment to free it from the 'membrane'. Let the segments drop into the sieve. Squeeze all the juice from the membrane into the bowl, then leave the segments to drain. Reserve 1 tablespoon of the juice for the dressing (and drink the rest!).

Mix the grapefruit juice and rind, grated ginger, salt, castor sugar, black pepper, mustard and olive or peanut oil together in a small bowl.

Scatter the grapefruit segments through the salad, then pour on the blended dressing. Toss gently and serve.

WINTER FRUIT SALAD

Serves 6

Oranges and grapes give this radicchio salad a welcome juiciness which contrasts nicely with the salty macadamia nut topping. Serve after a rich main course.

150 g green grapes, preferably seedless
150 g black grapes, preferably seedless
2 juicy oranges or tangelos
3 'balls' radicchio, trimmed (or use 6 heads witloof)
4 tablespoons olive oil or walnut oil
½ teaspoon salt
freshly ground black pepper to taste
1 large clove garlic, crushed (optional)
50 g salted macadamia nuts, coarsely chopped

Wash and dry the grapes and cut them in half (flick out any seeds). Prepare the oranges or tangelos as described in 'Filleting Citrus Fruits', page 257. Squeeze all the juice from the membrane into a bowl. Put the grapes in a salad bowl with the orange segments. Break the radicchio balls apart, wash and dry the leaves and add to the salad bowl. (If using witloof, trim the base, gouge out the core with a knife, then cut in half and break apart the leaves. Tear into bite-size pieces and add these to the oranges and grapes.)

Blend the olive or walnut oil into the reserved orange juice along with the salt, black pepper and garlic if used. Pour the dressing over the salad, toss well and sprinkle the macadamia nuts over. Serve immediately.

Something Extra with Watercress, Spinach and Grapefruit Salad

A tasty starter can be made with the watercress salad. Make a double quantity of the dressing and toss half of it with the salad. Arrange the salad on 4–6 plates, then top with small fillets or flakes of smoked fish. Anoint the fish with the remaining dressing and serve immediately with thinly sliced, buttered, grainy bread.

WITLOOF AND ORANGE SALAD WITH CHIVES

Serves 4–6

Another excellent winter salad that is as good to eat as it is to look at. Serve whenever something crisp and juicy is required, or as a palate cleanser after a main course.

2 large juicy oranges
6 firm witloof
1 tablespoon snipped chives
3 tablespoons olive oil
1 tablespoon white wine vinegar (or tarragon vinegar)
¼ teaspoon salt
freshly ground black pepper to taste

Prepare the oranges as described in 'Filleting Citrus Fruits', page 257. Squeeze all the juice from the membrane into the bowl.

Trim the ends of the witloof, then gouge out the core and remove any damaged leaves. Slice into chunks, separating the leaves. Place in the bowl with the oranges and scatter the chives over. The salad can be prepared an hour or so ahead to this point.

In a bowl mix the olive oil, white wine vinegar, salt and black pepper, then pour it over the salad. Toss well and serve.

PINEAPPLE AND CABBAGE SALAD

Serves 6–8

This easy-to-make, crunchy, juicy salad is good with spicy foods or in tacos.

½ small cabbage (or ¼ large cabbage)
440 g tin pineapple pieces, drained (choose an unsweetened brand)
½ cup soft raisins, soaked 30 minutes in a little pineapple juice
3 tablespoons mayonnaise (a commercial brand will do)
2 tablespoons sour cream
few pinches of salt
freshly ground black pepper to taste

Prepare the cabbage by chopping out any core, then slicing it very finely. Place it in a large bowl with the drained pineapple and drained raisins.

In a small bowl blend the mayonnaise, sour cream, salt and black pepper. Pour over the salad, toss very well and serve.

TANGY FRUIT SALAD

Serves 6

This is an interesting little salad, sweet and succulent, which teams up well with rich pastry and cheese dishes.

3 tablespoons walnut oil (or olive oil)
1 teaspoon lemon juice
¼ teaspoon salt
freshly ground black pepper to taste
pinch of castor sugar
small bunch seedless black grapes
2 juicy oranges or tangelos, peeled and segmented
1 buttercrunch lettuce, torn into bite-size pieces
1 tablespoon snipped chives

Mix the walnut oil, lemon juice, salt, black pepper and castor sugar in a salad bowl. Add the grapes (halved if large), orange segments and juice (do not use more than 2 tablespoons juice), lettuce leaves and chives. Toss and serve immediately.

Filleting Citrus Fruits

Filleting means to remove and discard membranes in between each segment of fruit. Carefully remove the peel with a serrated knife, using a gentle sawing movement, removing all the pith with the peel. Then make a cut on both sides of each piece of membrane and the segments will come away easily. Don't waste the juice in the membrane. Squeeze it into a glass and drink it if you don't need it in the recipe. After peeling, the fruit may be cut into slim rounds, instead of segments, if preferred.

Winter Salads

There's no rule that says salads should be confined to the warmer months. Winter, with its own assortment of vegetables, is as good a time as any to indulge in a salad; quick and light to accompany other foods, or substantial salads based on rice or starch vegetables.

NUTTY-TOPPED
RED CABBAGE SALAD

DIGBY'S KUMARA SALAD

RADICCHIO SALAD WITH CAPER
AND PARMESAN DRESSING

CAULIFLOWER AND
BROCCOLI SALAD

BOK CHOY SALAD

BLACK-EYED BEANS
WITH SPINACH

LETTUCE AND ORANGE SALAD
WITH TOASTED ALMONDS

CITRUS KUMARA SALAD

RICE SALAD

WHITE RADISH SALAD

NUTTY-TOPPED RED CABBAGE SALAD

Serves 4–6

Finely slivered red cabbage tossed with a flavoursome dressing makes an excellent winter salad.

½ large red cabbage (or a whole small one)
¼ cup finely chopped walnuts (make sure they are fresh and not rancid)
1 tablespoon coarsely chopped parsley

Dressing
¼ teaspoon salt
plenty of freshly ground black pepper
1 large clove garlic, crushed
¼ teaspoon castor sugar
½ teaspoon Dijon-style mustard
1½ tablespoons red wine vinegar
½ cup olive oil

Tear off any coarse leaves from the cabbage and chop out the core. Rinse well under running water and shake dry. Slice the cabbage very thinly and place it in a bowl. (If you want to prepare the cabbage in advance, put it in a plastic bag, exclude the air, tie it up and refrigerate until required.)

Put all the dressing ingredients, except the oil, in a bowl and blend together. Whisk in the olive oil. Pour over the salad and toss well. Cover and refrigerate the salad for an hour.

Before serving, toss again, transfer to a serving bowl and sprinkle over the nuts and parsley.

DIGBY'S KUMARA SALAD

Serves 6

I often warned my late, great mate, Digby Law, that one day I'd filch his kumara salad recipe. True to my word, here it is (in an altered version, of course).

700 g kumara, peeled and cut into chunks
salt
125 g streaky bacon
2 oranges
2 tablespoons raisins
freshly ground black pepper to taste
¼ cup mayonnaise

Position the pieces of kumara in a metal colander or steaming basket over a saucepan of boiling water. Sprinkle over a little salt, cover with a lid or tinfoil and steam for 12–15 minutes, or until just tender. Remove the colander or steaming basket from the saucepan and allow the kumara to cool. Cut into large cubes.

Place the bacon in a large, heated frypan. Cook over a low-medium heat until the fat runs, then increase the heat slightly and cook to a crisp. Tilt the pan and transfer the bacon rashers to a board and chop coarsely. Set aside.

Prepare the oranges as described in 'Filleting Citrus Fruits', page 257. Squeeze all the juice from the membrane into the bowl, then add the kumara and raisins. Sprinkle on a few pinches of salt and grind over some black pepper. Toss well, then stir in the mayonnaise. Transfer to a serving bowl and scatter over the bacon.

The salad keeps well, covered and refrigerated, for 1–2 days. The addition of one or two sticks of finely sliced celery provides a bit more crunch.

RADICCHIO SALAD WITH CAPER AND PARMESAN DRESSING

Serves 4–6

If I had to choose my 'last supper' this dish would certainly be part of it, served as a separate salad course. Magic is created when the garlicky Parmesan dressing hits the slightly bitter radicchio leaves. A drop or two of frisky Chianti merely accentuates the superb flavours.

1 teaspoon white wine vinegar
1 tablespoon capers, drained
1 clove garlic, crushed
1 tablespoon coarsely chopped parsley
½ cup olive oil
½ cup freshly grated Parmesan cheese
3–6 'balls' radicchio (use 3 large ones or 6 small ones)

Blend the white wine vinegar, capers, garlic and parsley together in a food processor fitted with the chopping blade. While the machine is running, dribble in the olive oil, then stop the machine, scatter the Parmesan cheese over and process briefly until blended.

The dressing can be prepared several hours ahead to this point; store it covered at room temperature.

If a food processor is not available, blend all the ingredients, except the olive oil, in a bowl with a fork. Slowly mix in the oil.

Wash and dry the radicchio, then tear it into bite-size pieces and place in a salad bowl. Pour over the dressing, toss very well, then serve.

Although this salad is at its best when freshly dressed, leftovers are always devoured enthusiastically in our household.

CAULIFLOWER AND BROCCOLI SALAD

Serves 6

This is a good winter salad to make when cauliflower and broccoli are plentiful, of good quality and inexpensive.

½ cauliflower
300 g broccoli
salt
½ cup homemade mayonnaise
1 tablespoon capers, drained and chopped
freshly ground black pepper to taste

Trim then cut the cauliflower and broccoli into small florets. Plunge the cauliflower into a saucepan of lightly salted, boiling water. Quickly bring it back to the boil, then drain the cauliflower and refresh with plenty of cold water. Leave to drain. Repeat the process with the broccoli. When well drained, dry off the cauliflower and broccoli florets on kitchen paper.

Turn the mayonnaise into a large bowl. If necessary, add a few drops of hot water to thin it down to a light coating consistency. Mix in the capers, ¼ teaspoon salt and a little black pepper. Add the cauliflower and broccoli and gently mix together. Transfer to a salad bowl or shallow dish and serve.

BOK CHOY SALAD

Serves 6

This is a light, refreshing 'green' that gives welcome relief from the rich sweetness of many Chinese dishes.

1–2 bunches bok choy (Chinese cabbage)
salt
sesame oil
soy sauce
sesame seeds

Prepare the cabbage by trimming off the root and shaving off most of the greenery (it is usually tough and bitter). Wash well. Plunge it into a saucepan of lightly salted boiling water and cook uncovered for 3 minutes. Drain and refresh with plenty of cold water. Shake and dry off on kitchen paper.

Slice the cabbage into chunks and place in a dish. Sprinkle over a little sesame oil and soy sauce, toss well, then sprinkle with sesame seeds and serve.

BLACK-EYED BEANS WITH SPINACH
....

Serves 6–8

Traditionally, silver beet is used in this Greek dish of black-eyed beans, but I prefer the lighter colour and more delicate flavour of spinach. Served with dishes made with tomatoes, feta cheese and eggplants, it makes a wonderful rustic lunch. Accompany it with pita pockets.

250 g dried black-eyed beans
300–400 g spinach, washed and finely chopped
½ cup olive oil
juice of 1 lemon
2 cloves garlic, crushed
1 teaspoon salt
freshly ground black pepper to taste

Pick over the beans, discarding any stones or damaged beans. Put them in a sieve and wash well under running water. Tip into a saucepan and pour on 1.25 litres of hot water. Leave to soak for 2 hours.

Bring the beans to a gentle boil, then immediately turn the heat down to a simmer. Cook for about an hour, partially covered, or until just tender. Add the spinach and cook for 5 minutes more, stirring occasionally. Drain well and transfer to a large bowl.

Mix the olive oil, lemon juice, garlic and salt in a small bowl. Add black pepper to taste. Pour over the beans, toss well, then leave to cool. Toss again before serving.

These beans improve after a day's rest; store them covered and refrigerated, but bring them to room temperature before serving.

LETTUCE AND ORANGE SALAD WITH TOASTED ALMONDS

Serves 4–6

This nutty, refreshing salad makes an excellent accompaniment to roasted chicken. Although I usually make it with blanched almonds, as they are easier to toast, toasted, unskinned almonds have a stronger almond flavour.

¾ cup blanched, or unblanched, almonds
1 small clove garlic, peeled
2 juicy oranges
1 buttercrunch lettuce, washed and dried
¼ teaspoon castor sugar
freshly ground black pepper to taste
salt
knob of butter
2 teaspoons lemon juice

Toast the almonds on a flat plate in an oven preheated to 180°C for 7–10 minutes, or until a light nut-brown. Cool, then store airtight until required.

Cut the garlic clove in half and rub both pieces around the inside of the salad bowl. Reserve the garlic.

Peel the oranges with a serrated knife, removing all the white pith with the peel. Cut the oranges into rounds and place them in the salad bowl. Tear the lettuce leaves into bite-size pieces and sit them on top of the orange slices. Sprinkle the castor sugar over the lettuce, grind over a little black pepper and sprinkle over a few pinches of salt. Scatter over the almonds.

Gently heat the butter in a small frypan with the pieces of garlic until the butter has melted and is warm (don't allow it to sizzle). Pour in the lemon juice, remove the garlic with a slotted spoon and pour the butter and lemon juice over the salad. Toss well and serve immediately.

CITRUS KUMARA SALAD

Serves 8

This is a delicious salad which brings a touch of summer into the winter months. It makes a perfect partner for fresh ham off the bone or smoked chicken.

1.5 kg kumara
salt
1 teaspoon grated lime rind
1 teaspoon grated orange rind
¼ cup freshly squeezed lime juice
½ cup freshly squeezed orange juice
2 teaspoons Dijon-style mustard
plenty of freshly ground black pepper
¼ cup peanut oil

Peel the kumara and cut into large chunks. Put them into a saucepan, cover with cold water, add ½ teaspoon salt, put on the lid and bring to the boil. Cook gently until just tender, for about 15 minutes (take care not to overcook them). Drain in a colander and when cool enough to handle, cut into cubes.

Meanwhile, make the dressing. Put the lime and orange rinds in a bowl with the juices. Add the mustard, ½ teaspoon salt and the black pepper. Whisk in the peanut oil.

Transfer the kumara to a large bowl and while it is still warm, pour over the dressing. Toss well, then leave to marinate at room temperature until cool. Chill before serving.

The salad keeps well, covered and refrigerated, for 2–3 days.

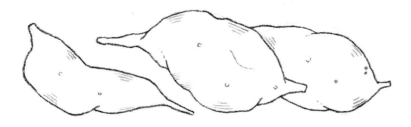

RICE SALAD

Serves 6–8

Gluggy or tasteless rice salads are unpalatable. But when the rice is cooked until just tender it is the perfect medium for a whole heap of flavourings. Although good as a summery lunch dish (providing cauliflower is still affordable; omit it if not), particularly with cold pork or chicken, this rice salad also makes excellent picnic fare.

250 g long-grain rice (use Basmati or jasmin rice for more flavour)
salt

Dressing
2 tablespoons white wine vinegar
½ cup olive oil
1 teaspoon salt
1 teaspoon freshly ground black pepper
1 teaspoon French-style mustard
2 tablespoons finely chopped parsley
1 tablespoon snipped chives

2 tablespoons raisins
6 dried apricots, chopped
1½ cups uncooked, stalkless cauliflower florets (cut very small)
1 large gherkin, sliced very thinly into rounds
6 pimento-stuffed olives, sliced into rounds
2 tablespoons pinenuts, toasted (optional)
a little grated nutmeg

Wash the rice in a sieve under running cold water until the water runs clear. Cook uncovered in a large saucepan of lightly salted boiling water until it is just cooked. Be careful not to overcook the rice, as it will quickly turn mushy. Tip it into a sieve and rinse under hot running water. Drain for several minutes, then shake off the excess water and tip the rice into a large bowl.

Whisk the dressing ingredients together and pour them over the hot rice. Carefully toss with a large fork or with your hands.

Place the raisins and apricots in a small bowl and cover with hot water. Leave to soak for 10 minutes, drain, then add to the salad.

Place the cauliflower florets in a pan of lightly salted, boiling water and leave for 30 seconds. Drain, rinse with cold water, shake dry and add to the salad. (This quick blanching makes the cauliflower more digestible, without destroying its crunch.)

Blend the salad together, adding the gherkin, olives, pinenuts, if using, and nutmeg. Leave to cool, then stir again before serving.

The salad will store quite happily for up to 2 days, covered and refrigerated.

WHITE RADISH SALAD

Serves 4–6

This salad works well with Asian foods.

2 large white radishes (about 500 g)
juice of ½ lemon
2 crisp apples
1½ tablespoons soy sauce
1 tablespoon salad oil
1 teaspoon sesame oil
3 tablespoons white wine vinegar
3 teaspoons sugar
¾ teaspoon salt
1 red chilli, deseeded and very finely chopped
2 tablespoons toasted sesame seeds

Peel the radishes and cut into julienne. Put them into a large bowl, cover with cold water and squeeze on the lemon juice. Peel the apples, cut into julienne and add to the radish.

In a small bowl whisk the soy sauce, salad oil, sesame oil, white wine vinegar, sugar, salt and chilli together.

Drain the radish and apple well, then return them to a dry bowl. Pour on the blended dressing and toss well. Cover and chill for 1–2 hours. Before serving, toss again, transfer to a serving bowl and sprinkle with sesame seeds.

Pepped-Up Salads

When I start getting bored with food I know it's because I've gone without chilli for too long — I suddenly crave a real chilli blast. If I haven't the time to do the 'works' (a full Indian blow-out) I'm more than happy to introduce a jot or two of chilli or spice into a salad to tide me over.

The following two carrot salads do the trick; they're definitely worth eating, but watch out for the Spinach Salad — you'll either love it or hate it. And if I say so myself, the two pumpkin salads are quite remarkable.

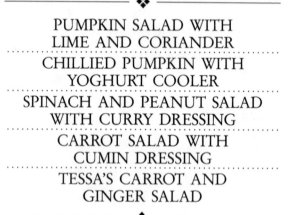

PUMPKIN SALAD WITH
LIME AND CORIANDER

CHILLIED PUMPKIN WITH
YOGHURT COOLER

SPINACH AND PEANUT SALAD
WITH CURRY DRESSING

CARROT SALAD WITH
CUMIN DRESSING

TESSA'S CARROT AND
GINGER SALAD

PUMPKIN SALAD WITH LIME AND CORIANDER

....

Serves 6

Pumpkin is a versatile vegetable, responding well to steaming, mashing, roasting and stuffing. But don't get caught up in convention. The sweet, delicately nutty flavour lends itself to sweet and sour treatments and pepped-up salads like the following intriguing blend. Try this as a sambal (side-dish) to accompany Indian food or spicy dishes.

½ large firm-fleshed pumpkin, cut into large chunks, deseeded and
   peeled
salt
1¼ cups plain unsweetened yoghurt
1 tablespoon sweet mango chutney (use the 'liquid' part only)
1 teaspoon fresh lime juice
1 red chilli, deseeded and very finely chopped
2 tablespoons coarsely chopped coriander leaves (substitute mint if
   coriander is not available)

Garnish (optional)
1 red chilli
few sprigs fresh coriander
twirl of lime rind

Position the pumpkin in a metal colander or steaming basket. Set it over a saucepan of boiling water (the colander or steaming basket should nearly fit the pan). Sprinkle lightly with salt, cover tightly with a lid or double thickness of tinfoil and steam it over vigorously boiling water until nearly tender. (Alternatively, boil gently until nearly tender.) Cool, then cut the pumpkin into large cubes. Pile it up in a dish.

In a bowl mix the yoghurt, chutney, lime juice, chilli, coriander and ¼ teaspoon salt together. Just prior to serving, pour the dressing over the pumpkin.

If you like, garnish with a whole red chilli, split in two, a little coriander and a twirl of lime rind.

CHILLIED PUMPKIN WITH YOGHURT COOLER

....

Serves 4

Spiced pumpkin with a cool, minty topping makes a good addition when a menu needs a little 'oomph'.

2 tablespoons oil
1 teaspoon ground cumin seeds
½ teaspoon chilli powder
1 teaspoon ground turmeric
2 cloves garlic, crushed
½ large grey pumpkin, peeled, deseeded and cut into cubes
½ cup water
½ teaspoon salt
freshly ground black pepper to taste
½ cup plain unsweetened yoghurt
1 tablespoon finely chopped mint

Heat the oil in a large frypan over gentle heat and add the spices and garlic. Cook gently for about 5 minutes, stirring often (take care not to let the mixture burn), then add the cubed pumpkin. Using a large spoon, gently toss the pumpkin cubes until they are well coated in the spice mixture, then pour in the water and add salt and black pepper. Cover with a lid and cook gently for 15–20 minutes, or until tender. Cool. (If there is a lot of liquid left, remove the lid for the last 5 minutes to evaporate it. If the pumpkin is tender, transfer it to a side-plate, then evaporate the liquid. When thickish, pour it over the pumpkin.)

Transfer to a serving dish and spoon over the previously mixed yoghurt and mint. Serve hot or at room temperature.

SPINACH AND PEANUT SALAD
WITH CURRY DRESSING

Serves 6

Spinach, peanut and apple salad, dressed with a mango chutney and curry dressing, might sound a bit of a mouthful ... but it works! Serve it as a separate salad course, after a barbecue, or team it up with a rice salad, or bean dish, as part of a vegetable meal.

450 g fresh spinach, trimmed (should yield about 200 g after
*   trimming)*
6 tablespoons peanut oil
3 tablespoons white wine vinegar
1 tablespoon finely minced mango chutney
½ teaspoon curry powder
½ teaspoon salt
2–3 tart apples
2 tablespoons lemon juice
3–4 spring onions, very finely sliced (optional)
½ cup dry roasted peanuts

Wash well and dry the spinach leaves, discard the stalks and tear the leaves into bite-size pieces. Place these in a large salad bowl, cover with plastic wrap and chill until required.

Put the peanut oil, white wine vinegar, mango chutney, curry powder and salt in a large bowl and set aside.

Just before serving time, peel the apples and grate them coarsely. Toss in a bowl with the lemon juice, then mix them into the spinach with the spring onions and peanuts.

Whisk the dressing, then pour it over the salad. Toss together (easiest done with the hands) and serve.

CARROT SALAD WITH CUMIN DRESSING

Serves 4

Carrots enlivened with cumin, paprika and garlic sounds good, doesn't it? And it is! Serve it as an accompaniment to pork dishes or meatballs, or with Middle Eastern fare.

350 g carrots, peeled and cut into short lengths, then into quarters
½ cup chicken or vegetable stock
salt
1 tablespoon olive oil
2 tablespoons white wine vinegar
1 large clove garlic, crushed
¼ teaspoon paprika
¼ teaspoon ground cumin

Put the carrots in a saucepan with the stock and cover with cold water. Add a few pinches of salt, then bring to the boil. Turn the heat to low and cook very gently for 10 minutes. Drain, then slice.

In a bowl whisk the olive oil, white wine vinegar, garlic, paprika and ground cumin with ¼ teaspoon salt. Add to the carrots. Stir well, then leave to cool, stirring occasionally. Serve at room temperature.

TESSA'S CARROT AND GINGER SALAD

Serves 4

This is an excellent salad from my friend, Tessa, to accompany spicy foods. If required, prepare it a day in advance; it remains fresh and crunchy.

¼ cup lemon juice
¼ teaspoon salt
freshly ground black pepper to taste
1 rounded tablespoon finely grated fresh ginger, or to taste
1 rounded tablespoon finely chopped mint
4–5 large, firm but not woody carrots, peeled and grated

Blend the lemon juice, salt, black pepper, ginger and mint together in a bowl. Mix in the carrots. Cover and chill until required.

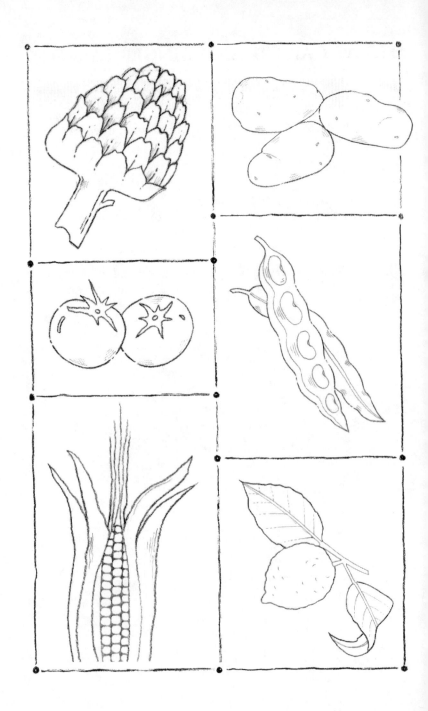

MISCELLANEOUS

Here's a disparate collection of recipes if ever I saw one. Still, they're all worthy of being in the book.

I couldn't leave out Pumpkin Pie, could I? And after raving about rich shortcrust pastry, I had to include it. And Pesto and Pistou are legendary. And it's handy to have a jar or two of chutney to jazz up a meal. And a few sauces and stocks and crumbs and croûtons never go amiss ... so I hardly need apologise for this miscellany of ideas.

❖

SOMETHING FOR THE STORE-CUPBOARD
ODDS AND SODS

❖

Something for the Store-Cupboard

Here are a few bits and pieces to fill in your spare culinary moments.

APRICOT AND CORIANDER
SEED CHUTNEY

MARINATED MUSHROOMS

SPICY TOMATO CHUTNEY

RHUBARB CHUTNEY

APRICOT AND CORIANDER
SEED CHUTNEY

Makes 3 x 500 ml jars

This is a fabulous chutney. When you bite into the coriander seeds they explode into a citrusy fragrance and taste. It makes the chutney fresh and exotic, and very moreish.

600 g dried apricots, washed
1 onion, finely chopped
3 cloves garlic, chopped
1½ tablespoons coarsely grated fresh ginger
120 g sultanas
300 g brown sugar
300 ml white wine vinegar
1 tablespoon coriander seeds

Soak the apricots in cold water for several hours. Drain, reserving the soaking liquid, then chop coarsely. Make the soaking liquid up to 450 ml with water.

Put all the ingredients, including the 450 ml of soaking liquid, in a large saucepan and set over gentle heat. Stir until the brown sugar has dissolved. Bring to the boil, turn the heat down and simmer gently for an hour, or until thick and pulpy. Stir often, especially once the chutney starts to thicken.

Ladle into hot sterilised jars, then run a clean knife through each jar to knock out any air bubbles.

For long-term storage (several months), cover with paraffin wax, then a damp cellophane jam cover or screw-on lid. For short-term storage (several weeks), cover with cellophane jam covers only. Store in a cool larder.

MARINATED MUSHROOMS

Makes 2 small jars

These mushrooms are always popular — just see how quickly a jar disappears after opening! Make them when mushrooms drop in price and either use them as an antipasto item, or as a 'nibble' with cold meats and salad.

1.5 litres water
salt
750 g small button mushrooms (they must be in prime condition), trimmed and washed well
¾ cup white wine vinegar
2 bay leaves
2 cloves garlic, peeled
1 teaspoon raw sugar
1 teaspoon black peppercorns
1 tablespoon coriander seeds
small piece cinnamon stick
olive oil to cover

Place the water and 1 tablespoon salt in a saucepan and bring to the boil. Add the mushrooms, return to the boil and boil rapidly, uncovered, for 3 minutes, pushing the mushrooms under the boiling liquid with a large spoon. Drain, reserving ¾ cup of the mushroom liquid.

Put the white wine vinegar, 1 teaspoon salt, bay leaves, garlic, raw sugar, black peppercorns, coriander seeds and cinnamon stick in the cleaned pan. Add the reserved liquid, then bring all to the boil and boil gently, uncovered, for 5 minutes.

Pack the mushrooms into hot, sterilised jars and pour over the hot marinade. Let the contents settle and cool, then pour over enough olive oil to cover.

When cool, cover the jars with corks, or seals and screw-bands, or seals and glass tops. The mushrooms should be left for a week for the flavours to develop, but they will last for several weeks providing the mushrooms are always covered with a layer of oil. If the weather is warm it is best to store them in the refrigerator.

SPICY TOMATO CHUTNEY

Makes approx. 750 ml

When tomatoes are cheap, whip up a batch of this very moreish chutney. It's excellent with avocados and taco chips, with cheese and crackers, or in tacos. It can be used immediately after making but it will keep several months providing it is refrigerated.

1 teaspoon cumin seeds
1 teaspoon coriander seeds
½ teaspoon fennel seeds
small knob of fresh ginger, peeled and sliced
6 cloves garlic, chopped
400 g granulated sugar
500 ml white wine vinegar
1½ teaspoons salt
½ teaspoon chilli powder
½ teaspoon garam masala
1 kg ripe tomatoes, skinned and diced
100 g raisins

Grind the cumin, coriander and fennel seeds. Add the ginger and garlic and process to a paste. Set aside.

Put the granulated sugar and white wine vinegar into a large saucepan and dissolve over a gentle heat. Add all the other ingredients. Stir well, then bring to the boil. Turn the heat down and cook gently for about 1½ hours, stirring often, or until the mixture is shiny, thick and pulpy. (During the last 15 minutes or so, stir often with a long-handled wooden spoon.)

Ladle into a hot sterilised jar, then run a clean knife through the jar to knock out any air bubbles. Cover with a damp cellophane jam cover and refrigerate when cool.

RHUBARB CHUTNEY

Makes 2 small jars

I grew up eating a lot of rhubarb, but it wasn't until recently that I encountered rhubarb chutney. It's great with cold meats, especially turkey, ham and chicken, but it is also good with firm, Cheddar-type cheeses, crackers and slices of crisp apple.

2 tablespoons oil
2 medium onions, finely chopped
¼ teaspoon ground turmeric
¼ teaspoon ground cumin
800 g rhubarb, trimmed, washed well and cut into short lengths
100 g brown sugar
60 ml white wine vinegar
salt
good grinding of black pepper

Put the oil in a large saucepan, set over a low heat and add the onions. Cover the pan and cook gently until the onions are very soft. (Take care not to let them catch on the base of the pan; add a tablespoon of water if it looks like catching.)

Add the spices to the pan, and stir well for a minute. Add the rhubarb, brown sugar, white wine vinegar, ½ teaspoon salt and the black pepper. Cover and bring to the boil over a medium heat. Turn the heat to low, take off the lid and continue cooking, stirring often, until the rhubarb breaks apart and the mixture becomes thick.

Pour the hot chutney into the hot sterilised jars, then run a clean knife through the jars to knock out any air bubbles. Cover with damp cellophane jam covers and refrigerate when cool.

The chutney will keep for several weeks providing it is kept refrigerated.

Odds and Sods

❖

FRESH TOMATO SAUCE
....
QUICK TOMATO SAUCE
....
GARLICKY TOMATO SAUCE
....
MORNAY SAUCE
....
HOLLANDAISE SAUCE
....
PESTO
....
PISTOU
....
MAYONNAISE
....
CHICKEN STOCK
....
VEGETABLE STOCK
....
CROÛTONS
....
BREADCRUMBS
....
GARLIC BREAD STICKS
....
HERB BUTTERS
....
CRÊPE BATTER
....
RICH SHORTCRUST PASTRY
....
PUMPKIN PECAN PIE

❖

FRESH TOMATO SAUCE

Makes approx. 400 ml

This delightful sauce captures the real sweet taste of tomatoes. Don't attempt it with hothouse tomatoes; they will make the sauce colourless and insipid. When sun-ripened, outdoor tomatoes are unavailable it is better to make a tomato sauce using tinned Italian tomatoes. Serve this sauce atop pasta noodles or with delicate stuffed pastas.

1 kg sun-ripened outdoor tomatoes, washed and roughly chopped
1 small onion, finely chopped
50 g butter
few pinches of salt

Put the tomatoes and onion in a saucepan and cover with a lid. Set over a medium heat and bring to the boil. Lift off the lid, lower the heat and cook gently for 30 minutes, stirring occasionally.

Pass the sauce through a mouli-légumes or coarse sieve. Wipe out the saucepan, drop in the butter and add the puréed tomatoes and onions. Sprinkle on a little salt. Bring back to the boil, then simmer gently for about 40 minutes, or until the mixture is thickish and pulpy, stirring often.

If the sauce is not for immediate use, cool, cover and refrigerate. Use within 2 days. Alternatively, freeze it in rigid containers. If you like, a little chopped fresh basil can be added to the sauce just before serving, or during reheating.

QUICK TOMATO SAUCE

Serves 4 atop pasta, or use on top of pizzas

This rich, red sauce is quickly whipped up with sieved, bottled Italian tomatoes (passata di pomodoro).

5 tablespoons olive oil
1 small onion, finely chopped
2 cloves garlic, crushed (optional)
700 g jar passata di pomodoro
few pinches of sugar
¼ teaspoon salt

Heat the olive oil in a medium-sized saucepan and add the onion. Cook gently until tender and a pale golden-brown. Add the garlic, if used, and cook for 2–3 minutes more. Pour in the passata di pomodoro, then stir in the sugar and salt. Bring to a gentle boil, then turn the heat down. Partially cover the pan and simmer for 15 minutes, stirring occasionally.

Use the sauce immediately or store, refrigerated, for 2–3 days, or freeze.

Don't Process Tomato Sauce

When tomatoes are processed the seeds, which are bitter, are also broken down. This can make the sauce bitter to taste. A mouli-légumes extracts the maximum pulp from the tomatoes, but traps the seeds. It produces a sauce with texture and good taste.

GARLICKY TOMATO SAUCE

Serves 4 atop pasta

An excellent all-purpose pasta sauce using tinned Italian tomatoes.

5 tablespoons olive oil
1 small onion, finely chopped
3 cloves garlic, crushed
600 g tinned Italian tomatoes, well mashed
¼ teaspoon salt
freshly ground black pepper to taste

Put the olive oil, onion and garlic in a saucepan. Cover with a lid and cook gently until the onion is a pale gold colour. Tip in the tomatoes, add salt and black pepper and bring to a gentle boil. Turn the heat down and simmer uncovered for 20 minutes.

Pass the mixture through a mouli-légumes or a coarse sieve, then return it to the cleaned pan. Cook for 5–10 minutes, or until the oil separates from the tomatoes and the sauce is pulpy.

Use the sauce immediately or store, refrigerated, for 2–3 days, or freeze.

Bruschetta ... There Ain't Nothing Like It!

We've got the Italians to thank for it — garlic bread like you've never had it before.

Toast some slices of country-style bread (or French bread) on both sides, preferably over a fire or barbecue. Rub each slice with a piece of cut garlic, then drizzle over a little extra virgin olive oil. Grind over some rock salt and black pepper and eat immediately.

For a change, top with sun-ripened, sliced tomatoes, or tomatoes and basil leaves, or tomatoes and chopped black olives.

MORNAY SAUCE

Some say it's passé, but I say great classics never die.

300 ml quantity	**450 ml quantity**
20 g butter	30 g butter
20 g plain flour	30 g plain flour
300 ml milk	450 ml milk
¼ teaspoon salt	scant ½ teaspoon salt
20 g finely grated cheese	30 g finely grated cheese

(if possible use Gruyère, or Cheddar and Parmesan cheese mixed)

optional flavourings: grinding of black pepper, grating of nutmeg, dab of prepared mustard

Gently melt the butter in a small saucepan, take off the heat and add the flour. Add the milk, a third at a time, stirring well. Return to the heat, add salt to taste and stir until the sauce comes to the boil. Cook for 2 minutes, stirring constantly. Take off the heat and beat in the Gruyère cheese. Check the seasoning, adding extra flavourings if you like. Use immediately.

If the sauce is to be prepared in advance, cover the surface with a piece of damp greaseproof paper; this prevents a skin forming. If the sauce is to be used within 1–2 hours, keep it at room temperature. For longer storage (overnight is maximum), cool, cover as described, then cover with a lid and refrigerate.

Reheat the sauce gently over a low heat, stirring constantly, but do not boil; boiling can cause the cheese to form strings. (To my mind, if the sauce is to be made in advance, it is easier to add the cheese after the sauce has been reheated.)

If you don't have scales to measure the butter, use a tablespoon measure: 1 tablespoon (flat measure) of butter = 15 gm. Therefore, use 2 tablespoons butter for the 450 g quantity of sauce and 1⅓ tablespoons butter for the 300 ml quantity of sauce.

HOLLANDAISE SAUCE

Although rich butter sauces are not presently in vogue, I think they still make a delectable treat, albeit a rich one. Try this sauce not only with the classics (asparagus, broccoli and cauliflower), but also with artichokes and green beans, or on top of stuffed mushrooms before grilling them (the heat of the grill browns the sauce . . . yum!).

3 tablespoons tarragon vinegar
6 peppercorns
small bay leaf
blade of mace
2 egg yolks, at room temperature
100 g butter, softened
pinch of salt

Put the tarragon vinegar, peppercorns, bay leaf and mace in a small saucepan and reduce over a medium heat to a dessertspoonful. Set aside.

Break the egg yolks into a smallish china bowl. Add a small 'nut' of butter and a generous pinch of salt to the yolks and beat with a wooden spoon until well creamed. Blend in the strained vinegar.

Pour very hot water into a roasting tin until three-quarters full and place it over an element. Set the element to medium-high. Sit the bowl in the water and stir until it thickens a little. Start adding the butter, by degrees, gently squeezing it through your fingers as you add it (yes . . . it is messy . . . but this softens it without oiling it). Blend well after each addition.

By the time it is all incorporated, the sauce should be thickish. Take care not to let the sauce get too hot, because it may curdle. If it does curdle, remove the bowl from the tin immediately and place it in a sink filled with cold water. Beat furiously (praying doesn't help!), then strain. Serve the sauce as soon as it is made.

It's worth noting that butter sauces are never served piping hot, as they may separate and become oily. Instead, serve them warmish. If left to stand they will thicken slightly; to 'loosen' a firmed sauce, rewarm it very gently in a bain-marie. Alternatively, store the hot sauce in a thermos flask until required; it will stay hot for several hours.

Mace

Mace is the lacy covering of the dried seed of a South-east Asian tree. The kernel of the seed is the nutmeg. Although the flavours are similar, mace is generally used in savoury dishes, while nutmeg is used in savoury and sweet dishes. Mace is sold in lacy shavings, called blades, and nutmeg is sold either whole, ready for grating, or already ground.

Tarragon Vinegar

Imported tarragon vinegar is expensive to buy. Try this simple recipe and save dollars.

6 clean, dry sprigs fresh tarragon
6 small sterilised bottles with corks
enough white wine vinegar to cover

Poke the tarragon sprigs in through the necks of the bottles, making sure the tarragon is low enough in the bottle to enable the vinegar to cover it easily. Heat the white wine vinegar in a stainless steel saucepan until very hot, but do not allow it to boil. Pour it immediately into the bottles, ensuring the tarragon stays immersed in the vinegar. Cool, then stopper with a cork, label and store. Leave for at least 2 weeks before using.

PESTO

Pesto comes from the Italian verb pestare, meaning to pound. In Italy it usually refers to a verdant green sauce made from fresh basil, garlic, pinenuts and Parmesan cheese, served atop pasta and gnocchi. But it can also mean a pounded sauce of varying herbs and nuts. The following version uses the classic 'Pesto' ingredients.

2 cups tightly packed, fresh basil leaves, washed and patted dry
  with kitchen paper
3–4 large cloves garlic, crushed
200 ml extra virgin olive oil
¾ cup pinenuts
70 g freshly grated Parmesan cheese

This pesto can be made quickly in a food processor. Put the basil leaves and garlic into the food processor bowl fitted with the chopping blade. Pour in 50 ml of the extra virgin olive oil and process to a smooth paste. Add the pinenuts, turn on the machine and pour in the rest of the oil through the feed tube. Process until the pinenuts are finely chopped. Transfer to a bowl and stir the Parmesan cheese through.

If the pesto is not for immediate use, drizzle a little olive oil over the surface, cover with a lid and store refrigerated for up to a week. For longer storage, freeze in small containers, or in cubes in an ice cube tray, for several months.

Some Other Ideas for Pesto

- Add a frozen cube of pesto to a piping-hot pan of vegetable soup like minestrone, minutes before serving; the hot soup quickly melts it. The pesto enriches the flavour and gives off a tantalising, spicy aroma.
- For a snack, spread pesto on crackers and top with sliced tomatoes, or firm cheese, like Cheddar, or with avocado slices.

PISTOU

Use this pounded mixture (it's similar to pesto) to add a burst of summer taste to vegetable soups or dishes of 'stewed' Mediterranean vegetables.

2 cloves garlic, chopped
1 cup tightly packed, fresh basil leaves
few pinches of salt
freshly ground black pepper to taste
3 tablespoons freshly grated Parmesan cheese
1 large tomato, skinned and diced
3 tablespoons extra virgin olive oil

Pound the garlic, basil, salt and black pepper in a mortar, then add half the Parmesan cheese, tomato and extra virgin olive oil. When smooth, work in the second portion of ingredients.

If preferred, the pistou can be made in a food processor or blender. Blend the chopped garlic, basil, salt and pepper, then add the Parmesan cheese and tomato. While the machine is running, pour in the olive oil through the feed tube.

Cover and refrigerate until required (use within 24 hours).

- Hollow out tiny cherry tomatoes and fill them with pesto; serve as a nibble.
- Dilute pesto with a little more oil and use it to dress new potatoes (good hot or warmish, even good cold).
- Add ½ teaspoonful pesto to a vinaigrette. Use it to dress a green bean salad, a dried bean or chick-pea salad, or a tomato salad.
- Serve a spoonful of pesto on top of jacket-baked potatoes.

Never Throw Anything Away

The adage 'never throw anything away' is good advice; take egg whites, for example. Store them, covered with a lid, in a container in the fridge for a week or two, or freeze them in small containers.

Make sure the chosen container is totally free of grease, as the egg whites won't whisk up if there is even a smear of grease present (a glass or china container is more easily made grease-free). Use them straight from the fridge, or thaw them an hour or two at room temperature if you have taken them from the freezer.

It is helpful to know that the contents of an average egg measure 60 ml and half of it is made up of egg white. Therefore, if a recipe calls for 4 egg whites you will need approximately 120 ml of egg white.

Mayonnaise

Homemade mayonnaise is rich and creamy and far superior to any commercial brand I have tasted. It's not difficult to make; it simply requires a little time.

It goes without saying that fresh egg yolks and good-quality oil are called for.

Both eggs and oil should be at room temperature to ensure they will blend easily; cold egg yolks will almost definitely curdle. If curdling does occur, start in a clean bowl with another egg yolk. Beat the yolk with a few pinches of salt, which helps thicken it and therefore gives you a better base to start with. Add the curdled mayonnaise to the new yolk, drip by drip, just as if you were making the mayonnaise from scratch.

Once the mayonnaise is made it can be used immediately or stored, covered and refrigerated, for up to a week.

Don't add herbs, spices or other flavourings until you are ready to use it, as they can turn the mayonnaise sour or cause it to go off.

MAYONNAISE

....

3 egg yolks, at room temperature
approx. ¼ teaspoon salt
300 ml olive oil (or use a quality light oil like canola)
1–2 tablespoons white wine vinegar or lemon juice
little dab of Dijon-style mustard (blend in with the egg yolks)
  (optional)

When I make mayonnaise, I prefer to use a wooden spoon first, then a hand-held electric beater (small quantities get lost in a food processor).

In a small bowl mix the egg yolks and salt. Use a wooden spoon or small whisk and beat until the yolks take on a darker colour and thicken slightly. Start adding the olive oil drop by drop, dropping it in off the tines of a fork, and beating with an electric beater. Don't hurry the process at this stage, as the fats won't blend; you can drop in the oil as fast as you can physically manage to dip the fork into the oil and dribble it into the bowl. Once you have added about half the oil, the mayonnaise will be considerably thicker; if it is very thick add a little white wine vinegar or lemon juice, say a teaspoonful.

Continue adding the second lot of oil more rapidly. Then sharpen it with more vinegar or lemon juice, and more salt if it tastes oily. If it is too thick, which it probably will be unless it is to be used for binding ingredients together, thin it with 1–2 teaspoonfuls freshly boiled water; the hot water blends in without causing separation.

Use as is, or flavour the mayonnaise with herbs, chopped olives, capers, etc.

STOCK

In the true sense of the word, stock consists of the strained liquid after bones, vegetables, herbs and seasonings have been gently simmered together. If you are a vegetarian, stock can be made without bones, or you can use vegetable cooking water, or the soaking liquid from either dried porcini mushrooms or seaweed. But there are a few points relevant to all stocks. Read the notes on Chicken Stock and observe the rules that are applicable to the stock you are making.

Chicken Stock

- The bones may be raw or cooked, but it is inadvisable to mix both in one stock, as the stock may not keep so well.
- The vegetables should be cut into thick chunks (onions in quarters, etc.). If they are too small they will break down during the long cooking and make the stock cloudy.
- No one vegetable should predominate. The main vegetables — onion, carrot and celery — should be in equal quantities to produce a balanced flavour.
- Certain vegetables should be avoided: tomatoes, as they can cause the stock to go sour; and starch vegetables, such as potatoes, as they can make the stock cloudy.
- Extra flavourings like mushroom peelings and bacon rinds may be included in small quantities for added flavour.
- The bones and vegetables should fill the saucepan by one-third; top up with water, so choose the saucepan according to the amount of bones and vegetables you have.
- Cold water should be used, as this takes longer to come to the boil and forces more 'scum' to the surface. The scum should be skimmed off during this process to produce a clearer stock.
- The stock should only be very lightly salted because reduction takes place, concentrating any seasonings and flavourings; also, the dish the stock is added to may already be seasoned.
- The stock should be brought to the boil to kill bacteria and to commence cooking, then must only simmer (simmering means the surface in one spot only may be erupting into bubbles). Boiling will make the stock cloudy.
- After cooking, the stock should be drained immediately. Never store stock with bones and vegetables in it; the vegetables may turn sour and ruin the stock.

- The stock must be cooled down very quickly, as it is a perfect breeding spot for bacteria. The easiest way to cool it is first to strain it into a clean bowl or bucket. Wash the saucepan. Return the stock to the saucepan. (It will cool down more quickly in a metal pot than in a china bowl or plastic bucket, as the metal loses heat more quickly.) Place the saucepan in the sink and fill the sink with icy cold water (put some ice in to speed it up) and keep on changing the water until the stock is tepid. Chill the stock for several hours in the refrigerator, after which time any fat will have settled on the top and can be scooped off.

The stock is now ready to use. It can be stored, refrigerated, for up to two days, or it can be poured into containers, covered with lids and frozen for several months.

CHICKEN STOCK

chicken carcasses, bones, skin
carrots, celery, onions, mushrooms
to every 3 litres of water: ½ teaspoon salt, 12 black peppercorns,
  2 bay leaves, several parsley stalks, several sprigs of thyme

Rinse the chicken carcasses, bones and skin and put them in a saucepan with the remaining ingredients. Bring to the boil slowly. Skim off any fat or scum that rises to the surface. Simmer the stock for 2–3 hours with the lid partially on (this prevents boiling over but minimises reduction). Strain and cool as described, then leave it to set in the refrigerator. Scoop off any fat and use as required. (If it is to be stored for longer than 2 days the stock *must* be frozen.)

VEGETABLE STOCK

1 large onion, peeled and cut into thick chunks
2 small carrots, peeled, trimmed and cut into chunks
2 sticks celery, cut into chunks
1 leek, trimmed, coarsely chopped then washed well
8 button mushrooms, washed
several pieces dried porcini mushrooms or ½ teaspoon Vegemite
10 stalks parsley
8 sprigs thyme
2 bay leaves, fresh if possible
several blades of mace
1 teaspoon salt
1 tablespoon black peppercorns
2 short leaves fresh lemon grass or 2 strips lemon peel

Prepare the vegetables; they should roughly total 5 cups. Put them in a large saucepan with the remaining ingredients and pour on 10 cups cold water. Bring to the boil, lower the heat, partially cover with a lid and simmer gently for 1½ hours. Strain and cool.

Refrigerated, the stock will stay fresh for 2–3 days, but it may be frozen for longer storage.

Porcini/Cèpe

Porcini or cèpe *(Boletus edulis)* is an edible fungus, available fresh in Europe during the autumn months, or dried at other times of the year. Usually only dried boletus are exported. Dried, they possess a woodsy aroma, with a savoury (almost like Vegemite) concentrated flavour. They give a full mushroom flavour to everything they are cooked with.

Reconstitute them by soaking for 30 minutes in warm water.

CROÛTONS

Croûtons add a little crunch and flavour when added to soups or salads. Use bread which is at least a day old; it contains less moisture, therefore minimising spitting, and browns more evenly. If you have old bread but don't require croûtons, rather than feeding the bread to the ducks or birds, cut it into croûtons, wrap in a plastic bag and freeze until required.

slices of day-old bread (white, wholemeal or grainy) cut into small cubes
approx. 100 g butter (or approx. ½ cup oil) per 3 slices of bread
salt

Heat a large frypan over a medium heat. Drop in the butter (or oil) and allow it to sizzle. Add the cubes of bread and cook, turning once, until a light golden-brown. Take care not to let them burn.

Wholemeal or grainy bread croûtons will take longer to colour and crisp than white bread croûtons.

Use a slotted spoon to transfer the croûtons to a plate lined with absorbent paper. Sprinkle with salt and toss them in the paper. Serve hot.

If the croûtons are to be prepared ahead of time, cool them quickly, then store airtight until required.

Lift them out of the liquid (reserving the soaking liquid) and rinse well under running water. Chop finely, discarding any woody bits. Strain the liquid into a bowl through a sieve lined with a piece of kitchen paper.

Use with other mushrooms to improve their flavour, in casseroles, or vegetable medleys, in pasta sauces, crêpe fillings and chicken or meat dishes, incorporating the soaking liquid whenever possible.

BREADCRUMBS

Soft white crumbs are used in stuffings and fillings to absorb liquids and flavours and to give body and a light texture. They do not stay fresh very long, as, like bread, they ferment. They will stay fresh in the refrigerator for about a week, or they may be frozen — then there are crumbs to have on hand when time is short (thaw for about 10 minutes at room temperature).

Use a loaf of white bread, remove all the crusts and blend the soft crumbs in a food processor or blender until smooth. Store in a plastic bag. Fresh white crumbs may be dried.

DRIED WHITE BREADCRUMBS

Dried white crumbs are used primarily for coating foods that are to be fried. Usually the items for frying are floured and dipped in beaten egg, which makes a sticky base to which the crumbs adhere. The protein in the egg coagulates when the food is immersed in the fat and this makes an impenetrable wall. For this reason 'egging and crumbing' should be done with great care, because if it is patchy, the fat will enter the food, making it greasy. Dried white crumbs are used to thicken this protective wall and to give food a crisp, crunchy exterior, which is also appealing to the eye. Fresh white crumbs should not be used, as they contain moisture that will cause the fat to spit and the crumbs may not adhere. Dried browned crumbs (available commercially) are unsuitable for frying, as they will be overbrowned and possibly burnt before the food is cooked through.

Spread the fresh white crumbs in a baking dish and bake in an oven at 120°C until crisp and dry, but not coloured. Turn them from time to time to ensure they dry evenly. They may take as long as 45 minutes, but don't be tempted to increase the heat. When they are very dry, take them out of the oven and push them through a metal sieve or blend in a food processor or blender again until a fine crumb is achieved. If they feel at all moist, return them to the baking dish and continue drying in the oven. When completely cool, store airtight. Dried crumbs will last many months, as the moisture has been driven off and they will not ferment. (Homemade crumbs are far superior to commercially made crumbs. The latter often have a musty smell and are usually pulverised and powdery.)

GARLIC BREAD STICKS

Makes 24 bread sticks; serves approx. 6

Most people enjoy garlic bread, but it is filling and rich and doesn't suit all menus. The following idea transforms the three elements — bread, butter and garlic — into something just as irresistible but far more stylish.

50 g butter, softened
2 cloves garlic, finely crushed
12 thin slices fresh white bread

Mix the butter and crushed garlic together in a small bowl. Roll out the bread with a rolling pin until it is evenly compressed. Spread it with garlic butter.

Trim away the crusts. Working with one slice of bread at a time, tightly roll one side of the slice to the centre, turn, then roll from the other side until the rolled pieces meet. Cut through the centre of the slice with a sharp bread knife, forming two bread sticks from each slice.

Lay the bread sticks, seam-side down, in a shallow oven dish, packing them in tightly to stop them unrolling. Smear any remaining butter over the surface. Cover them with plastic wrap and set aside until required. The rolls may be prepared a day ahead to this point; wrap and chill, or freeze.

When you are ready to cook, remove the wrapping and bake the bread sticks in an oven preheated to 200 °C for approximately 15 minutes, or until golden. Serve hot.

HERB BUTTERS

Herb butter can transform a plainly cooked vegetable into a taste treat. The possibilities are endless, but here are a few suggestions.

mint butter: carrots, potatoes, baby beetroot, peas, zucchini
chive butter: potatoes, baby beetroot, asparagus, zucchini, kumara, parsnip
tarragon butter: green beans, potatoes, leeks, zucchini, cucumber
chervil butter: carrots, celery, fennel, peas, green beans, butter beans, broad beans
basil butter: artichokes, butter beans, peas, zucchini
parsley butter: carrots, potatoes, zucchini, parsnips, celery
summer savory butter: broad beans, carrots, potatoes, zucchini, broccoli
marjoram butter: butter beans, leeks, potatoes, fennel, cabbage, zucchini, broccoli
rosemary butter: pumpkin, potatoes
coriander butter: potatoes, carrots, cauliflower, parsnips
dill butter: red cabbage, potatoes, cucumber, carrots, marrow, baby beetroot
lemon thyme butter: carrots, zucchini, leeks, fennel, butter beans, broccoli, parsnips, kumara
sage butter: green beans, butter beans, broad beans
thyme butter: marrow, zucchini, onions

HERB BUTTER (HOW TO MAKE IT)

200 g softened butter
1–2 tablespoons finely chopped fresh herbs (with pungent herbs, like sage and rosemary, use the lesser quantity)
salt
freshly ground black pepper to taste

Blend the butter and herbs with a few pinches of salt and a little black pepper. Transfer to a small container, smooth the top and chill until required. (For long-term storage freeze the herb butter.)

Other flavourings, such as crushed garlic, freshly grated nutmeg, grated lemon, orange or lime rinds, caraway seeds, ground cumin, cumin seeds, chilli powder, finely chopped chilli, etc, can also be used in combination with herbs, or alone.

Fresh Herbs Versus Dried

Whenever possible use fresh herbs; they have a liveliness of aroma, taste and colour that can't be beat. That's not to say that dried herbs don't have their place — they do — it's just a matter of knowing which ones are successful in their dried state.

When they are dried, feathery herbs like dill and fennel lose their colour and some aroma and their worst qualities are often accentuated. Basil becomes brittle, loses colour and aroma and takes on a musty smell and taste.

Dried rosemary falls apart, the spikes separating from the stems, but it retains good flavour. Just use the spikes chopped, that way you won't spear yourself and your guests with sharp spikes when you eat it.

Thyme, oregano, marjoram and sage all dry well, keeping good strong flavours.

Parsley is not even worth considering; it should always be on hand, growing in the garden or in a pot, to provide a splash of colour, a clean grassy taste and a valuable jot or two of iron in the diet (if you live in a hot climate grow parsley in the shade during summer months and water very well; pick out any bits that start going to seed to prolong the plant's life).

Mint is another funny one. Like fennel and dill, the worst qualities of mint, when it is dried, are often drawn out and exaggerated (it becomes excessively minty and overpowering).

Chives, dried, are miserable too.

CRÊPE BATTER

Makes 25–30 crêpes

This batter is easy to make and turns out light, crisp crêpes. If you're in the mood, make a double batch and store them in the freezer; they come in handy for producing a quick meal.

115 g plain flour
pinch of salt
1 whole egg and 1 extra egg yolk
325 ml milk, maybe a little more
1 tablespoon melted butter

Making the crêpes by hand

Sift the flour and salt into a deep mixing bowl and make a well in the centre. Drop in the egg and egg yolk. Use a wooden spoon to blend the eggs together, gradually drawing in the flour as you go, then start adding the milk, keeping the mixture the consistency of thick cream. Continue stirring until all the flour is drawn in (you will have used about half the milk by this time). Beat well together, then add the melted butter and remaining milk.

Cover the batter and leave it on one side for 30 minutes to soften the starch grains in the flour (this makes the crêpes lighter). Before making the batter into crêpes, check the consistency (it should be like a thin cream). If necessary, thin with a little milk.

Making the crêpe batter in a food processor

Use the same quantities. Put the egg, egg yolk, melted butter and milk into the processor bowl fitted with the chopping blade. Whizz for a few seconds, stop the machine, sprinkle the flour and salt over and whizz again for 30 seconds. Pour into a bowl and rest for 30 minutes as above.

Making up the crêpes

Choose a small, heavy pan, 12–18 cm in diameter, preferably one with sloping sides to make turning over easier. Lightly oil or butter the pan and heat it on a medium-high heat until the oil just starts to haze. Pour in a spoonful of batter and quickly swirl it around the pan, coating the entire base, then pour any excess batter back into the bowl.

It should take about a minute to cook the first side. Loosen with a palette knife and either flip or turn over and cook the second side. Put the crêpes on a cooling rack as they are made.

If necessary, oil or butter the pan occasionally, but if bad sticking occurs, wipe the pan with a piece of kitchen paper dipped in oil and salt, wipe clean and start again.

When all the crêpes are made, wrap them in plastic wrap and refrigerate until required. Otherwise, layer them up, separating each crêpe with a sheet of waxed paper, wrap and freeze (the waxed paper makes it easy to peel off the crêpes when required). To thaw, separate the number of crêpes you want, and leave them at room temperature for 5–10 minutes. Use as directed.

PASTRY NOTES

The recipes in this book call for a 20 cm flan ring or dish to be lined with pastry. This requires 170 g of pastry (i.e. pastry made with 170 g flour), but I prefer to make a 225 g quantity of pastry (or otherwise a double batch which is no more difficult to do) because the ingredients are easier to work with (ever tried splitting an egg?). Any leftover pastry can be used to line a smaller flan, or tartlet tins or a small pie dish. A double batch of pastry, made with 450 g flour, will line three 20 cm flan rings or dishes.

If you want to freeze the pastry, it is more convenient to do so after lining the flan ring or tins. Once frozen, the pastry/pastries can be slipped out of the rings or tins (thus freeing them for other uses), and stored in a sealed plastic bag in the freezer for 6 months. This allows you to collect tartlet bases until you have enough for a recipe, and if you have made a double batch of pastry you will have extra flan bases to have on hand when you want to put a quick meal together. Thaw the pastries for 5 minutes only, and return to their rings or tins before baking.

Remember to work in a cool atmosphere when making pastry, as warmth and steam can quickly turn the pastry limp and sticky. Cold metal utensils, a chilled china bowl and ice-cold water all help to keep the temperature of the ingredients cool.

Be careful with the amount of water you add: too much and the pastry will shrink — too little and it will be dry to eat.

RICH SHORTCRUST PASTRY

This is a useful pastry which can be used to line flan rings, pie dishes or tartlet tins. It is crisp, thanks to the egg yolk, and deliciously 'short' (melt-in-the-mouth) and buttery to taste. It's superior in every way to any commercially made pastry I've tasted.

225 g plain flour
pinch of salt
170 g butter, pliable (see notes at end of recipe)
1 egg yolk
3–4 tablespoons ice-cold water (put the water to chill in the freezer)

Sift the flour with a pinch of salt into a large mixing bowl. Cut the butter into large lumps and drop it into the flour. Using two knives, cut the butter through the flour until the pieces of butter are like small marbles. Use your fingertips to rub the butter into the flour until the mixture resembles coarse breadcrumbs.

Mix the egg yolk and water together and add it all at once to the flour mixture (use 3 tablespoons water to begin with; if the pastry seems a little dry and flaky during mixing, sprinkle over the extra water, or part of it, on the dry flakes). Stir with a knife to combine. Lightly knead with your hands and turn out onto a cool, dry, lightly floured surface. Knead briefly until smooth. Wrap in plastic film and refrigerate for 30 minutes. (This is important, as it allows the fat to cool and firm, which will prevent sticking during rolling out, and it relaxes the gluten in the flour, which will help minimise shrinkage.)

Roll out thinly, using a smooth rolling pin, with short rolls, rolling away from your body. Occasionally flour the rolling pin and the board underneath the pastry to prevent sticking. Don't flour the top of the pastry, as the flour gets rolled in and can make the surface of the pastry dry. Cut and shape as required.

PUMPKIN PECAN PIE

Serves 6–8

I'm not a lover of sweet gooey things, so I've subjected the 'trad' pumpkin pie to a little doctoring. The result? The sweet pumpkin takes back seat, allowing the welcome tang of apricots and nutty taste of pecans to come to the fore. But be warned; this is very moreish!

½ cup chopped, dried apricots, soaked for several hours in hot water
1 cooking apple, peeled and grated
grated rind and juice of 1 lemon
1 cup golden raisins
2 eggs
½ cup soft brown sugar
¼ teaspoon allspice
½ teaspoon ground cinnamon
¾ cup cooked mashed pumpkin
1 cup evaporated milk
20 cm pie dish lined with rich shortcrust pastry, chilled
   (see page 302 for pastry recipe)
1 cup pecan nuts
200 ml cream

Drain the apricots after soaking. Mix the grated apple in a bowl with the lemon rind and juice, then blend in the raisins and drained apricots.

In a separate bowl beat the eggs with a fork, and blend in the brown sugar, allspice, ground cinnamon and mashed pumpkin. Then add the evaporated milk. Blend in the apple mixture, then pour it into the pastry case. Arrange the pecans on top, then bake the pie in an oven preheated to 200°C for 15 minutes. Lower the heat and continue baking for 25–30 minutes, or until the pastry is golden-brown. Remove the pie from the oven and cool.

Lightly whip the cream and either spoon it on top of the pie in soft 'dollops' or fill it into a piping bag fitted with a rose nozzle, and pipe rosettes on top of the pie. Serve cut in wedges.

INDEX